Women and
Culture Series

*The Women and Culture Series is dedicated to books that illuminate the lives, roles, achievements, and status of women, past or present.*

Fran Leeper Buss
*La Partera: Story of a Midwife*

Valerie Kossew Pichanick
*Harriet Martineau: The Woman and Her Work, 1802–76*

Sandra Baxter and Marjorie Lansing
*Women and Politics: The Visible Majority*

Estelle B. Freedman
*Their Sisters' Keepers: Women's Prison Reform in America, 1830–1930*

Susan C. Bourque and Kay Barbara Warren
*Women of the Andes: Patriarchy and Social Change in Two Peruvian Towns*

Marion S. Goldman
*Gold Diggers and Silver Miners: Prostitution and Social Life on the Comstock Lode*

Page duBois
*Centaurs and Amazons: Women and the Pre-History of the Great Chain of Being*

Mary Kinnear
*Daughters of Time: Women in the Western Tradition*

Lynda K. Bundtzen
*Plath's Incarnations: Woman and the Creative Process*

Violet B. Haas and Carolyn C. Perrucci, editors
*Women in Scientific and Engineering Professions*

Sally Price
*Co-wives and Calabashes*

Patricia R. Hill
*The World Their Household: The American Woman's Foreign Mission Movement and Cultural Transformation, 1870–1920*

PATRICIA R. HILL received honorable mention in the Hamilton Prize competition for 1982. The Alice and Edith Hamilton Prize is named for two outstanding women scholars: Alice Hamilton (educated at the University of Michigan Medical School), a pioneer in environmental medicine; and her sister Edith Hamilton, the renowned classicist. The Hamilton Prize competition is supported by the University of Michigan and by private donors.

*The World Their Household*

# The World Their Household

The American Woman's
Foreign Mission Movement
and Cultural Transformation,
1870–1920

*Patricia R. Hill*

Ann Arbor    The University of Michigan Press

Copyright © by The University of Michigan 1985
All rights reserved
Published in the United States of America by
The University of Michigan Press and simultaneously
in Rexdale, Canada, by John Wiley & Sons Canada, Limited
Manufactured in the United States of America

1988  1987  1986  1985    4  3  2  1

**Library of Congress Cataloging in Publication Data**

Hill, Patricia Ruth.
    The world their household.

    (Women and culture series)
    Bibliography: p.
    Includes index.
    1. Women in missionary work. 2. Women missionaries—
United States. 3. Missions, American. 4. Protestant
churches—Missions. 5. United States—Church history—
19th century. 6. United States—Church history—20th
century. I. Title. II. Title: American woman's foreign
mission movement and cultural transformation, 1870–1920.
III. Series.
BV2610.H55 1985        266'.023'73        84–13206
ISBN 0-472-10055-6

# Acknowledgments

For the part they played in changing cultural assumptions about what women can accomplish, I am indebted to these missionary women. There are other, more immediate debts of gratitude for me to acknowledge. The deepest is to William R. Hutchison, teacher and advisor, who sparked my interest in the history of missions and encouraged me to pursue this study. To Barbara Miller Solomon, who has shaped my understanding of the experience of women in American history, I owe a very special thanks. Friends and colleagues in the New World Church History Colloquium at the Harvard Divinity School have read parts of the manuscript in various stages and offered instructive criticism as well as warm support. Without them all, I could not have seen this project through to its conclusion.

I am grateful to the program in the History of American Civilization at Harvard for a research grant in the summer of 1980. I also wish to thank members of the Alice and Edith Hamilton Prize Committee at the University of Michigan for the recognition accorded my manuscript in the 1982 competition. I am especially grateful to Louise Tilly for her valuable suggestions for final revisions.

My appreciation for access to the collections and archives of the following libraries must certainly be recorded here: Houghton Library, Harvard University; Andover-Harvard Library, Harvard Divinity School; Boston University School of Theology Library; The Mission Research Library, Union Theological Seminary, New York; and the Presbyterian Historical Society, Philadelphia. The Program Agency of the United Presbyterian Church graciously granted me permission to consult missionary manuscript collections and papers of the Commission on Ecumenical Mission and Relations on deposit at the Presbyterian Historical Society. Quotations from the correspondence on deposit in the Houghton Library between Jean Kenyon Mackenzie and her editors at Houghton Mifflin are used by permission of the Houghton Library.

Finally, to John Klause for help in editing and proofreading and for sustaining moral and emotional support, I owe an enormous debt.

# Contents

# Introduction

America became in those days the leading nation in the sending out of Protestant missionaries. Prior to 1880 missions had been maintained by relatively small and specially dedicated groups of believers, but now they blossomed into a major interest of the churches and a significant interest of the nation. The number of American foreign missionaries, which stood at 934 in 1890, reached nearly 5,000 a decade later and over 9,000 in 1915. In support of those workers large movements were organized not only in the churches but in the nation generally.[1]

The blossoming of missionary enthusiasm in late-nineteenth-century America has frequently been attributed to the rise of lay movements dedicated to the cause. Indeed, Kenneth Scott Latourette describes as a "distinctive feature of the expansion of Christianity in the nineteenth century...the extent to which Christian missions became an enterprise of the rank and file of the membership of the church." Building upon Latourette's observation, historians have credited the Student Volunteer Movement for Foreign Missions (SVM) and the Laymen's Missionary Movement, as well as individual lay leaders like John R. Mott, with the spectacular spurt in the growth of American Protestant missions that occurred between about 1880 and the First World War.[2]

To Latourette, widespread lay support for missions was evidence of "the permeation of the masses by the Christianity which had been adopted hundreds of years before under the leadership of the aristocracy." He saw the fact that "so many hundreds of thousands were willing to contribute to the propagation of their faith" as an "indication that increasingly the large body of professing Christians were devoting themselves seriously to their faith and were not merely passive recipients of it."[3] Current interpretations are less flattering; they link missions to imperialism or, more kindly, offer vague assertions that in their expansiveness and optimism about world conquest "foreign missions matched the national mood." Ministers and lay leaders have been accused of adopting strategies and mirroring attitudes of the business world in order to prove themselves men among businessmen. According to such theories, the result in the mainline, liberal denominations was the professionalization and secularization of the mission enterprise; social service and social reform superseded personal religious conversion on the Protestant mission agenda. The overt cultural imperialism of modern missions proved embarrassing to liberal reformers after the horrifying spectacle of the First World War had exposed the hypocrisy of the Christian West. This embarrassment, coupled with changes in mission policy designed to accommodate burgeoning nationalism in the non-Western world, encouraged the major Protestant groups in America to scale down their missionary activities in the twenties and thirties.[4]

What is missing from this version of the story of American Protestantism's crusade to evangelize the world is any mention of the largest of the lay movements organized to support the missionary enterprise, the woman's foreign mission movement. As so frequently happens in the writing of history, the women have simply disappeared. Latourette does note their increased numbers on the mission field (without linking this phenomenon to the organization of female missionary societies), and Charles Forman observes that "an improvement in the position of women was always first and foremost" among the "cultural advantages that, it was presumed, Americans had to offer"; but such observations have not led historians to revise the history of missions outlined above. Some denominational histories have included accounts of denominational women's societies and particular missionary heroines, but only one historian of missions has felt that women's societies merited treatment as an interdenominational phenomenon.[5]

Women, however, constituted a majority of the rank and file membership of the churches. Much of the credit for generating the missionary revival of the late nineteenth century belongs to the woman's foreign mission movement. The purpose of this study is to make that movement visible again, as it was to contemporaries, as a cultural and religious phenomenon. Doing so will force a reevaluation of the sources and character of the much-vaunted activism of American religion and a reconsideration of the nature of religion's "feminization" in the nineteenth century. And, as the phrase *cultural transformation* in the subtitle to this study suggests, the woman's foreign mission movement will be examined for both the role it played in the cultural imperialism that aimed at transforming the non-Western world and its symbiotic relationship with changing cultural paradigms of ideal womanhood in America.

Foreign missions gripped the imaginations and enlisted the support of hundreds of thousands of middle-class churchwomen in the late nineteenth century. By 1915 there were more than three million women on the membership rolls of some forty denominational female missionary societies. The interdenominational woman's foreign mission movement eclipsed the Student Volunteer Movement and the Laymen's Missionary Movement in size, and was substantially larger than any of the other mass woman's movements of the nineteenth century. This study examines the cultural and ideological climate that made foreign missions an especially congenial object for female benevolence in the years immediately following the Civil War. It then charts a changing philosophy of woman's work as the movement mushroomed and became increasingly professionalized at the administrative level. The rhetoric of the movement reveals ideological changes that, when translated into practice, contributed to the redefinition of ideal womanhood and the emergence of the New Woman in the 1890s. Yet despite the apparent elasticity of its definition of woman's proper sphere, the movement was unable to sustain either its appeal to a massive constituency or even its continued institutional existence after the First World War. Sketching the interplay between the mission movement and the cultural and religious milieu in which it existed suggests why the movement flourished and why it faded into obscurity in the 1920s.

The images of female missionaries created by three popular novelists serve to illustrate the history of the movement and provide evidence of the hold that foreign missions had on the female imagination when the movement was at its height. Following this fictional frontispiece, the study turns to the movement's initial formulation of a special and limited mission to women and children. The notion of a special mission, consonant with the Victorian sanctification of motherhood, reflected the organizers' assumptions about the nature of woman and her proper role in society and served as a justification for women's missionary societies when they encountered opposition from conservative ministers and denominational mission boards.

The rapid proliferation of women's foreign missionary societies in virtually every branch of American Protestantism and the spectacular growth of the movement in its first twenty years testify not only to the imaginative appeal of its mission but also to the organizational genius of it leaders. They successfully planted auxiliaries in cities and villages across the continent. Local auxiliaries, like temperance groups and women's clubs, offered conservative women a forum for developing skills in public speaking, fund-raising and organizational management that could be easily transferred from these semiprivate spheres to the public arena. And when the women of small-town America embarked upon the systematic study of foreign mission fields, their cultural horizons were considerably broadened. Women who served overseas as missionaries or who headed denominational societies at the national level carved out careers for themselves in mission service. Thus, paradoxically, this eminently respectable, religiously conservative movement fostered a wider sphere of responsibility for ordinary churchwomen and opened up new professional opportunities for several thousand American women.

With professionalization (stimulated by the emergence of other female professions in the 1890s) came a redefinition of woman's role in missions that separated professional from amateur and distanced the movement's leadership from its broad-based constituency. The very presence of female missionaries in foreign fields had necessitated broadening the meaning of evangelism to include social service; women, denied ordination, were sent as teachers, doctors, nurses, and social workers rather than as preachers. On the home front, the leaders of women's missionary societies began to conceive of themselves as experts in the new "science" of missions. As membership lists lengthened and receipts climbed, these officers were taken ever more seriously by their male colleagues. In the climate of collaboration that developed, the women adopted the style and strategies employed by male mission administrators. They began to press their claim to an equal voice in the administration of the vast Protestant missionary enterprise, a claim that went far beyond jurisdiction over work with women and children.

The new direction taken by the leadership is apparent in a change in the tone that characterized the magazines published by all the major women's societies. The magazines constitute the collective voice of the movement's leadership. Accepting the premise that the message may be in the metaphor, that figures of speech as well as statistics are appropriate measures of a social movement, this study pays particular attention to the rhetorical content of editorials and short stories published in women's missionary magazines. Movement leaders relied from the beginning on the printed word to stir the emotions of women and forge the bonds of sympathy that drew masses of middle-class women to the mission cause. By comparing the manner in which the cause was presented in the early years with the appeal made later, one can partly understand the failure of the movement to sustain the support of its female constituency.

In the mid-nineteenth century, American evangelicals had adopted a theology of missions that attached special significance to the conversion of "heathen " mothers as the most efficient means of Christianizing heathen lands. Since it was widely accepted that only women could reach the secluded females of the Orient, this emphasis on the conversion of mothers elevated the importance of woman's mission and made American women peculiarly responsible for the success of the Protestant mission crusade. Victorian ideology buttressed this definition of woman's duty by suggesting that her nature made her peculiarly fitted for the task.

The theory of modern missions replaced the argument for woman's special responsibility with an assumption that in the regeneration of non-Christian cultures the lives of women would be transformed; the new theory offered no rationale for a distinctive mission of women, to women. But while the rhetoric of a special mission was abandoned, the rhetoric of domesticity was retained—and recast in light of pronouncements issued by practitioners of the new science of sociology. The functional role of mothers in the critical process of socializing children justified efforts to improve the condition of women through education and with protective legislation. A new paradigm of ideal womanhood, described by Sheila Rothman as "educated motherhood," replaced Victorian notions about the sacral quality of maternal love and the instinctually religious tendencies of the True Woman. Both the new theory of missions and the new paradigm of womanhood reflect the influence of those forces of modernization that were transforming the world of the American bourgeoisie from a Protestant to a predominantly secular culture.[6]

The leaders of the woman's foreign mission movement embraced modernity as the product of social and material progress, not realizing the secularization that accompanied modernization would eventually undermine their movement. Without the melodramatic

appeal that worked so effectively on the sensibilities of Victorian females, the women's societies experienced difficulties in recruiting
new members in the era of modern missions. Their work overseas
continued to attract volunteers until the whole missionary enterprise
foundered in the 1920s, a victim of postwar isolationism and fundamentalist attack, but the home base operations of the women's societies could not be adequately staffed even before the war. Young,
single women of the middle classes were less likely to choose a career
in poorly paid mission work as business and professional opportunities for college-educated women multiplied. Ordinary churchwomen
continued to be at least nominally active in their support of missions, but devotion to female missionary societies as manifestations
of a vast, interdenominational movement among women waned.

Without the rationale of a distinctive mission, the administrators of the women's societies failed to resist mergers with denominational boards after the war. Mergers fragmented and dissolved the
power base that women working for missions had established within
American churches. The women's foreign missionary societies of
the four largest Protestant denominations, on which this study con-
centrates, lost institutional autonomy. The women of these churches
also lost any sense of belonging to an ecumenical movement among
women. Ties with the women of smaller denominations, ethnic immigrant churches, and Black churches who had also formed female
missionary societies were severed. The remnant in the mainline
churches who devoted their energies to the mission cause became
again the small and specially dedicated groups of believers that had
fostered Protestant missions in the years preceding the rise of vast
lay movements.

Leaders of women's societies who protested against forced
mergers with denominational mission boards or consolidation into
all-purpose women's associations within denominations discovered
that both ordinary churchwomen and the secularized culture of postwar America were indifferent to the plight of the Protestant woman's foreign mission movement. Like the other mass women's
movements of the nineteenth century that barely survived the First
World War, the woman's foreign mission movement was rooted in
ideologies of domesticity that defined a "public" dimension of appropriate female influence in society. Victorian women were encouraged to exert themselves in moral and religious causes. In the

Progressive era, women were applauded for involving themselves as "public housekeepers" in campaigns for civic reform and the enactment of social legislation. The retreat from Progressive reform in the postwar period had a cultural parallel for women in a new ideology of domestic bliss that focused on the private, conjugal relationship. The new ideology posited, in its celebration of companionship in the marital relation, a greater equality between men and women. Its lack of any public dimension meant, however, the erosion of female spheres of public influence. The redefinition of ideology in the direction of equality between the sexes made gender-based mass movements seem, from the perspective of the dominant culture of the twenties, as antiquated as religious movements.

# Chapter 1

# The Romance of Missions

Eclipsing even the Woman's Christian Temperance Union (WCTU) in size, the woman's foreign mission movement counted more than three million American women as dues-paying members of female foreign missionary societies by 1915.[1] It would be surprising if this largest of all the late-nineteenth-century women's crusades had left no trace of its existence in popular fiction. In fact, vignettes drawn by novelists illustrate more graphically than do official records the movement's history and the nature of the romance between American women and foreign missions.

Emma Dorothy Eliza Nevitte Southworth, in her 1868 novel *Fair Play*, sketches the relationship of women to missions before the formation of denominational female missionary societies in the 1870s. Kate Douglas Wiggin, writing her *Rebecca* books in the first decade of the twentieth century when the woman's foreign mission movement was in its ascendancy, paints a picture of little girls in rural Maine whose imaginations are fired with missionary enthusiasm. And Ellen Glasgow's *Barren Ground*, published in 1925 after the movement had faded into obscurity, includes a remarkable portrait of the heroine's mother as a woman on whose heart and mind the missionary dream had been indelibly engraved. None of these novelists was herself involved in the movement; that they wrote about it at all testifies to the imaginative significance of foreign missions in the female world at the turn of the century.

The years from 1880 to 1920 were the golden age of missionary expansion in the history of American Protestantism; one might conclude that women were simply caught up in the general missionary fervor of the churches. But in their very choice of missions as material for fiction, these novelists suggest that the involvement of women with foreign missions had a special character. As women writing for a largely female audience they present a perspective on missions that is sex-specific; one cannot call to mind any male novelist of the period writing a book for boys that employs images of missionaries in a similar manner. Foreign missions were the focus of ambition and the stuff of dreams for young women. Insofar as popular fiction records them, young men dreamed other dreams. What then was the romantic appeal that foreign missions held for women, and why did it wane in the twenties? In their fiction, these three novelists have indicated some answers.

Mrs. E. D. E. N. Southworth, "the most popular authoress in the annals of American publishing," took up writing (along with schoolteaching) to support herself and two children after her marriage foundered.[2] Her literary talents are decidedly meager. Her plots are contrived and largely derivative—pastiches of Defoe, Richardson, and Scott. Her characters are implausibly good, implausibly bad, or simply implausible. Herself an avid reader of fiction, Southworth had a knack for isolating in other and better novelists' work those features that most appealed to the sensibility of her audience. She shared with her predominantly female readership a taste for melodrama and saccharine sentimentality. Unlike more serious writers of the period who used fiction as a medium for exploring the ramifications of political and theological issues, Southworth confined herself to domestic arrangements—and derangements—with their attendant romantic entanglements. Her opinions on social questions are expressed obliquely, if at all, in her novels. In her Civil War novel, *Fair Play,* the war itself remains a subplot; more crucial to the central romance of the novel is the effect that the feminism espoused by the heroine has on the course of true love.

Through Britomarte Conyers, the implausible heroine of *Fair Play,* Southworth displays familiarity with the concerns and demands of the woman's rights movement at midcentury. Her inclusion of feminism as a prominent issue in the novel reflects the widespread (and largely negative) publicity this movement received in the popular press. Southworth is perhaps not entirely unsympathetic toward her heroine's complaints against men, but the novel treats feminism as deviance. Britomarte Conyers, man-hater, is a strong and attractive woman, intelligent and virtuous as well as a good Christian. Yet some mystery shrouds her origins (in true Gothic fashion), and Southworth hints that something in her dark past has warped her attitude toward the male sex. The secret of this mysterious past is never fully revealed to the reader—primarily, one suspects, because Mrs. Southworth dropped that particular thread in the complicated task of unraveling her convoluted plot. But whatever the source of the problem, Southworth does tell us that Britomarte has a wounded spirit; that in some mysterious way her intellect has been divorced from her affections. The purpose of Southworth's tortured and improbable plot is to confront Britomarte with the error of her ways and, not incidentally, to build toward the sequel, *How He Won Her.* It is Southworth's linkage of this feminist protagonist with the missionary enterprise that makes this novel an illuminating document for a study of the role women played in the Protestant mission crusade.

Suspending disbelief, as the reader must to accept a heroine who, though a graduate of a Southern female seminary, spouts feminist propaganda, let us look at Britomarte's manifesto:

> so long as the barbarous law in changing a woman to a wife makes her a nonentity, I will not marry. . . . so long as your barbarous customs close half of woman's legitimate field of labor, and open the other half only to admit her to work at degrading rates of wages, I will not work for any wages whatever. . . . so long as man continues to wrong woman, I will never accept assistance from any man whomsoever.[3]

If she will not marry and will not work for wages, what then is she to do? What other means of support can she find? Our heroine has no hesitation in supplying an answer.

> The Board of Foreign Missions are in want of teachers to join a company of missionaries. . . to Farther India. I shall offer my services to go with them. It is better to labor for nothing in the vineyard of the Lord among the heathen, than to slave here where your cruel laws and customs in regard to women dishonor Christianity. (*FP,* 125–26)

Britomarte apparently sees no conflict between her feminist faith and evangelical Christianity; on the contrary, she believes that a truly Christian society would be organized according to her feminist principles. To Southworth, Britomarte's feminism represents an aberration of the mind, potentially curable; her adherence to Christianity testifies to the soundness of her heart and indicates to the reader that she is ultimately redeemable.

The content of Britomarte's Christianity, although adequate for Southworth's purposes, would surely have raised qualms on the part of any genuine mission board. Her theology is nebulous and only semi-Christian by evangelical standards. Her sympathies lie with both sun worshipers and Catholics. The only sense of mission that Britomarte expresses is her desire to save other women. In reaching her decision to leave America, she ends a long lament on the plight of women by exclaiming, "Oh, my sisters! my sisters! as Christ died to save the whole human race, so I would die to free you!" (*FP,* 124). When women organized societies to send female missionaries to foreign fields their specific purpose was, like Britomarte's, to aid their heathen sisters; but they offered spiritual salvation—and took care to dissociate themselves from the woman's rights movement. Britomarte's goal as a missionary was to use all her influence to prevent other women from marrying. When she announces this resolve to her friends, they react with horror.

> But Britomarte, you shock me beyond measure! Prevent women from marrying! prevent women from fulfilling the very first law of God given to man! Why, the very first Divine institution on earth was that of marriage. And the very first command given to man was to increase and multiply and replenish the earth. Why, what are you thinking of? You—a Christian missionary to the heathen! (*FP,* 184).

Southworth's own sympathies lie with the speaker in this passage. She has the entire missionary party aboard ship for the South Seas aiding and abetting the suit being pressed by Justin Rosenthal, Britomarte's ministerial admirer, who has followed her to sea in the hope of winning her hand. Marriage, at least in theory for Southworth and her readers, is a divinely ordained and desirable state. Indeed, whatever personal ambivalence Southworth may have had toward the conjugal state, it constitutes the heart of her faith as a sentimental novelist. Hers was not a naive faith; women in her novels suffer when they contract marriages for the wrong reasons or when they are tied to bad husbands, but the standard of happiness against which the plights of these women are measured is the good marriage.

Baptized a Roman Catholic and raised an Episcopalian, Southworth had no deeper interest in the evangelical missionary cause than her heroine had. For the purposes of her story, the mission field was a useful device. What else in the mid-nineteenth century could one do with a heroine who would neither marry nor work, and who had no money? And how else was she to get both Britomarte and her lover on board ship so that they could be shipwrecked and cast ashore on a desert island with only their Girl Friday, the ship's Irish washerwoman, as a chaperone? Precisely because Southworth was not an insider in mission circles, we can assume that her portrayal reflects what was then common knowledge about foreign missions.

Southworth was clearly aware that mission boards preferred married missionaries. She has the board suggest to Britomarte that she marry one of the young clergymen headed for the field. Southworth writes that the board members

> urged upon her that such was the custom, that it was expedient, and that young ladies called to the work not only married missionaries here, where they had a full opportunity of knowing them beforehand, but that many of them also went out with the express understanding that they should marry, on the other side, missionaries that they had never set eyes on before. (*FP,* 131)

In this description of board practice and policy regarding the marriage of female missionary candidates, Southworth is historically accurate; virtually no single women were sent overseas as missionaries until after women's societies were organized to recruit and support them. Southworth's own distaste for this practice of arranging marriages is apparent when she sends the entire party out from Boston in unseasonably dreary weather—chilly and rainy—that mirrors the misgivings and tears of the two young wives who are embarking as strangers not only to each other but also to their husbands. Southworth suggests that they are already regretting the "fever of enthusiasm" that led them to see their duty in board-sponsored marriages.

Mary and Martha are, however, as their names suggest, types eminently suited to the role of missionary wife. One is an orphan, and the other is the child of a pious merchant willing to sacrifice his daughter on the altar of missions. Southworth gives the reader a keen sense of the sacrifices these women are making in leaving home and friends, and we do not wonder that "they wept bitterly behind their veils" (*FP,* 138). Yet romance triumphs; even these girls grow into satisfied wives and ardent proponents of the married state. We know that they have won the Southworth seal of approval when we learn that they and their husbands miraculously survived the shipwreck and are sending home cheery reports from Farther India.

Meanwhile Britomarte and her suitor lead a Crusoe-like existence on their island, blissfully ignorant of the Civil War raging in the states, until they are rescued by a Union ship. Saving the Union strikes them as a more worthy cause than converting heathen, so they head home to take up arms on the side of righteousness. Britomarte returns to American soil without having soiled her reputation or changed her mind on the question of marriage; but neither has she undergone the desired " 'sea change into something new and strange,' namely a woman free from the fraility of love" (*FP,* 137). Instead, Southworth hints that in the sequel Britomarte's love for Justin will grow strong enough to overcome her intellectual reservations against marriage.

*Fair Play* presents the missionary enterprise in a favorable light as a respectable undertaking for a virtuous woman. It shows, however, no place for single women on the mission field. Britomarte conveniently never reaches India. This is fortunate indeed, for one can scarcely imagine what Southworth would have done with her had she been deposited anywhere but on an uninhabited desert isle. Even on board ship, Britomarte's only contribution to the spiritual life of the missionary party had been to raise her glorious voice in hymns of praise. The other women had not even done that much, but they were clearly fulfilling their entire duty simply by being wives to their missionary husbands. They were not required to "do" anything in order to "be" missionaries.

Southworth's novel was written just as the woman's foreign mission movement was beginning. The first women's boards were organized in the late 1860s and early 1870s. When Kate Douglas Wiggin published *Rebecca of Sunnybrook Farm* in 1903, the situation had changed radically. Single women, largely recruited and supported by women's societies, had swollen the ranks of female mis-

sionaries to the point that more than 60 percent of all mission personnel were women. In several denominations the wives of missionaries were no longer counted as missionaries unless they also
functioned as teachers, doctors, nurses, evangelists, or social workers. The woman's role in the missionary enterprise was no longer
passive in any sense. Indeed, more broadly speaking, passivity was
no longer a characteristic of the ideal woman; the New Woman who
emerged in the 1890s was a doer. What a woman could do remained
circumscribed by notions of women as naturally oriented toward
service, but missionary service obviously met the criteria of a nurturing profession suited to feminine propensities. The emergence of
this New Woman in the nineties affected the portrayal of women in
fiction. Child heroines became active sprites like Rebecca, not
models of the good dying young like little Eva in *Uncle Tom's Cabin.*
Wiggin's Rebecca is characterized as "not perfection, for that's a
post afraid to move, but a dancing sprig of the tree next to it."[4]

Wiggin was a kindergarten educator of no little renown when
she wrote the first Rebecca book. Rebecca was created not only to
entertain girls but also to instruct them. Wiggin's didacticism is
charmingly concealed—and therefore particularly effective. Her
prose has a comfortable, homely tone. Her characters are skillfully
drawn to expose both the provinciality and the basic decency of the
villagers. As readers, we understand that Rebecca in growing up
will transcend the boundaries of small-town lives and minds, but we
see that she has much to learn from them. The incidents of her life in
Riverboro teach the reader as well as Rebecca the lessons that she
must learn if she is to achieve the gracious maturity that her bright,
girlish charm promises. Wiggin makes it clear that she considers a
well-cultivated religious sense an important element in the character
of a truly lovely woman. What constitutes this necessary religious
sensibility in Wiggin's view is especially apparent in the three chapters devoted to the visit of a Syrian missionary family to Riverboro.

Rebecca's involvement with the missionaries begins when she
represents her maiden aunts at an Aid Society meeting that illness
obliges them to miss. Wiggin's depiction of the meeting itself is an
accurate representation of village church life at the turn of the century, a vivid illustration of what has been termed the feminization of
American religion.[5] The meeting is attended by about a dozen ladies
and a deacon. The missionary couple occupies the platform in the

Sunday School room together, but Mr. Burch takes responsibility for running the meeting. He opens with prayer and leads in the singing of a missionary hymn that Rebecca accompanies on the melodeon.

The centrality of missions in local church affairs is evident in this scene, but so are some of Wiggin's reservations about missions. Evidence of the villagers' parochialism surfaces in the comments whispered to Rebecca during the meeting.

> That's Mrs. Burch on the platform with her husband. . . . She's awful tanned up, ain't she? If you're goin' to save souls seems like you hev' to part with your complexion. . . . They're poor as Job's turkey, . . . but if you give'em anything they'd turn right round and give it to the heathen. His congregation up to Parsonfield clubbed together and give him that gold watch he carries. I s'pose he'd 'a' handed that over too, only heathens always tell time by the sun 'n' don't need watches.[6]

Mrs. Burch is described as slim, tired, and frail looking, dressed in worn black silk. To the village women she is an object for pity and condescension as well as a model of religiously inspired selflessness. Wiggin seems to share their attitude. Missionaries are impractical, but appealing—especially to children. Wiggin describes Mr. Burch's talk as "much the usual sort of thing" with its plea for money (*RSF*, 183). But she gives him credit for being more appealing than most; this explains why he touches Rebecca's sensitive and romantic soul so deeply. Wiggin stresses the educational value of his talk.

> He interwove his discourse with stories of life in a foreign land,—of the manners, the customs, the speech, the point of view: even giving glimpses of the daily round, the common task, of his own household, the work of his devoted helpmate and their little group of children, all born under Syrian skies. (*RSF*, 183)

The significance of the missionary visit, as far as Wiggin is concerned, lies largely in its role in stretching Rebecca's imagination and sympathies beyond the narrow confines of the village, in giving her a sense of living in a large and diverse world. What is significant for us is that Wiggin used missionaries home on furlough as a natu-

ral way of introducing this perspective into a rural town in New England.

If to the ladies this is "much the usual sort of thing," to Rebecca it comes close to an epiphany.

> Rebecca sat entranced, having been given the key of another
> world. Riverboro had faded;...and she saw blue skies and
> burning stars, white turbans and gay colors; Mr. Burch had
> not said so, but perhaps there were mosques and temples and
> minarets and date-palms. What stories they must know, those
> children born under Syrian skies! Then she was called upon to
> play "Jesus shall reign where'er the sun." (*RSF* 183–84)

Called abruptly back to reality, Rebecca realizes with horror that
none of the good ladies is responding to the missionaries' request for
a place to spend the night and to hold a parlor meeting. (A parlor
meeting, Wiggin informs us, was customarily held to display native
costumes and handicrafts.) Reminded that in her grandfather's time
missionaries were never allowed to sleep elsewhere, Rebecca offers
the hospitality of her aunts' home.

The visit of the missionaries to the brick house proves a great
success. The Burches are charmed by Rebecca. Mrs. Burch tries to
recruit her for the mission field—not for her spiritual gifts but for the
temporal ones of language facility, musical talent, and executive
ability. Employing such temporary criteria in choosing candidates
for mission service was increasingly common in the era of "modern
missions" that was in full flower by the time Wiggin wrote the first
Rebecca book.

The effect of the Burches' visit on Rebecca is compared to an
outward and visible sign (like wearing a new dress or bowing one's
head in prayer) that has a positive influence on the inward spiritual
state. It is an effect, Wiggin claims, "not easily described." Yet, she
says, "from the vantage ground of after years, she [Rebecca] felt
that the moment...marked an epoch in her life" (*RSF* 209). Wiggin's description of that "moment" reflects a liberal, Bushnellian
view of Christian nurture.

> Her spirit soared towards a great light, dimly discovered at
> first, but brighter as she came closer to it. To become sensible

of oneness with the Divine heart before any sense of separation
has been felt, this is surely the most beautiful way for the child
to find God. (*RSF,* 210)

*Rebecca of Sunnybrook Farm* proved so popular that a sequel was
almost inevitable in a children's book market that relied heavily on
serials. In *New Chronicles of Rebecca,* published in 1907, Wiggin returned to the missionary theme. Rebecca's "Thought Book," repro-
duced for her faithful fans, reveals that being a missionary was,
along with painter, writer, and teacher, among the careers that Rebecca considered seriously—and discarded. Wiggin devotes an entire chapter to the incident that led Rebecca to give up her
missionary ambitions. The Burches' visit is recalled, and we are told
that "the romance of that visit had never died in [Rebecca's] heart"
(*NCR,* 38). We learn that Mrs. Burch has kept in touch with Rebecca, and has encouraged her to form a children's branch of the missionary society in Riverboro. (By 1907, children's missionary bands
were a firmly established subsidiary of the woman's missionary
movement.) Mrs. Burch's motive, aside from garnering a few extra
pennies for the cause, is to instill the habit of supporting missions
early in life.

The little girls, however, decide on more active participation
than Mrs. Burch had anticipated. They hold a meeting in a barn loft
while their mothers are attending their quarterly missionary meeting, and they constitute themselves as the Daughters of Zion. Rebecca, with her natural executive talent, emerges as president. The
meeting itself is a gentle parody of adult behavior. The girls address
issues ranging from the troubling question of the "accountability of
the heathen" (which had been much debated in the churches during
the nineties) to whether or not it would be permissible to draw lots at
a missionary meeting.

Believing that they are not yet ready for foreign missions, the
girls decide to start with a home mission project. They pick the
"very most heathenish and reperrehensiblest [*sic*] person in Riverboro" (*NCR,* 46) as their first target and send out one of their number as an emissary. She is chased away by the outraged old man who
threatens to set his dog on her the next time. This episode considerably dampens the girls' enthusiasm for mission work. And, Wiggin
tells us, for Rebecca the incident was particularly instructive be-

cause "all at once the adult point of view dawned upon Rebecca" (*NCR,* 55). The little society disbands. Rebecca retreats to the brick house

> to do overcasting as hard as I can, because I hate that the worst. Aunt Jane must write to Mrs. Burch that we don't want to be home missionaries. Perhaps we're not big enough anyway. I'm perfectly certain it's nicer to convert people when they're yellow or brown or any color but white; and I believe it must be easier to save their souls than it is to make them go to meeting. (*NCR,* 57)

The adult point of view that Rebecca has encountered is, one suspects, Wiggin's own view. The brick house is a bastion of civilized manners and New England reserve; Rebecca's retreat to the brick house marks her assent to her aunts' strictures against meddling in others' private lives. While Wiggin does not exactly disapprove of efforts to Christianize—and thereby civilize—other cultures, she obviously has a certain distaste for unbridled emotionalism in religion. She is teaching her audience that impulsive behavior proceeding as it may from the best of motives must be curbed in maturity; passionate natures like Rebecca's must be disciplined.

Wiggin's attitude toward missions is ambiguous. Despite the fact that she makes the little girls fail in their efforts and has Rebecca discard as childish her notion of being a missionary, Wiggin portrays Rebecca's interest in missions as evidence of the fineness of her spirit. (When she finally transcends the parochialism of Riverboro and achieves the level of worldly wisdom and sophistication of a Kate Douglas Wiggin, Rebecca will, the novel hints, marry rich and handsome Adam Ladd—a poor boy made good—who has been watching over Rebecca, waiting for this charming child to grow into a nearly perfect specimen of American womanhood. It does not matter, finally, how many childish careers Rebecca abandons; she is destined, like Wiggin herself, to end up as a businessman's wife.) The missionary episode is a catalyst, moving Rebecca morally and spiritually closer to full womanhood. That a writer not particularly sympathetic to the missionary crusade would use missionaries to introduce her heroine to broader cultural and spiritual horizons testifies to how deeply missions had penetrated the lives and imaginations of American women.

If a career as a missionary was still "thinkable" for Rebecca in 1907 and if the inculcation of at least a generalized religiosity was an important part of becoming a woman for the girls who read the Rebecca novels, then Elllen Glasgow's *Barren Ground* of 1925 reflects a drastically secularized culture. Glasgow's novel offers a fascinating contrast between the generations of her protagonist Dorinda and of Dorinda's mother. Dorinda, we are told, grew up browsing "happily among the yellowed pages in [her grandfather's] library, returning again and again to the Waverley Novels, or the exciting Lives of the Missionaries."[7] At age fifteen Dorinda joined the church, experiencing grace as "a softly glowing ecstasy, which flooded her soul...while the prosaic duties of life were infused with a beauty, a light" (*BG,* 60). So far her life fell into a conventional and accepted pattern, the same pattern that had made religion the central and sustaining force in her mother's drab existence. Then, for Dorinda, for no apparent reason, "suddenly, as mysteriously as it had come, the illumination in her soul waned and flickered out like a lamp. Religion had not satisfied" (*BG,* 60).

Love does not satisfy Dorinda either. She rejects men and marriage not, like Britomarte, innocently and for political reasons, but in reaction to betrayal by a man she loved deeply. To love too hard is, Glasgow informs us, a trait of the women in Dorinda's family. Dorinda's great-aunts were both crossed in love. One attempted suicide, survived, sobered up, and married sensibly. The other went insane and had to be confined to a locked room for a time. When she recovered her wits she went overseas as a missionary, saying that "anybody could be a fool once, but only a born fool was ever a fool twice" (*BG,* 103). A pattern of marriage or missionary service was then part of Dorinda's family tradition. And Dorinda's own mother was haunted throughout her life by her recurring dream of being a missionary in Africa. At times it threatened her sanity and drove her to the brink of suicide. Her story as she told it to Dorinda is worth repeating in full.

"But when I was just a girl, not more than sixteen or seventeen, I felt the call to be a missionary, and I wanted it, I s'pose, more than I've ever wanted anything in my life. I reckon it started with my favorite hymn, the missionary one. Even as a little child I used to think and dream about India's coral strand and Afric's sunny fountains. That was why I got engaged to

Gordon Kane. I wasn't what you'd call in love with him; but I believed the Lord had intended me for work in foreign fields, and it seemed, when Gordon asked me to marry him, that an opportunity had been put in my way. I had my trunk all packed to go to the Congo to join him. I was just folding up my wedding-dress of white organdie, when they broke the news to me of his death." She gasped and choked for a moment. "After that I put the thought of the heathen out of my mind.... Your great-grandfather said I was too young to decide whether I had a special vocation or not; and then before I came out of mourning, I met your father, and we were married. For a while I seemed to forget all about the missionary call, but it came back just before Josiah was born, and I've had it ever since whenever I'm worried and feel that I'll have to get away from things or go clean out of my mind. Then I begin to have that dream about coral strands and palm trees and ancient rivers and naked black babies thrown to crocodiles. When it first came I tried to drive it away by hard work, and that was the way I got in the habit of working to rest my mind. I was so afraid that folks would begin to say I was unhinged. Sometimes in my sleep [it comes back still]. When I'm awake I never think of it now except on missionary Sunday when we sing that hymn.... I used to know all those pictures by heart in your great-grandfather's books about Asia and Africa. It was a wild streak in me, I reckon," she conceded humbly, "but with the Lord's help, I've managed to stamp it out." (*BG,* 120–21)

The enchantment the mission field held for Dorinda's mother as a child is strikingly similar to its effect on Rebecca. Yet Glasgow portrays Dorinda's mother as a sick woman, one with a troubled and disturbed mind, who struggles to maintain her sanity. But we are not meant to assume that this woman's troubles stem from her thwarted missionary ambitions. Rather we are to understand that for a woman of her generation, from a family so closely tied to the missionary enterprise, the particular form that her delusions take is not surprising. Dorinda fears the same wild streak in herself—with some justification. She, too, spends much of her life "stamping out" her great passion. The significant difference is that missions are not a natural focus for Dorinda's passionate imagination.

The specific, religious form of the mother's fantasy never troubles Dorinda. The relegation of religious concerns to an older generation is made explicit in Dorinda's encounter with a Gospel Wagon. The elderly evangelists she finds busily nailing texts to trees are retired African missionaries. To Dorinda this shabby, broken-down pair represent her mother's missionary dream "come to life" (*BG*, 59). It has no appeal for her. As the couple drives off, the words of a hymn—one of her mother's favorites—float back to her "growing fainter and thinner as the distance widened" (*BG*, 60). The images of decline and diminishment that mark this passage reflect both Dorinda's and Glasgow's estimation of the place of religion in the modern world. When Dorinda's crisis comes, she never considers the mission field an escape as her great-aunt had. Instead, she takes the first train to New York City. She supports herself in the city as a doctor's receptionist. Rather than marry the doctor's partner, she takes night classes in scientific agriculture and eventually returns to Virginia to take on the ordinarily masculine task of subduing the land. She wrests a living from the land and satisfaction from becoming the most successful farmer in the county. Dorinda lives in a world in which women had more choices than were available to either Britomarte or Rebecca; becoming a missionary no longer functions in the same way as a romantic and exotic alternative to marriage or teaching. Dorinda is free to reject romance as well as religion because she can support herself. Only in middle age does she relent enough from her determination to stamp out romance in her life to marry a man who shares her progressive agricultural views— and who is physically and sexually a clownish figure willing to submit to her domination. Obviously neither the Waverley Novels nor the Lives of the Missionaries left a permanent imprint on Dorinda's psyche. The missionary impulse that had driven her mother is transmogrified in Dorinda into a mission to reclaim the land from the broomsedge that had overgrown it. Her mission deals only with concrete, physical realities.

> All her trouble, she felt, had come to her from trying to make life over into something it was not. Dreams, that was the danger. Like her mother she had tried to find a door in the wall, an escape from the tyranny of things as they are; and like her mother, she had floundered among visions. (*BG*, 182)

The trouble with religion—and with daydreams of romance—was that they were evasions of cold, hard realities. And so Dorinda rejected the romantic and sentimental in life just as Glasgow rejected it in literature. The light that science shed on the modern world had, for Dorinda and Glasgow, discredited religion and made obsolete the romance of missions that had moved earlier generations of women.

The progress traced here, from the heroine of a sentimental novel to a heroine who rejects sentiment, parallels the changing role of women both within the Protestant mission movement and in middle-class American culture. Each of these bright and vibrant protagonists embodies a set of cultural attitudes that had important ramifications for the woman's foreign mission movement. Southworth's heroine, with her burning sense of a mission to women, is separated only by her feminism from the ideology that informed the woman's mission movement at the formative stage. The following chapter examines that Victorian ideal of womanhood and demonstrates how, reinforced by a theology of missions that attached special significance to the conversion of mothers as the most efficient means of Christianizing heathen lands, it made foreign missions a more attractive object for female benevolence than any of the other causes promoted by female voluntary associations in late-nineteenth-century America.

# Chapter 2

# A Congenial Object

Fiction frequently reflects social reality. It is not merely coincidental that Britomarte Conyers, the heroine of Mrs. Southworth's vacuous romance, rejected an arranged marriage and insisted upon being sent to the mission field as a single woman at precisely the time women were organizing themselves into societies to send single women overseas as missionaries. Spurred on by the formation of the Woman's Union Missionary Society in 1860, female missionary societies proliferated in the evangelical Protestant churches in America in the final third of the nineteenth century. American women, responding to appeals made by returned missionaries and their wives, mobilized on behalf of their heathen sisters; they shared Britomarte's sense of a mission to women, but not her man-hating feminism or her rejection of American culture. Their goal was to uplift heathen woman, to elevate her to the heights inhabited by Christian womanhood in America. Their efforts in this direction constituted, as the persistence of a missionary theme in popular fiction testifies, more than a minor current in the history of women as well as in the history of missions.

Historians of American religion, when they have not ignored the ladies altogether, have tended to place their activities in footnotes to denominational histories.[1] In this case to divide is to trivialize. If the organization of women's foreign missionary societies is considered—as it was by the participants—as an interdenominational movement, it emerges as the largest of the great nineteenth-century women's movements and as perhaps the largest nineteenth-century religious movement in America. In the history of missions, women's societies have been pointed to as a manifestation of missionary expansion in the last decades of the century; but their role in generating enthusiasm for missions as well as collecting money and recruiting candidates for foreign service has been largely overlooked in studies that focus on the activities of denominational mission

boards and of a handful of prominent missionary statesmen. Yet
sheer numbers alone would argue that the woman's movement be
given serious consideration; by the turn of the century, women enjoyed a numerical advantage on the mission field as they long had on
the membership rolls of America's Protestant churches. If the activism that is said to characterize American religion and American missions is to be fully understood, surely the activities of churchwomen
and female missionaries must be examined. From the perspective of
women's history, it is equally important that a movement which enlisted millions of women be placed in the tradition of female voluntary associations to which historians of women in nineteenth-
century America have assigned considerable significance.

The importance of voluntary associations in American society
has attracted comment since Alexis de Tocqueville first published his
observations on the subject. Tocqueville was particularly impressed
with the variety of ends for which Americans formed associations.

> Americans of all ages, all conditions, and all dispositions con-
> stantly form associations. They have not only commercial and
> manufacturing companies, in which all take part, but associa-
> tions of a thousand other kinds, religious, moral, serious, fu-
> tile, general or restricted, enormous or diminutive. The
> Americans make associations to give entertainments, to found
> seminaries, to build inns, to construct churches, to diffuse
> books, to send missionaries to the antipodes; in this manner
> they found hospitals, prisons, and schools. If it is proposed to
> inculcate some truth or to foster some feeling by the encourage-
> ment of a great example, they form a society.[2]

Tocqueville, traveling in America in the 1830s, observed that individuals in a democratic society obtained and exercised power by
combining in associations. As he points out, this was a technique
that could be adopted for practically any purpose. At least it was a
method that men used for many purposes. The particular—and
more restricted—nature and function of voluntary associations
among women has engaged the attention of historians writing about
the female experience in America.

Nancy Cott notes that in the early years of the nineteenth century, while men formed associations for every conceivable reason,

women organized primarily for religious and charitable ends.[3] Yet women clearly shared the American propensity for joining societies; Kathryn Sklar estimates that in New England, "at the peak of the Great Revival in the 1830's a significant proportion—at least one-third and probably a majority—of adult women were members of one or more such [female religious, charitable, or reform] associations."[4] Historians have concluded that membership in such societies had a profound effect on the women involved; Carroll Smith-Rosenberg's influential article on the American Female Moral Reform Society argues that in the tenets of evangelical religion women found the legitimation they needed to leave the confines of the home on a crusade to enjoin upon men the standards of sexual morality by which they, as pious women, abided. She suggests that these women were motivated by frustration at their powerlessness as well as by piety and that they discovered a source of power and emotional satisfaction in female solidarity. Ruth Bordin, in her recent study of the Woman's Christian Temperance Union (WCTU), has uncovered a strikingly similar dynamic. Unlike the earlier Moral Reform campaign, however, the WCTU gradually incorporated explicitly feminist goals into its national program. In that respect it resembles the secular woman's club movement of the late nineteenth century which, according to Karen Blair, demonstrated an increasingly feminist orientation as it shifted its emphasis from self-culture to municipal reform. Ordinarily, participation in benevolent associations did not transform middle-class women into radical feminists; instead, these female voluntary associations served as a bridge between the domestic sphere and the male-dominated arena of public life. Crossing that bridge eventually changed women's estimation of themselves and their capabilities, but they initially ventured out of the home on missions suited to their notions of woman's nature and her special talents.[5]

The view of woman's nature formulated in the early years of the nineteenth century constituted a profound departure from traditional religious and philosophical evaluations of the female of the species. Historians have offered various explanations for the change, but their descriptions of the content of this new understanding of woman's nature are remarkably consistent.[6] Women, under the new scheme, were valued for a primary and sacred function as mother. Ideal motherhood encompassed a full complement of virtues and responsibilities. Mothers reigned supreme in the domestic sphere; their responsibility was to make the home a training ground for future citizens and a haven for beleaguered husbands seeking refuge from the brutalities of the new industrial order. It was believed that women had been endowed by nature with special qualities that fitted them for these tasks. Their sensitivity and innate compassion made them naturally susceptible to the teachings of religion—especially a religion that featured a gentle Jesus and a benevolent Father anxious for His children to find salvation. Women were judged, as a result of both nature and training, peculiarly capable of the self-denial and self-sacrifice that Christianity demanded. Hence, as mothers, they were regarded as the natural nurturers of religion and morality in their offspring. As models of piety and moral virtue they were also expected to exert moral guidance in the culture at large through their influence over fathers, husbands, sons, and brothers.

The elevation of woman to the office of moral guardian in the society reflected the radically revised estimation of woman's essential nature. Gender differentiation in Puritan society had been a matter of function and convention, not of moral theology; the doctrine of original sin granted women equality of depravity with men. Women were not considered naturally religious. The Puritans used marriage as their primary analogy for the relationship of the individual—and the church—to God, but this analogy applied equally to men and women. The higher conversion rate among women in New England after the first generation may reflect the fact that training for housewifery inculcated patterns of behavior and response appropriate for a relationship with God; or it may be that, as Gerald Moran has argued, the life experience of married women—particularly the occasions for reflection upon mortality provided by frequent pregnancies—encouraged conversion; but nothing in Puritan theology suggests that woman's nature was closer than man's to that of the Divine Nurturer. Indeed, the nurturing aspect of God was not one that the Puritans emphasized. The marriage analogy of which they were so fond firmly establishes the masculinity of the Deity. Puritan men, who were expected to adopt a feminine, wifely role when they turned to God, exercised a God-like function within their earthly families as husbands and fathers. The Puritan male was responsible for the moral governance of his household. Theology placed him on an equal moral footing with his wife, but practice made him the moral arbiter in his family as the minister was in society.[7]

In the eighteenth century, as Puritan theology loosened its grip on the minds of Americans, certain Enlightenment ideas about the nature of male and female began to replace the concept of moral equality before the judgment seat of God. Enlightenment thought not only separated reason and emotion—and devalued the latter—it also associated reason with men and emotion with women. Women were judged emotional and sensual creatures, ruled by their appetites and lacking higher rational faculties. They were considered not only scarcely educable, but also incapable of moral reasoning. It was imperative therefore that they be subjected to the moral guidance of fathers and husbands. Eternally children, they were governed, for the good of society, by male relatives who embodied rational authority.[8]

The glorified vision of womanhood that characterized Victorian ideology was indebted to the *philosophes* for its broad outlines; like them, the Victorians assigned distinctive natures to male and female. Women remained associated primarily with emotion rather than reason. In important ways, however, the Victorian vision reverses Enlightenment notions. The emotions, under Romantic influences, no longer had attached to them the negative connotations that the Enlightenment had fastened upon them. To the Romantic, a sensual and emotional nature was one receptive to beauty in all its aspects. The Romantics redefined beauty itself, rejecting the formal, ordered qualities central to Enlightenment concepts of beauty. In the Romantic view, beauty could be apprehended intuitively rather than appreciated for its conformity to rigorously applied formal standards.

When the discussion of beauty is transposed from the aesthetic to the theological realm, the new ideas concerning beauty have far-reaching implications for women. If moral beauty is apprehended intuitively rather than intellectually, then women with their emotional natures are peculiarly capable of appreciating moral virtues. As more emotional creatures, women are more susceptible than men to religious emotion. As early as the First Great Awakening of enthusiastic revivalism in the eighteenth century women had, of course, been deemed especially prone to religious enthusiasm, but it had not been generally counted to their credit in an age suspicious of enthusiastic religion. In contrast, evangelical Protestantism in the nineteenth century unabashedly employed emotional revivalism, applauded emotional conversions, and celebrated woman's religious receptivity.[9]

The influences of evangelical Christianity and Romanticism converged in the early nineteenth century to reinforce and reinterpret the special role assigned woman in the wake of political and economic revolution. The reorganization of labor that accompanied industrialization separated the home from the workplace, effectively confining middle-class women to a newly restricted domestic sphere and limiting their economic functions. Evangelical religion glorified this limited sphere of activity by placing new emphasis on the sanctity of the home. Simultaneously, republican ideology spawned what Linda Kerber calls "Republican Motherhood," which assigned women the critical task of training their sons to be citizens. The influence of the home was expected to have its effect on the public sphere through the agency of husbands, brothers, and sons.[10] This indirect method of controlling and raising the moral tone of society was supplemented, increasingly as the century wore on, by more direct participation of women in reform as members of female voluntary associations.

The persistence of the idea of woman's special nature, however, determined the particular reforms in which women heavily involved themselves. Through voluntary associations dedicated to ends in which female interest was considered natural, women brought their influence to bear on social problems that excited their sympathies. They were encouraged to join charitable associations not only by their ministers, but also by the women like Sarah Hale, editor of *Godey's Lady's Book,* and Catharine Beecher, of the famous Beecher clan, who most vigorously urged their sisters to accept a subordinate status in political and public life in exchange for dominion over the newly glorified domestic sphere.[11]

Catharine Beecher's *Treatise on Domestic Economy,* so popular with the American housewife that it was reprinted annually for many years after its initial publication in 1841, devotes an entire chapter to the topic "On Giving in Charity." Beecher argues that as "self-denying benevolence" was "the grand peculiarity of the character of Christ" so anyone who hopes to attain a Christ-like character must practice benevolence.[12] The theology is Hopkinsian, but its application is strictly feminine: Beecher urges women to keep strict household accounts in order to eliminate superfluities from their budgets, thus freeing small sums for charity. Acutely aware that women did not control large amounts of money, Beecher realized that for the funds at their disposal to be used effectively they would have to be pooled. Administering such funds through voluntary associations was the solution she endorsed—in language that suggests her fondness for organization and her complacency with the social order.

> Another point to be attended to, is the importance of maintaining a system of *associated* charities. There is no point, in which the economy of charity has more improved, than in the present mode of combining many small contributions for sustaining enlarged and systematic plans of charity. . . . In a democracy, like ours, where few are very rich. . . this collecting and dispensing of drops and rills is the mode by which, in imitation of Nature, the dews and showers are to distil on parched and desert lands. And every person, while earning a mere pittance to unite with many more, may be cheered with the consciousness of sustaining a grand system of operations, which must have the most decided influence in raising all mankind to that perfect state of society, which Christianity is designed to secure.[13]

In constructing this perfect society, women have, according to Beecher, specific tasks that reflect their natural concern with matters of nurture, religion, and morality. They have "no interest or concern," she announces, in "civil and political affairs"; but "in matters pertaining to the education of their children, in the selection and support of a clergyman, in all benevolent enterprises, and in all questions relating to morals or manners, they have a superior influence."[14] The ends for which women organized in the early part of the nineteenth century—to rescue indigent women from forced prostitution, to curb the sale of distilled spirits, to distribute tracts and Bibles, to establish orphanages, and to contribute their mites to the growing missionary movement—met with Beecher's approbation. The goals of these associations were, by her criteria, appropriate concerns for women as mothers and as the moral guardians of society.

Beecher, however, refused to countenance the participation of women in antislavery agitation. In the controversy that raged over the promiscuous behavior of the Grimké sisters in addressing mixed audiences in New England in 1837, Beecher sided with the Congregational ministers who warned of "the dangers which...threaten the female character with wide-spread and permanent injury." Refraining from attacking the Grimkés specifically, the ministers explained that the New Testament itself indicates that woman's power and influence ought to be private and unobtrusive. The Congregational clergymen approved "all such associated effort as becomes the modesty of her sex," but expatiated on the evils that would befall women who became public reformers.

> When she assumes the place and tone of man as a public reformer, our care and protection of her seem unnecessary;... she yields the power which God has given her for protection, and her character becomes unnatural. If the vine, whose strength and beauty is to lean upon the trellis-work and half conceal its clusters, thinks to assume the independence and the overshadowing nature of the elm, it will not only cease to bear fruit, but fall in shame and dishonor into the dust. We cannot, therefore, but regret the mistaken conduct of those who encourage females to bear an obtrusive and ostentatious part in measures of reform, and countenance any of that sex who so far forget themselves as to itinerate in the character of public lecturers and teachers.[15]

Catharine Beecher accorded woman somewhat more backbone than the clerics' clinging vine image suggests, but she was in essential agreement with the Congregational pastors in defining the very private sphere in which woman's influence ought to operate. Beecher was as outraged by the Grimkés' behavior as the clergymen. Angelina Grimké had been Beecher's pupil and protégé for a brief period in 1831; perhaps this personal connection encouraged Beecher to take pen in hand. Whatever the compelling reason, Beecher published an extended "Essay on Slavery and Abolitionism" in 1837 which she addressed to Miss A. D. Grimké. Beecher devotes nearly one hundred of her one hundred fifty pages to her general objections to abolitionism; she finds its methods inflammatory, "contrary to the dictates of common sense,...the rules of good breeding

and the laws of the gospel." Having demolished the abolitionist
cause on general principles, she turns to a consideration of "the
just bounds of female influence, and the times, places, and manner
in which it can be appropriately exerted." She rehearses the argument, developed more fully in her *Treatise,* for female subordination
in social relations. Such subordination, she claims, is not dependent on or reflective of inferiority "either in intellectual or moral
worth." Indeed, Beecher felt herself the intellectual equal and the
moral superior of most men, but she believed it expedient—and ultimately beneficial—for women to choose a subordinate role in
society.[16]

Beecher argues that the divine design was not that woman's influence should be less than man's but that the mode of exercising it
should be "altogether different and peculiar." The peaceful and benevolent principles that Beecher considered the essence of Christianity are to guide and govern woman's behavior. In contrast—and
without explanation beyond gender differentiation for their exemp-
tion from the dictates of Christianity—men may lawfully engage in
activities that women must eschew in Beecher's scheme.

> A man may act on society by the collision of intellect, in public
> debate; he may urge his measures by a sense of shame, by fear
> and by personal interest; he may coerce by the combination of
> public sentiment; he may drive by physical force, and he does
> not overstep the boundaries of his sphere.

Women, on the other hand, were "to win everything by peace and
love." They were to make themselves so loved and respected that
their male relatives would gladly defer to their wishes. This was,
however, "to be all accomplished in the domestic and social circle,"
for Beecher firmly believed that "all the sacred protection of religion, all the generous promptings of chivalry, all the poetry of romantic gallantry, depend upon woman's retaining her place as
dependent and defenceless, and making no claims, and maintaining
no rights."[17]

Having relegated her sex to wresting power from dependency,
Beecher explores the limits of the sphere inhabited by those who
must strike a delicate balance between cultivating weakness and exercising influence. The limits Beecher prescribes for women are specifically behavioral.

A woman may seek the aid of co-operation and combination among her own sex, to assist her in her appropriate offices of piety, charity, maternal and domestic duty; but whatever, in any measure, throws a woman into the attitude of a combatant, either for herself or others—whatever binds her in a party conflict—whatever obliges her in any way to exert coercive influences, throws her out of her appropriate sphere.

By Beecher's standards the abolition cause was clearly beyond the pale for women; she objected to the methods even of the men who led the movement. But abolitionism was only a case in point for Beecher; she opposed the exercise of any political role by women. The one political right allowed women in Jacksonian America, the right to petition, seemed to her "IN ALL CASES, to fall entirely without the sphere of female duty."[18]

The only role in which Beecher felt it appropriate for a woman to step outside the domestic sphere was as a teacher; she was herself an educator and the founder of several female seminaries. But she argued that it was precisely because America would soon be "distinguished above all other nations, for well-educated females, and for the influence they will exert on the general interests of society" that American women needed to be especially careful to "appreciate the wisdom of that ordinance that appointed her subordinate station." Catharine Beecher had spent years persuading prospective donors for her schools that educating women would not make them unwomanly. It was an article of faith with her that "while intellectual culture in the female mind, is combined with the spirit of that religion which so strongly enforces the appropriate duties of a woman's sphere," American women would continue to be models for the rest of the world of "retiring modesty, virtue, and domestic faithfulness." Christianity, in her view, could countenance the education of females so long as they remained submissive to male domination of political and commercial realms.[19]

Women did, according to Beecher, have a special role to play in the agitation over the slavery question; they were to be mediators and advocates of peace. Beecher pled for *"calm rational Christian discussion"* to persuade the South that relinquishing slavery would be in its own highest interest. Well aware in 1837 of the explosive potential of the controversy, she called on women to pour oil on troubled waters.

The question of slavery involves more pecuniary interests, touches more private relations, involves more prejudices, is entwined with more sectional, party, and political interests, than any other which can ever again arise. It is a matter which, if discussed and controlled without the influence of these principles of charity and peace, will shake this nation like an earthquake, and pour over us the volcanic waves of every terrific passion. The trembling earth, the low murmuring thunders, already admonish us of our danger; and if females can exert any saving influence in this emergency, it is time for them to awake.[20]

Beecher believed that the key to salvation did lie in the hands of Christian women who were peculiarly suited to embodying the graces of a gentle Jesus. And she did not deny that women had the rational capacity to discuss this matter with men; but she feared that women would lose the power to exert their Christ-like influence if they discarded their peculiar, domestic access to moral virtue and joined the ranks of partisans in public disputation.

Angelina Grimké answered Catharine Beecher in a series of letters that elaborate the radically different lesson that she drew from Christianity on the nature and duty of women. Grimké's religious perspective as a Quaker provided her with a basis for dissenting from the prevalent view of woman's nature that Beecher held and promulgated. Grimké objected strenuously to the religion Beecher espoused (and that Grimké feared might indeed be the character of Christianity in America in 1837).

Thou seemest to think...that Christianity is just such a weak, dependent, puerile creature as thou hast described woman to be. In my opinion thou hast robbed both the one and the other of all their true dignity and glory. Thy descriptions may suit the prevailing Christianity of this age, and the general character of woman; and if so, we have great cause for shame and confusion of face.[21]

Grimké was persuaded that a radical moral equality among individuals—regardless of sex or race—was the central message of Christianity. Beginning with this premise, she argued that it is untenable to define a "different rule of acting" for women than that which obtains for men. She objected specifically to Beecher's suggestion that women cooperate and combine for appropriate ends. Grimké felt the impossibility of marking out "Appropriate offices!" and demanded rhetorically,

> Who has ever attempted to draw a line of separation between the duties of men and women, as *moral* beings, without committing the grossest inconsistencies on the one hand, or running into the most arrant absurdities on the other?[22]

Beecher and Grimké, in their public controversy, defined the parameters of the debate over the appropriate role for women that racked the abolition movement. This dispute not only precipitated an organizational split in the ranks of the American antislavery crusade, but also led indirectly to the crystallization of a woman's rights movement in America. It was the exclusion of the female American delegates to the World Antislavery Convention in London in 1840 that sparked the feminist fires smoldering in the breasts of Elizabeth Cady Stanton and Lucretia Mott and eventually led them to call for a Woman's Rights Convention at Seneca Falls, New York, in 1848. The Declaration of Principles drawn up at Seneca Falls transposed Grimké's assertion of absolute equality from the moral to the political realm.

The woman's rights crusade attracted adherents among Quaker women who shared the religious assumptions of Grimké and Mott and among political liberals and freethinkers who, like Stanton, adopted the rhetoric of the revolutionaries of both America and France and applied it to the situation of women. Both groups shared a belief in the radical equality of individuals regardless of sex or race. The number of women who espoused such radical egalitarianism and became actively involved as abolitionists or crusaders for woman's rights remained relatively small. The bulk of middle-class American women found themselves more nearly in accord with Beecher. They confined their activities to prayer groups, temperance, tract, and benevolent societies. Female abolitionists and woman's rights advocates of either the Quaker or the freethinking variety converted few women; they failed entirely to dislodge the entrenched notion that woman's peculiar nature fitted her for the domestic sphere—and for particular types of reform and moral suasion.

Despite the rather small number involved, the woman's rights crusade attracted a great deal of publicity, especially in the years after the Civil War. Much of the attention it received was highly critical, particularly within the ranks of evangelical Protestantism. (Only when, toward the end of the century, the movement narrowed its goal to woman's suffrage and dropped radical egalitarianism for the argument that giving women the vote would raise the moral tone of the nation's political life did it begin to find advocates among evangelical women.)

American Protestantism in the nineteenth century heartily endorsed the view of women that Beecher held. Women who took up the cause of foreign missions after the Civil War were explicit in their rejection of egalitarianism and felt compelled to dissociate themselves and their movement from the woman's rights crusade. An editorial in the first issue of *Woman's Work for Woman,* the journal of the Woman's Foreign Missionary Society of the Presbyterian Church (North), offers an extended comparison of the "two very different movements going on at this time among the women of our country." What the writer gives as a descriptive account of the woman's rights crusade uses language that reveals her negative attitude toward that movement.

> One [of the movements] insists upon what its promoters call the equality of woman with man. It seeks to give to her whatever advantage in the battle of life is supposed to belong to man; to afford her the opportunity (and more than this, to lay it upon her as a duty) to push her way into public life, to the polls and the rostrum. She is to let no man come between her and any right which she can fight for and win, no matter how much of womanliness or delicacy she must lose in gaining the victory.... They insist on *rights,* they talk of the down-trodden position of women in this free and happy land, and call upon her to take and keep the place which these dissatisfied few claim to be rightly hers.

The editorialist is clearly not among the dissatisfied few, and the movement she is promoting does not ask any woman to jeopardize her womanliness and delicacy. Instead it calls upon woman *qua* woman to join the most selfless of all benevolent causes:

The simultaneous effort among women, in several denominations of Christians, to take a more active part...in extending
the blessings which they enjoy to their less favored sisters in
heathen lands. These women feel that to the Gospel they owe
the place of honor and of dignity which is theirs in this Christian land....So they...reach forth to the other side of the
world to bring love and hope to those who are wasting their
lives in idle ignorance of the capabilities of true womanhood
...the blessings of wifehood...the holy responsibility of motherhood.[23]

Could any movement more perfectly fulfill the criteria set forth by
Beecher in her discussion of the "appropriate offices" for which
women might consociate?

That the woman's foreign mission movement embodied the
ideal of organized evangelical womanhood does not by itself explain
the inception of the movement or its rapid growth in the decades immediately following the Civil War. Its embodiment of a conservative
ideal does, however, suggest that those who have seen the mass
women's movements of the postwar period as offshoots of the abolitionist and woman's rights crusades are mistaken. One must look to
such diverse factors as war and education to uncover causative explanations for these phenomena. The war itself certainly had a more
pervasive effect on the lives of ordinary women than had the example of a handful of militant female reformers.

The exigencies of war required many women to fill the civilian
roles of absent husbands and fathers; women were also called upon
to act publicly in collective as well as individual capacities. War relief
efforts challenged women to exercise organizational and managerial
skills not ordinarily attributed to them. Their performance under
the auspices of the celebrated Sanitary Commission, itself "an out-
growth of the Women's Central Association for Relief of the Sick
and Wounded of the Army" was especially creditable.[24] Women emerged from the war years with an enlarged sense of their responsibilities and their capability. That did not mean, however, that their
basic assumptions about themselves and their special gifts had
changed; ideology rarely keeps pace with reality. After the war
women were relegated once again to the home. The relinquishment
of wartime power and responsibility, was, some women found, not

an unmixed blessing. Accustomed to fuller utilization of their talents and energy, they now felt a void in their lives and sought for ways to fill it. It is scarcely surprising then that the mass women's movements of nineteenth-century America were postwar phenomena.

Certainly the women who organized denominational foreign mission societies viewed their wartime experiences as providential preparation for mission work. The lead article in the first issue of *Heathen Woman's Friend,* the magazine published by the Woman's Foreign Missionary Society of the Methodist Episcopal Church (North), cites indications of the Lord's preparation for the commencement of this new work; one of the signs pointed to is that "the efforts of our sex during our late war exhibited, as never before, [woman's] latent and unemployed power to labor for great and noble ends."[25] Ten years later, in 1879, an editorial in the same publication summarized a similar assessment of the relationship of the war to the female missionary movement in the opinion of "a gentleman acquaintance, not uninterested in our work."

His idea seemed to be that the present is the golden opportunity, and in all probability the golden age of woman's missionary work. The exigencies and inspirations of the great civil war were the best of preparations. These evoked from the heart and brain of American women undertakings of national significance, and gave us, for the first time in our history, some adequate consciousness of our power...[and] a sense of corresponding responsibility. ...Thus it happened that when, with the cessation of the war, the need of woman's work for the soldier ceased, a new and yet one of the mightiest of the moral forces of a mighty nation was suddenly set free for new and different employment. Being a spiritual force, it naturally sought in the field of spiritual interests and aims a worthy and congenial object. The needs and claims of unevangelized women just met the demand...a cause fitted to call out all of woman's devotion to duty, all her pity for the unfortunate, all her motherhood of the weak, all her enthusiasm for Christ's kingdom. The sudden upspringing of the new Foreign Missionary Societies of the women of the great national churches of the land signalized the new direction which the whole power of organized womanhood had taken.[26]

The editor rejected her friend's further conclusions that other claims such as temperance work and eventually the franchise and full citizenship would inevitably draw women away from the missionary enterprise, and she quibbled with assigning full credit to the war for mobilizing the power of organized womanhood; but she had no quarrel with his view of woman's nature as peculiarly suitable for "benevolent and reformatory work." She agreed that woman's power had been unleashed in the war, but objected to the suggestion that this power was finite. She believed that women need not drop mission work in order to undertake new tasks. Like Frances Willard, head of the WCTU, whose "Do Everything" policy embraced a multitude of reforms and affirmed woman's capacity to meet any call to service, the editor of *Heathen Woman's Friend* was convinced that the whole power of organized womanhood was sufficient for every challenge. The war had been a testing ground on which women proved themselves.

War, of course, is not a sufficient explanation for the proliferation of women's organizations in the latter half of the nineteenth century. A combination of other factors created a salubrious climate for the growth of female societies. Analysis of nineteenth-century demography reveals that the birth rate declined more rapidly than the infant mortality rate, with the net result that life expectancy increased while the size of the average family shrank. As Daniel Scott Smith has pointed out, the decline in marital fertility made a significant difference "in structuring the possibilities open to the average woman."[27] Despite declining fertility, there was only a slight increase in the number of women in the labor force. Middle-class women who figured in the labor force at all did so primarily as teachers and rarely worked after marriage. In addition, the increasing affluence of the middle class (in the North and West), coupled with the availability of unskilled immigrant women as domestic servants, meant that many women were relieved of their most strenuous household chores. Technology also relieved women of arduous tasks; Eleanor Flexner cites a string of advances.

> The development of gas lighting, municipal water systems, domestic plumbing, canning, the commercial production of ice, the improvement of furnaces, stoves, and washtubs, and the popularization of the sewing machine aided growing numbers of women to escape from the domestic treadmill.[28]

Freed from heavy household chores, less burdened with the care of large families, and with their health not strained by incessant pregnancies, middle-class women had more time and energy as well as more money at their disposal in the years after the war. Demographic, economic, and technological factors explain why women had time, energy, and resources available, but do not in themselves offer any clues that would enable one to predict how women would choose to use their new leisure. Because the woman's foreign mission movement embodies a conservative ideal, it might be tempting to assume that women simply organized in response to an urgent call from the churches for their support of a burgeoning overseas mission crusade; that the wives and daughters of the Protestant bourgeoisie, like docile sheep, were herded by their pastors into a new field of pious endeavor. Such an explanation, however, ignores historical realities. In the years immediately following the Civil War, foreign missions remained the concern of small and dedicated groups; by and large, the churches and the clergy were indifferent, if not actually hostile, to foreign mission efforts. Evangelical women—and the popular press—had been gripped by the dramatic stories of Ann Judson and other suffering missionary heroes and heroines in exotic places, but most ministers and denominational leaders preferred to emphasize parish work and missions to American Indians and freedmen. Women organized for foreign missions in the face of opposition from existing missionary boards not anxious to send single women to the field and uneasy at the prospect of women's societies siphoning off some of the all-too-scanty giving for missions. Indeed, far from being passive tools of church policy, evangelical women were instrumental in popularizing foreign missions. The massive foreign mission crusade mounted by the Protestant churches in the late nineteenth century owes its existence as much to the "harrowing" of the churches by female missionary societies as to the imperialistic mood with which it has been causally linked by historians of American religion.[29]

But if bourgeois Protestant women can be said to have exercised a certain freedom of choice in selecting foreign missions as "their" sacred cause, it must be admitted that the options available to them fell within parameters defined by prevailing religious and cultural ideologies. The importance of the sanctification of motherhood in Victorian culture, reinforced by the sanctions of evangelical religion, has already been noted. Other significant influences

shaped the lives of middle-class women in the course of the nineteenth century. The experiences of women in prewar benevolent societies and prayer circles and in wartime relief efforts had their
impact. When one turns to the expansion of educational opportunities for women and examines the content of female education, it appears almost inevitable that the causes women judged worthy and
congenial, like foreign missions, represented extensions of domestic
concerns and the enlargement of woman's maternal role in the
world.

Beginning well before the war and continuing at an ever-
increasing pace afterward, educational opportunities for women
grew with the proliferation of seminaries and academies for young
women, the founding of normal schools and women's colleges, and
the opening of state universities to women. Increased access to
higher education, however, generally meant more thorough preparation for teaching or enlightened domesticity. As Catharine Beecher
argued, the mere assertion of intellectual equality with men need not
disrupt the divinely designed social order in which women "choose"
a subordinate role befitting their maternal natures. Advocates of female education challenged only that aspect of the definition of woman's nature that questioned her capacity to reason and her ability to
withstand physically the rigors of the classroom; few of them
doubted that woman's nature was essentially different from man's.
Indeed, denominational colleges and state universities that opened
their doors to women typically instituted separate female departments. Resistance to enrolling women in professional courses or in
professional schools remained high, even after arguments that
higher education could permanently damage female reproductive
and nervous systems had been discredited. The purpose of educating women was largely confined to making them better wives and
mothers or training them as teachers.

Catharine Beecher's theory of female education included preparing women for the teaching profession as well as for motherhood
and housewifery. Significantly, her campaign to train teachers for
the West was essentially a secular mission aimed at regenerating society. It is in her conception of woman's role in the regeneration of
the world that Beecher's thinking most closely parallels the rationale
of the women who organized foreign mission societies. She states,
without qualification, that, "the principles of democracy, then, are
identical with the principles of Christianity." That being so, Ameri-

cans are the ones to whom "is committed the grand, the responsible privilege, of exhibiting to the world, the beneficent influences of Christianity, when carried into every social, civil, and political institution." And because women have charge of "the formation of the moral and intellectual character of the young," it is women on whom the outcome of this "great moral enterprise" rests. On these grounds Beecher argues that the proper education of women is of paramount importance.

> Let the women of a country be made virtuous and intelligent, and the men will certainly be the same. The proper education of a man decides the welfare of an individual; but educate a woman, and the interests of a whole family are secured. If this be so, as none will deny, then to American women, more than to any others on earth, is committed the exalted privilege of extending over the world those blessed influences, that are to renovate degraded man.[30]

Beecher's scheme assigns woman a role that is socially and politically subordinate to man's but, in the final analysis, more critical.

A similar bifurcation characterizes the rationale of the woman's foreign mission movement. The organizers of the female missionary societies defined for themselves a special mission to women and children in other lands that would not duplicate or usurp the work of denominational mission boards. The women's societies were designed to function as supplemental and auxiliary forces in the great missionary endeavor of the evangelical churches. Yet female missionary society leaders firmly believed that the key to Christianizing other cultures lay in converting women. An appeal for members made by the newly organized Methodist Episcopal (North) Woman's Foreign Missionary Society in 1869 spells out the argument.

> Dear Sister! shall we not recognize, in this emergency, God's voice as speaking to us—for who can so well do this work as we?...We well know how close is the relation of the mother to the child, and how important it is that the mother's heart be filled with the love and grace of God if her child is to grow up under Divine influence....How then can we more successfully

cooperate with our missionaries, and better insure the rapid extension of the knowledge of the truth...than by opening the hearts of the mothers....We know too how inestimable is the value, and how incalculable the influence of a pure Christian home; and if the influences of such homes are so indispensable in a Christian land, what must be their importance among a people, the depth of whose degradation is, as we are often assured, altogether beyond our realization?[31]

Female missionaries sponsored by women's societies were messengers from the Christian mothers of America to the women of heathen lands. Their mission of religious regeneration corresponds to the social regeneration that Beecher expected her teachers to work in the American West. Both sorts of emissaries, by inculcating the virtues of Christian womanhood, were to transform entire cultures.

If Catharine Beecher formulated the rationale on which the woman's foreign mission movement rested, another educator in the first half of the nineteenth century developed a model for evangelical education for women. Mary Lyon, in founding Mount Holyoke Female Seminary in 1837, enunciated a specifically evangelical counterpart to Beecher's democratic and semisecular theory of education. Lyon's stated purpose at Mount Holyoke was "to cultivate the missionary spirit among its pupils; the feeling that they should live for God, and do something as teachers, or in such other ways as Providence may direct." Mount Holyoke was to do for women what denominational colleges springing up at the time were doing for young men in training them for the ministry. She was convinced that her task was equally important, and she appealed to evangelical women who were supporting denominational colleges to supply funds for training evangelical teachers.

Fill the country with ministers, and they could no more conquer the whole land and secure their victories, without the aid of many times their number of self-denying female teachers, than the latter could complete the work without the former.... This work of supplying teachers is a great work, and it must be done, or our country is lost, and the world will remain unconverted.[32]

Lyon was enormously successful; a huge majority of Mount Holyoke graduates became teachers and a significant number were recruited as wives by young men headed for foreign mission fields in
the 1840s.

Education for women created a problem for the college graduate who had internalized an ideal of service consistent with notions
of woman's natural propensity for self-denying benevolence. There
had developed with the growth of educational opportunities for
women no concomitant enlargement of their place in economic and
political spheres. Consequently, the only uses many educated
women with minimal family responsibilities found for their skills
and training were in the various female organizations that
mushroomed after the Civil War.

The leaders of these organizations were usually graduates of female seminaries or women's colleges, but their constituency was, of
course, largely composed of women who had not enjoyed the advantages of higher education. Nevertheless, nearly all middle-class,
white women had benefited from the establishment of free public education; by 1850 native-born white women were almost universally
literate—a dramatic change from the pre-Revolutionary era when
fewer than half of the native-born, white females in America could
read.[33] The emergence of women as readers, coupled with advances
in printing that made mass circulation of newspapers and magazines
economically feasible and priced books within the reach of the middle classes, resulted in the informal "education" of masses of
women. Sentimental novels written by women for a female audience, as well as ladies' magazines, promoted the ideal of self-
denying female benevolence.

Possibly the most influential of these informal educators was
Sarah Josepha Hale, editor of *Godey's Lady's Book*.[34] As the editor for
more than forty years of the most widely circulated magazine of its
day, she was the arbiter of taste and manners for several generations
of American women. She used the pages of *Godey's* to promote her
chosen causes as well as the latest fashions. Female education was
one of her favorite causes; she publicized the work of both Catharine
Beecher and Mary Lyon, urging that they be supported and imi-
tated. She fought for property rights for married women and even
argued that women ought to sit on school boards, although she did
not sympathize with woman's rights crusaders and saw no other appropriate role for women in public life.

A staunch supporter of foreign missions, Hale served as the first president of the Philadelphia branch of the Woman's Union Missionary Society. In the editorial column of *Godey's,* she reported the founding of that society and described its "plan of sending Christian women, as teachers, to christianize and civilize heathen households."[35] An early proponent of medical education for women, she was one of the first to urge the sending of female medical missionaries to foreign fields. In 1851 she organized the Ladies' Medical Society of Philadelphia to finance the medical education of women who would pledge themselves to the mission field. At the time, no denominational mission board would agree to send an unmarried woman overseas; female doctors could go only as the wives of male missionaries. Not until 1869, when Dr. Clara Swain sailed for India under the auspices of the Woman's Foreign Missionary Society of the Methodist Episcopal Church (North) did one of Hale's lady doctors make it to a foreign field. Despite her frustration on this point, Hale continued to promote the cause of foreign missions. In the summer of 1865 she suggested that the time was ripe to enlist women in the crusade. She wrote,

> Philadelphia has, for the last four years, been the city of hospitals. In the care and for the relief of the sick and wounded from the battle-fields, the ladies of Philadelphia have given their time, their thoughts, their means. With the blessed return of peace and union, there will come a time for other charities. We hope that many Christian hearts will then be warmed, and many helping hands held out with aid for the poor oppressed victims of the great heathen rebellion against God, which has caused rebellion also against his righteous Bible-laws for the protection, the honour and the happiness of women.[36]

Hale anticipated that many charities would compete for the time and talents of "demobilized" women; she hoped that her endorsement of foreign missions would carry some weight with her readers as they chose among competing causes.

If Sarah Hale's words were not enough, there was the shining example of the saintly Sarah Doremus, founder of the Woman's Union Missionary Society, to inspire the fainthearted and to rebuke those who used other benevolent activities as an excuse for not supporting foreign missions. The wife of a wealthy New York businessman and the mother of nine children, Mrs. Doremus was a guiding light of practically every benevolent project in New York City.[37] Prisons, hospitals, foundling and old-age homes, and industrial schools as well as individual families were the beneficiaries of her personal, meticulous care; but it was on the missionary enterprise and especially on her own Woman's Union Missionary Society that she lavished her deepest love. Her concern for sending out female missionaries was inspired by the plea of the Reverend David Abeel in 1834. Abeel, a returned missionary from China, had recognized a need for female workers in the field and had issued a call for them in both England and America. Doremus attempted to organize a society to send such workers in the 1830s but was thwarted by denominational opposition to sending single women overseas.

By 1860 overt opposition to the idea had lessened considerably, and Doremus organized the interdenominational Woman's Union Missionary Society. For fifteen years it operated out of her home, under her personal supervision of every detail of the work. Eulogizing her in 1877, *The Missionary Link* described her relationship with the society's missionaries.

> She was literally a mother to the dear representatives of our Society. . . . How many touching tokens of personal self-denial she surrounded them with! Her correspondence among them was immense, in which she carefully avoided business details, but wrote as a mother might have done. She would glean items of daily interest and sketches of lectures to send them, that something fresh from their native land might give variety to their lives of arduous toil. No event of public importance transpired that she did not send copies of newspapers to all the stations. Then she was always on the outlook for inspiring books, which she sent to them by mail, feeling all that cheered their lives would strengthen them for duty.

The eulogy dwells on Mrs. Doremus's womanly and motherly qualities. Her delicate tact is stressed as strongly as the magnitude of her achievements. The point is made twice that she never neglected her home and family.

With all her world-wide usefulness, it is peculiarly sweet to recognize that her home was the scene of her tenderest cares. No
outside duty was undertaken until that first claim had been dis-
charged. The mind that could have ruled a kingdom, gave its
best energies to the ordering and beautifying of that dearest
realm of a true woman.

Never, the reader is assured, were her benevolent projects "prose-
cuted by her at the expense of her home life," and furthermore "her
household was managed by her as admirably as if, instead of having
so many public cares upon her, she had been simply and only a
housekeeper."[38] (No credit is given in the eulogy to the servants who
enabled Mrs. Doremus to manage these miracles.)

    This housekeeper extraordinaire exemplified in her person and
in her work the highest ideal of Christian womanhood. Her Union
Society was the direct antecedent of the denominational women's societies; the founders of the denominational societies invariably cited
Mrs. Doremus as a source of inspiration. If the denominational
women's groups lacked the institutional independence and ecumenical character of the Union Society, they shared its sense of a special
mission to women in other lands. Each in turn would issue to the
women of its own denomination a plea like that made in the first
number of Mrs. Doremus's *Missionary Crumbs*.

> If we believe that it is Christianity alone which the elevated
> woman from her former abject position...can we rest in the
> enjoyment of these benefits without a single desire to elevate
> our poor heathen sisters?[39]

    The first of the denominational women's foreign missionary
societies, the Woman's Board of Missions (Congregational), was
formed in Boston in 1868 as an auxiliary to the American Board of
Commissioners for Foreign Missions. The stated purpose of the
Woman's Board was "to co-operate with the American Board in its
...labor for the benefit of women and children in heathen lands, to
disseminate missionary intelligence and increase a missionary spirit
among Christian women at home and to train children to interest
and participation in the work."[40] This mild statement, accompanied
by a commitment to support all single women sent as missionaries,

masked a major shift in American Board policy. Congregational women, aware of the opposition of longtime foreign secretary of the American Board, Rufus Anderson, to sending single women to foreign mission fields, had judiciously waited to organize their society until after his resignation in 1866. N. G. Clark, Anderson's successor, was a firm supporter of both female mission societies and single women missionaries; he actually invited women in Boston to form an auxiliary to the American Board.[41]

Despite Clark's active support, the women felt compelled to issue a disclaimer as they launched their new society. The first issue of their journal, *Life and Light for Heathen Women,* made it clear that they did not "profess to be commencing a new work," but were "entering into their [the American Board's] labors." The basis of their appeal for support, however, reflected their special, feminine perspective on the evangelization of the world. They wrote of "being more and more convinced that Protestantism cannot flourish until the women are thoroughly renovated, and their old superstitious notions are rooted out." Converting women was, in their view, more important than reaching heathen men in realizing the ultimate goal of Christianizing whole cultures. And the conversion of women was a mission for women. In undertaking to support all single women sent out as American Board missionaries, the Woman's Board queried, "Ought we not to do it? On whom does it so appropriately devolve as ourselves: Who shall comprehend woman's woes and degradation like woman?"[42]

The women of Boston and the Northeast were not alone in feeling a responsibility for Christianizing women in foreign lands. In the same year that the Boston ladies organized the Woman's Board of Missions, a second Congregational body sprang up in Chicago using the name Woman's Board of the Interior. The two boards worked cooperatively from the beginning; both shared in the publication of *Life and Light for Heathen Women.* Initially both boards welcomed the women of the Presbyterian and Reformed churches as partners in a common enterprise; but eventually women of other denominations withdrew to form their own denominational societies, and the Congregational groups lost their ecumenical flavor.

Following the lead of the Congregational women, female foreign missionary societies were formed in the major Protestant churches in rapid succession. The rather dramatic story of the organization of the Woman's Foreign Missionary Society of the Methodist Episcopal Church (North) features a handful of women who fought their way through a raging storm to the Tremont Street Church in Boston in March, 1869. The "intrepid eight" met in response to an appeal made by returned missionary wives for the Christian women of America to meet their obligation to their heathen sisters. The message was clear: women workers were essential if the Gospel were to penetrate to the secluded women of India. The response was swift: the eight women meeting in the Tremont Church scheduled an organizational session for the following week. The first issue of the new society's journal, *Heathen Woman's Friend*, was published in May. The society's first missionaries, Isabella Thoburn and Dr. Clara Swain, sailed for India in November.[43]

Methodist women, incorporating for the specific purpose of sending single women to the foreign mission field, acknowledged a debt to the female missionary societies that preceded theirs, but devised an organizational structure that set their society apart from the others. Theirs was the first denomination-wide woman's foreign missionary society. They divided their organization into geographic regions with branch headquarters in each region. Eventually eleven branches blanketed the entire country. (The WCTU adopted a strikingly similar organizational structure under Frances Willard's leadership; it is perhaps more than mere coincidence that Willard was raised a Methodist, graduated from Methodist-affiliated North Western Female College, taught at a series of Methodist schools, served as secretary of the American Methodist Ladies Centenary Association, and was named president of a Methodist college for women shortly after the Methodist Woman's Foreign Missionary Society was formed.[44]) This decentralized structure allowed women in local societies to feel more closely connected to and in control of the movement they supported with their pennies and their prayers. A policy of assigning the task of supporting specific missionaries, schools, or hospitals to a particular branch or local society reinforced a sense of direct participation in the missionary endeavor. This method of enlisting the support of churchwomen was highly successful. The Methodist group rapidly became the largest of all the women's missionary societies, not only in absolute numbers but also in the percentage of church members recruited. By 1895, more than 150,000 women had joined the Methodist society; by 1910, the figure had risen to 267,000 and reached more than half a million in 1920. A study done in 1913 reported, in somewhat admonitory tones, that only one out of every eight female church members was enrolled in the society, and that receipts for 1912 ($840,000) constituted only 35 percent of the total receipts for foreign missions in the Methodist Episcopal church that year. [45] Confronted with the enormous task of evangelizing the whole world, the record of Methodist women may have seemed inadequate; but in retrospect it looks like a triumph of mobilization of both people and resources—particularly when one remembers that women's gifts to missions ordinarily represented a "second gift," given on top of a family's contribution to the church's general mission board.

Methodist women, through their society, assumed "primary responsibility . . . for the evangelization of women in the fields where the Church has established missions." The rationale for the necessity for a special campaign to evangelize women was that a permanent church could not be built without women. "A man's church will last for one generation. Mothers are the conservators of religion, bringing up their children in their own faith." [46] The rhetoric used by the Methodist women echoes Beecher's estimation of woman's importance in shaping and perpetuating cultural values; it is a rhetoric that, as we have seen, was common in evangelical mission circles. The Methodist women, however, did not accept quite so quietly a subordinate status within the missionary enterprise. They exercised a greater degree of autonomy in allocating and disbursing funds they collected than did most of the other denominational women's societies. Yet even Methodist women applied to the general board for confirmation of missionaries under appointment, and submitted appropriations to the board for approval. This seems to have been a formal rather than an actual act of submission, however, as the approval of the board was never withheld. Nevertheless, the formation of a woman's foreign missionary society was not accomplished without confronting considerable opposition, most of it couched in terms of the danger of fragmenting fund-raising efforts for missions.

The corresponding secretary of the General Missionary Society, John P. Durbin, felt strongly that the women should confine their efforts to raising money for the General Society. The First Annual Report of the Woman's Foreign Missionary Society glosses over the negotiations with Dr. Durbin in its account of the society's formation, but its constitution incorporates his demand that the general board review and approve all appropriations and appointments and that fund-raising be restricted to avoid competition with the General Society for gifts. Section III of Article VIII spells out the details.

> The funds of the Society shall not be raised by collections or subscriptions taken during any church services or in any promiscuous public meeting, but shall be raised by securing Members, Life Members, Honorary Managers, and Patrons, and by such other methods as will not interfere with the ordinary collections or contributions for the treasury of the Missionary Society of the Methodist Espiscopal Church.[47]

The women had refused to become simply a collecting agency for the General Society, but tactful compromise was clearly the order of the day; they agreed to confine their work to a restricted sphere. Making a virtue out of necessity, they encouraged women to make a habit of systematically giving small gifts, the fruit of small, daily acts of self-denial. The *Heathen Woman's Friend* instructed local auxiliaries that

> no public collections should be taken, but an effort made to interest every lady of each congregation.... This may require self-denial and sacrifice, but as the ladies worked during the war, to relieve the suffering of soldiers, so let them work now for their suffering, perishing sisters in foreign lands.[48]

The acceptance of the private rather than the public sphere as the appropriate forum for woman's work and the comparison of this new cause to the war work for which women had been so universally praised are measures of how perfectly the mission movement meshed with the prevailing ideology of womanhood. And the appeal to woman's capacity for self-denial, to her innate desire to relieve suffering, proved enormously successful. As it turned out, Dr. Durbin's fears were unjustified; general receipts for missions rose significantly as women's groups popularized and championed the cause. Friction over the scope of woman's prerogatives continued in the years that followed, but Methodist women maintained greater administrative control over their work for women than did the corresponding societies in other denominations. The Methodist women's society was recognized in 1884 as an official arm of the church and retained its structural autonomy even when other women's missionary societies were merged with denominational mission boards in the 1920s.

The Woman's Foreign Missionary Society of the Presbyterian Church (North), founded in Philadelphia in 1870, offers a sharp contrast to the relative autonomy of the Methodist women's group. The Philadelphia society was the first of several Presbyterian women's foreign missionary societies; it remained the largest until the formal consolidation of all seven societies in 1920. However, the several societies worked cooperatively from the beginning, communicating freely among themselves and engaging in joint publication ventures. The Philadelphia society began publishing *Woman's Work for Woman* in 1871. Originally the organ of the Philadelphia society alone, it merged with *Our Mission Field,* the journal of the Ladies' Board of Missions of New York, in 1885, and thereafter made arrangements to share its pages with the other Presbyterian ladies' foreign missionary societies. The cooperation between the societies was coordinated and systematized after 1885 by a Central Committee of Women for Foreign Missions that met yearly in conjunction with the denomination's General Assembly. All of these Presbyterian women's societies were auxiliaries to the assembly's Board of Foreign Missions, which made all appropriations and disbursed all funds. The women's groups had no official status within the church structure, although it became the board's practice to assign responsibility for raising funds for certain parts of the work to women's societies. Women took over the support of female missionaries, built and sustained girls' schools, medical colleges and hospitals for women, and assumed that share of a married male missionary's salary that exceeded the sum allotted a single man.

While Presbyterian women exercised virtually no control over appropriations, they played a crucial role in recruiting candidates for the mission field. Their recommendation of candidates to the board was never overruled. Nevertheless, the women were not entirely happy with the arrangement. As early as September of 1871, the minutes of the executive committee of the Philadelphia society reported dissatisfaction with the necessity of always working through the board.

The Foreign Secretary presented some of the difficulties attending our work hitherto, particularly in regard to getting the
information we need from missionaries. Thought the time had
come when we should take up certain fields, and conduct the
work there ourselves; always with the approval of the Board
and yet in such a way as to give us constant communication
with such fields without needing to consult the Board about
everything connected with them.[49]

The foreign secretary may have felt the time had come for women to
take charge of the work, but she was clearly a woman ahead of her
times in a church where women had to be encouraged to pray publicly and to conduct women's meetings. In 1875, the pages of *Woman's Work for Woman* contain a letter from an organizer of local
women's missionary societies that indicates the attitude of ordinary
churchwomen toward active participation in even such a patently respectable organization as a female missionary group.

Few are aspirants to office, but when it becomes their duty to
assume such responsibility, they "wear their blushing honors"
gracefully, and are learning to conduct affairs according to par-
liamentary rules. Many, shrinking from this work because of
the publicity it may involve, have yet to learn that there is a
wide distinction between the bold advocacy of Woman's Rights
(so-called), and the modest testimony of a woman nerved to
duty in religious work by the strength of the Master whom she
serves.[50]

*Woman's Work for Woman* repeatedly reassures women that their
homes are their first responsibility and that participation in the
woman's foreign mission movement is entirely within the province
of a Christian mother precisely because she is a mother and a Christian. The specter of neglected homes is banished and the taint of
woman's rights abjured.

We do not ask you, dear Christian sister, to neglect any clear
home duty. But we are apt to do many unnecessary things for
our families. . . . Your family will better realize the power of the
unseen and the eternal, if they see that in order to attend some

missionary meeting for prayer, or for business; or that you may have more to give to this great cause, you are ready to save upon some rich article for the table, or do without some extra tucking or embroidery even for "the household pet;" and even though the enticing sewing-machine urges you on to further labor.[51]

The implication is here made plain; women who join the missionary movement are better mothers, more completely fulfilling their obligation to provide moral and religious guidance to their families. If Presbyterian women were not allowed to determine policy in the foreign field, they were, as befitted their role as mothers, encouraged to assume responsibility for missionary education at home and to set an example of sacrificial giving. They did well on both counts, and in 1877 their work received an accolade from the General Assembly.

Without stepping beyond the sphere of a refined Christian womanhood, they are making their power in prayer and in gifts felt unto the ends of the earth. *We rejoice in their good works and bid them God speed.*[52]

Women of the American Baptist Association (North) formed their Baptist Woman's Missionary Society in 1871. Its territory was limited to all the churches east of Buffalo, while the Woman's Baptist Missionary Society of the North-West, organized later the same year, covered the western states. The Society of the West, as it came to be called, remained the smaller of the two groups. The two societies united in 1914 as the Woman's American Baptist Foreign Missionary Society. The Baptist women's groups, like the Congregational and Presbyterian societies, were subordinate and auxiliary to the denomination's general missionary society, the American Baptist Missionary Union. The Union directed all mission work; it appointed and assigned missionaries, controlled appropriations, and divided responsibility for specific projects among the various organizations channeling funds into its coffers.

Despite their rather limited institutional power, Baptist women worked aggressively for missions. They published their own missionary magazine under the appropriately modest title, *The Helping*

*Hand*. They carried on an extensive program of missionary education in their churches—especially among children. And, perhaps because Baptist polity and practice had accustomed women to taking a more active role in the leadership of their congregations, Baptist women produced a disproportionate share of the most prominent and vigorous leaders in ecumenical and interdenominational women's foreign mission projects.

Rapidly following the example set by the women of the four largest Protestant groups in America at midcentury, women organized female missionary societies in virtually all of the Protestant fellowships in the country. Before 1880 there were more than twenty women's foreign missionary societies; by 1900 the number had doubled. The proliferation of separate denominational societies partly reflects the pressure put on women by denominational leaders to support denominational mission activities rather than contribute to nonpartisan efforts. It was with some reluctance, for example, that Presbyterian women withdrew from the women's boards established as auxiliaries to the American Board of Commissioners for Foreign Missions. But when Francis Ellinwood, secretary of the Presbyterian board, asked for help from the women and offered firm support for the female missionary movement in Presbyterian circles, the women felt compelled to answer their denomination's call.

The proliferation of women's missionary societies was a desirable phenomenon from the perspective of each denomination for obvious reasons. It is harder to explain why hundreds of thousands of ordinary churchwomen found it so desirable to join such societies. Why did they find this particular cause "a worthy and congenial object" above all other benevolent projects? The specialness of the mission movement can perhaps best be seen in examining the relationship of the woman's foreign mission movement to other nineteenth-century women's movements. The attitude of the missionary ladies toward woman's rights has already been indicated. The egalitarian rationale underlying the woman's rights crusade challenged the very assumptions about the sanctity of the Christian home that fueled other nineteenth-century female benevolent and reform movements. It is scarcely surprising that the woman's foreign mission movement would abjure a crusade for woman's rights. The relationship of the mission movement to other causes that shared its underlying assumptions is more revealing.

The women of the missionary societies saw the Woman's Christian Temperance Union (WCTU) as the other great movement of their day, and they both sympathized and cooperated with it. To a certain extent, membership in the two groups overlapped. The WCTU was itself interested in the foreign mission field; it eventually organized a special department for Missions and Temperance to implement its goal of establishing a temperance society on every mission station. Nevertheless, there was an element of competition between the two movements. The WCTU was the only organization that approached the woman's mission movement in size; as it grew, some of the organizers of the woman's foreign mission movement feared that it might divert attention from the foreign field. Jennie Fowler Willing, a frequent contributor to *Heathen Woman's Friend* and also editor of the *Woman's Temperance Union,* warned readers of the Methodist periodical in 1875 that woman's interest was being divided by competing causes and that extra effort would have to be exerted to keep the missionary movement afloat.

> The woman's temperance movement, a grand home missionary scheme, has come to the front, claiming the lion's share of the strength of Christian women. The church has always thrust the icy end of the plank toward foreign missions.[53]

Actually, although the temperance movement received the lion's share of the publicity in the 1870s, it never enlisted as many women as the foreign mission cause attracted. That Willing would support both movements is natural and consistent, since both shared a common ideology, assuming that Christian womanhood would be the effective agent in the salvation of the world. Willing's evenhandedness, however, is atypical. Temperance reform was regarded by most mission society advocates as simply one manifestation of the beneficent influence of evangelical women on the social order; they believed that woman's help was more desperately needed in heathen lands than in Christian America.

The women's club movement was viewed with rather more ambivalence than temperance work. The duty of the Christian woman was less apparent in a movement that combined civic reform with self-culture. Self-culture, while not precisely immoral, was not clearly virtuous. A paper read at an annual missionary meeting in

Trenton in 1898 summed up the position of the missionary ladies on the club movement.

> We have no quarrel with the women's clubs, literary, social, philanthropic or patriotic. Many a woman, finding her voice in them, has brought it back to her Master's service. I do plead for fairness in distribution of the time and talent of our Christian women. Many a woman giving a tenth of the time to church work which she gives to whist would be a power and inspiration.[54]

The tone conveys the message; women's clubs are all very well, but card playing is a paltry employment for talent that could be consecrated to nobler ends. This comment, of course, gives short shrift to the municipal reform work taken up by women's clubs in the 1890s; the speaker perhaps felt more hostility than she expresses. Women's clubs, however, did not pose a serious threat to the missionary movement as competitors for potential members until the twentieth century. As Karen Blair's recent study demonstrates, the women's clubs appealed to a limited constituency; the typical clubwoman was mature, married with grown children, and generally from the upper reaches of the socioeconomic ladder.[55]

It was in fact in the home mission movement that the women dedicated to the foreign mission cause perceived the greatest threat. The vexed relationship of the woman's foreign mission movement to the woman's home mission movement throws into relief that aspect of foreign mission work that made it special. It was not simply that mission work was an appropriate task for self-denying Christian women. Home missions, after all, would do equally well if that were the only criterion. What foreign work offered women was a special mission to women and children. Like Catharine Beecher, the women involved in foreign mission work discovered the power they could wield by carving out a special, albeit subordinate, task that they alone were suited to carry out. As early as 1878 *Woman's Work for Woman* reprinted a leaflet circulated by the Woman's Board of Missions (Congregational) arguing against combining home and foreign missionary work. The writer of the leaflet claims a providential origin for foreign mission work that ought to protect it from tampering and tinkering, but she obviously adduces that argument to legitimate her desire to preserve the role she has found for herself in missionary work. She describes home missions as not calling women to participate in any "new work which shall be peculiar to them and which they only can do . . . ; it offers them no new responsibilities in administration. They are to be chiefly collecting agencies." In distinct contrast, she writes,

> in the foreign work the raising of funds is only a part of the labor laid upon the Woman's Boards. They look out candidates to go abroad. Their counsel is sought, and their judgment has weight as to the fitness of such persons. They keep up a close correspondence with the lady missionaries on the field. They publish a periodical, print documents, circulate information, hold meetings, and direct the movements of their missionaries at home on furlough. In short, while everything is done through the channels and by the counsel and consent of the American Board, the women have a real responsiblity in the management of the work. And the feeling that they are *trusted with an important department* of the great cause, which will prosper or fail as they prosper or fail, has given them an inspiration, a steadiness of purpose, a business tact, and an executive ability which have awakened admiration on every hand.[56]

The women's foreign missionary societies clearly felt they had much to lose by being lumped into a single organization with home missions. (Opposition to combining home and foreign missions was not a universal attitude among American Protestant women. Some of the smaller denominations, especially the so-called immigrant churches, never organized separate home and foreign mission societies. In the South, where female missionary societies were organized somewhat later than in the North and West, home mission work seems to have been more often combined—sometimes forcibly—with foreign mission efforts. The relatively greater popularity of home missions in the South may reflect the fact that Southern women were usually not allowed as active a role in foreign mission work as their sisters in Northern denominations played.)

One can speculate that the home mission field lacked the exotic appeal of foreign lands; the task of furnishing parsonages in the West or even teaching freedmen or Indians on reservations may well have seemed less dramatic than converting heathen. It is clear that home work was considered less demanding and much safer. In later years, as the emphasis on professional training for missionary candidates grew, the home mission field was often pointed to as an appropriate training ground for foreign stations. Like the little girls in the *Rebecca* books who organized a home mission band because they felt they were not yet ready for foreign work, many mission volunteers were required to test their vocations in home mission work.

The real key to the resistance of women to subsuming foreign missions in a general mission organization lies in the special nature of the role they had defined for themselves in foreign work: a role that justified them in assuming the functions and powers that the anonymous writer of the leaflet quoted above so obviously relished. There was a special category of and need for woman's work in evangelizing non-Christian cultures. In the mid-nineteenth century, American evangelicals adopted a theology of missions, consonant with the Victorian sanctification of motherhood, that attached special significance to the conversion of mothers as the most efficient means of Christianizing heathen lands. Only female missionaries could witness to women in cultures where women lived in seclusion. And since no culture could be successfully Christianized until the women were reached with the message of the Gospel, here was a task of ultimate importance that could be accomplished only by women. It appealed to them as evangelical Christians and as true women.

It was also a mission that promised tangible results in the transformation of heathen households into Christian homes. As Ellen Parsons, editor of *Woman's Work for Woman,* pointed out at the World's Colombian Exposition in Chicago in 1893 when she reported on the history of the woman's foreign mission movement,

> it is more difficult to point to what is distinctively the fruit of woman's work in missions at home than abroad because the peculiar barriers of the East are wanting here. . . . Let a European light down upon any village in Asia Minor, or the Chinese Empire, and the tidiest house there, with the cleanest tablecloth and the most inviting bed, is the house of a mission-school graduate. The transformation appears in the deaths they die. . . . These women are transformed by happiness. Christianity encourages them, wakes their intellect, kindles aspiration, as well as offers peace. . . . As women rise they bring the home up with them.[57]

This transformation of heathen homes was possible precisely because, according to Victorian theories of the primacy of gender-determined characteristics, heathen women—despite their systematic degradation—had essentially the same nature as their Christian sisters in America. Evangelical women believed, when they looked on their heathen sisters, quite literally in the cliché, "There, but for the grace of God, go I." An editorial in 1873 in *Woman's Work for Woman* reminded them of that fact.

> Nor are these other lives those of beings of altogether different, inferior, and less sensitive natural organization than ours, as we are too apt to comfort ourselves by thinking. Certainly their position and manner of life for generations past has deadened their sensibilities, and limited their capacities for joy and sorrow somewhat. But they are women exactly like ourselves in nature and in original capabilities—they have in them what can be by the grace of God nourished and cultivated into true Christian womanhood.[58]

From this perspective it appears that the blessings of Christianity have made all the difference between American women and their heathen sisters; any wrongs that American women suffer—or fancy they suffer—must pale beside the intolerable treatment of women of other cultures and other religions.

As Ellen Parsons presented the case in Chicago, the motive force behind the massive woman's foreign mission movement was woman's nature, her tenderness and motherliness responding to the appeal of her own sex.

> What was it that shook the Church, roused the women to united systematic, concentrated action, that moved on and on, a compelling force, until we now have in this country the spectacle of hundreds of thousands of women, representing every branch of the Christian Church, banded together in chartered societies and disbursing from one to one-and-a-half million dollars every year? Only one other movement, that of the Temperance Union, compares with it in numbers and moral power. Whence came that powerful voice which evoked so much energy and action? It was not patriotism warning of the menace

of an incoming tide of immigrants; that came later. It was not
national remorse demanding reparation for the exiled Indian.
It was not even the last command of Jesus, "Disciple all nations," like a clarion call to the conscience. It was a *human cry*
appealing expressly to a woman's tenderness, and it pierced
her heart. It sounded from out black heathenism, ages old,
lost, vast, awful—the heartbreak of motherhood, the stifled cry
of distorted childhood; *this* was what happy women heard in
their happy, protected homes.[59]

In answering the cry of heathen women, evangelical womanhood in
America had found its highest calling. The woman's foreign mission
movement was a worthy and congenial object for the benevolent impulses of several generations of American women who needed to
find a use for their time and their talents in the years between the
Civil War and the First World War. It offered them a role in a world-
wide enterprise that claimed ultimate significance yet was entirely
consistent with their ideology of home and motherhood and their
theology of sacrificial service. In undertaking a mission to women
and children in other cultures, evangelical women did not venture
out of the domestic sphere; they simply enlarged it. In the words of
one of their favorite missionary hymns,[60] their goal was

> To stretch our habitations,
>     Lengthen cords and strengthen stakes,
> Till Christ's kingdom, of the nations
>     One unbroken household makes.

Despite the self-sacrificial character of their rhetoric, evangelical women were not wholly altruistic in their mission to their heathen sisters; they fully expected that in the process of stretching their
habitations they would improve the quality of their own spiritual
lives. The following chapter explores the activities these women engaged in as the means of extending their households to the nations
and examines their theory of "reflex influence," the supposedly
beneficial effect that supporting foreign missions would have on the
homes and churches of America.

*Chapter 3*

# Sanctified Female Talent

The rationale underlying the phenomenon of the woman's foreign mission movement was not designed to justify the usurpation of male prerogatives. Instead, the theory that women had a special and natural responsibility for reaching out to their heathen sisters reflects, as we saw in the last chapter, the belief of those who spearheaded the movement that Christian women had a particular part to play in the "great work of evangelizing the world." Their portion in this world drama was to extend "the sphere of Christian wifehood and motherhood" to include degraded heathen mothers.[1] These women shared with Mrs. C. F. Wilder of Kansas in the "desire for a deeper, broader life [that] has developed the art societies, the reading clubs, the scientific circles, and the home and foreign mission work," but they never imagined that such activities might require them to leave the familiar confines of their domestic world. With Mrs. Wilder, they felt that the attraction of missionary work lay in its suitability for mothers.

> The house-mother's position is the highest in the world and *need* not be the narrowest, and what makes this missionary work for heathen women so peculiarly adapted to our needs is, that it enlarges our lives in our own sphere. It does not call us from our homes to other fields of labor.[2]

The idea expressed here, that in answering the needs of their heathen sisters American women would also find some of their own needs met and their own lives enlarged, is a consistent theme in the literature of the woman's foreign mission movement. The deeper, broader life stemming from participation in missionary societies and reading clubs alike was to be made manifest in a deepened spirituality and a broadened intellectual outlook; the concern of those who encouraged woman's work for foreign missions was with the interior

lives of women. The changes anticipated as the result of woman's efforts on behalf of her heathen sister would have, according to this
theory of the "reflex influence" of foreign missions, no effect on the
external circumstances of the lives of women in Christian America.
Spiritual renewal would strengthen home and family life; it would
not call women out of the home to labor in fields ordinarily tilled by
men.

If they were not to labor in the field alongside men, what specifically was the nature of the work women were to do? Actually, at
the denominational level, women did imitate the men. The organizational structures of the large denominational women's societies
roughly duplicated those of denominational mission boards. Home
and foreign corresponding secretaries handled the bulk of each society's administrative work, implementing decisions made by an executive committee that met weekly or biweekly. In the smaller societies
and in those attached to Southern churches, however, such executive
committees met less frequently and exercised less influence over
such matters as the review of candidates' credentials and their assignment to specific stations, the building and administration of
girls' schools, hospitals for women, and orphanages. But in the
larger societies, the officers—who were usually the wives of ministers (frequently of those ministers who officered denominational
mission boards) or of prominent businessmen in the city where a society had its headquarters—did work that was not so very different
from that done by their male colleagues. It was at the congregational
level that the woman's foreign mission movement took on a character distinct from any available male models.

The program embarked upon at the local level can be broken
down into two categories: support and education. Women's groups
offered three types of support: financial, emotional, and spiritual.
Indefatigable fund-raisers, women systematically collected dues and
planned bazaars, fairs, and missionary teas. They pinched pennies
from their household budgets and, following the admonition of
Catharine Beecher, collected "the drops and rills...to distil on
parched and desert lands." In the four largest Protestant denominations, between one-fourth and one-fifth of the total receipts for foreign missions were contributed through the women's societies—and
this at a time when women rarely controlled more than small sums
of money. (The systematic approach women used for fund-raising

was so successful that their example was employed by the leaders of
the Laymen's Missionary Movement in the early twentieth century
to shame businessmen into contributing to missions.) To stimulate
giving, "special objects" were assigned to particular local societies.
This practice encouraged women to feel a personal responsibility for
"their" missionary, "their" scholar, or "their" Bible woman (a native employed as an itinerant Bible reader).

Women provided emotional support to female missionaries
through direct personal correspondence between local societies and
individual missionaries. Women's missionary magazines frequently
published articles advising churchwomen about the sort of letter one
ought to write to a missionary and reminding them of the tremen-
dous importance of maintaining close contact with their missionaries. Letters exchanged were to replicate the confiding and
affectionate tone of communiqués between mother and daughter,
sisters, female kin and intimate female friends. Missionaries were to
be made to feel that they were never far from the thoughts and prayers of a supportive sisterhood in America.

The most important task of the women's societies, as they understood their mission, was to offer spiritual support to the crusade
to evangelize the world. Regular, informed prayer—both public and
private—was the consecrated duty of every member of a female missionary society. Some societies asked each woman to set aside the
hour from five to six on Sunday afternoon for prayer for missions.
Methodist women called for "Prayer at Noontide Encircling the
Earth." Women's mission journals urged women to use their mission year-books or prayer calendars to intercede for individual missionaries and specific objects by name. Some societies encouraged
the practice of remembering a missionary in special prayer on her
birthday. In the 1870s the power of organized womanhood was perceived as virtually equivalent to the power of female prayer. The
temperance crusade that swept through the Midwest in the winter of
1873–74 was launched and sustained by bands of praying women; in
this woman's crusade for temperance, the WCTU had its origin. It
is no accident that the two largest women's movements of the late
nineteenth century relied so heavily on the efficacy of female prayer
in the regeneration of the world. While some might question
whether public prayer was altogether womanly, it was almost certainly more acceptable to conservatives than any other activity in

which a woman might publicly engage. And private prayer was unquestionably appropriate for woman with her naturally religious bent.

The educative function of the woman's missionary movement had two components. First, women were concerned with informing themselves; then they sought to communicate what they called missionary intelligence. Mission study provided women with the information they needed in order to pray intelligently and effectually. It was primarily to keep women abreast of developments on the mission field that the denominational societies followed the lead of the Woman's Missionary Union in issuing journals. These journals typically offered news from the mission field, interspersed with advice on other mission books and articles worth reading, and detailed suggestions for exciting interest in local auxiliary society meetings. The information gleaned from mission magazines and papers read at regular auxiliary meetings constituted the missionary intelligence that it was woman's solemn duty to share with family and friends. Because women believed that those who could be made to understand the desperate plight of the heathen would be moved to join the missionary crusade, they felt it was imperative to seize every opportunity to promote their cause. Doing so might be hard or awkward work, but in urging women on to the task one writer in *Heathen Woman's Friend* promised that it would pay spiritual dividends to American women as well as to their heathen sisters.

> I know it is hard to start the random flow of playful conversation, which is wont to ripple lightly along the weather, the spring styles, Miss Phelp's last book, and our fancy work, into serious and rugged channels; but it will pay in widening our outlook into life, in deepening the channels of our being, in making our souls grow.[3]

Missionary education not only created the awareness of need that led to monetary commitment and informed prayer on the part of the faithful; it also led the young to dedicate their lives to missions. A central focus of women's concern with missionary education was on work with children. Most of the women's mission magazines, for instance, included a special section of stories for children designed to whet their appetite for more "missionary intelligence.'' Women were encouraged to feel a sacred responsibility to offer their children—particularly their daughters—for the mission field since they could not go themselves. Missionary work among the young was viewed as a primary tool for recruiting candidates for the foreign field and for instilling the principle of stewardship for missions at an early age. (Women were proud, when the Student Volunteer Movement emerged in the late nineteenth century, of having prepared the soil.) Interested in training as well as recruiting candidates, women's societies sometimes assumed the cost of schooling—often of medical education—for potential missionaries.

To carry out these vital functions, the founders of the woman's foreign mission movement worked to establish an auxiliary society in every local church. Their tactical strategy for accomplishing this was to enlist pastors' wives and to encourage the engrafting of missionary concerns on existing ladies' aid societies or female prayer meetings. Enlisting pastors' wives and ordinary laywomen would be easy, they believed, if the mission cause could be presented graphically. No true woman could resist the appeal if she understood the dire need of her heathen sisters. Organizers were not above playing upon the fears and guilt of Christian women in order to enforce the claims of the heathen. Women were chastised for wasting money on dress and frivolous entertainment and warned that

> we will have to answer exactly for our stewardship. Our wastefulness will be our Nemesis. . . . How fearful it will be in the last day, to have our Master point to the cowering, wretched, pagan women, and say to us, ''Ye knew your duty toward these, but ye did it not.''[4]

The fearful responsibility for the souls of their heathen sisters devolved upon Christian women precisely because women alone could enter the harem and the zenana. As a missionary wife writing from Persia told Presbyterian women,

> None but women can reach Mohammedan women. . . . So *we* have a solemn duty in this matter that we cannot shift. The blood of souls is on our skirts, and God will demand them at our hands.[5]

Finally, having appealed to woman's natural altruism and pointed to her solemn and awful responsibility in this matter, the leaders of the woman's foreign mission movement urged that self-interest, too, dictated the formation of local auxiliaries in churches throughout America. Methodist women were assured in the first issue of *Heathen Woman's Friend* that "apart from all considerations of duty to others, it will be profitable to ourselves to unite together in such associations as are contemplated by this Society."[6] The beneficial effect that supporting foreign missions would have on the spiritual life of the churches of America was a powerful, albeit standard, answer to critics who suggested that foreign missions not be undertaken until American Protestantism had put its own house in order. The reflex influence of foreign missions on the church at home was the keystone of the argument for organizing local auxiliaries of the women's foreign mission societies. Regular meeting at the local level for prayer and the dissemination of missionary intelligence would presumably—together with systematic, self-sacrificial giving—deepen the spiritual lives and broaden the commitment to the church of all women involved.

This enormously successful, multi-faceted argument for the participation of evangelical women in the foreign mission crusade was made directly in editorial appeals and indirectly through short pieces of didactic fiction sandwiched into the journals between editorials and reports from the field. Fiction, once roundly denounced in evangelical circles, had been adopted by the late nineteenth century as a form peculiarly suited for teaching moral lessons to women and children.[7] Women, it was popularly believed, responded to graphic portrayals of concrete dilemmas more readily than to abstract argumentation. Fictional embodiments of editorial rhetoric and prescription abound in mission journals. A typical example of such fiction, the story of "The Hillerton Auxiliary" depicts the formation of a small-town auxiliary in the early years of the movement. Read at the Semi-Annual Meeting of the Woman's Foreign Missionary Society of the Presbyterian Church in 1879 and subsequently serialized in *Woman's Work for Woman,* "The Hillerton Auxiliary" is a vehicle for rehearsing the arguments for female missionary societies. As fiction, the story has little to recommend it; as a convenient sketch of the functions of an auxiliary and of that most ambiguous of reasons for forming auxiliaries, the doctrine of reflex influence, "The Hillerton

Auxiliary" will serve our purposes as well as it served those of its author and publishers.

That the ladies of Hillerton need to undergo spiritual transformation is apparent from the opening paragraph. The reader is asked to view Hillerton society through the eyes of the new pastor's wife, since the ladies themselves, in their smug and settled complacency, do not recognize the spiritual deficiencies obvious to a newcomer.

> Mrs. Preston was the young wife of the new pastor at Hillerton. Timid and inexperienced, she was yet an earnest and thoughtful Christian; it troubled her to find no missionary society and no prayer meeting among the ladies of the church. They met often in social life; picnics and festivals were frequent in their respective seasons; but there was no coming together for praise and prayer, or to hear and tell of God's gracious work among the nations, and to consider what they, His children, could do to spread the good news. As Mrs. Preston mused, "the fire burned" until she could no longer hold her peace; so, in the orthodox way, she sought counsel of her husband.[8]

The implicit message to earnest Christians is clear: if their church life has come to revolve around social events rather than spiritual and evangelical concerns, they ought, like Mrs. Preston, to search out a way to recall church life to its true purpose. A missionary society is not a social club; picnics and festivals are inferior to praise and prayer.

The anonymous author of this story, presumably an officer of the Woman's Foreign Missionary Society of the Presbyterian Church, suggests that Mrs. Preston is somewhat quaint and old-fashioned in her timidity and deference to her husband's guidance in church affairs, but there is a double edge to the phrase "in the orthodox way." The association of Mrs. Preston's demure orthodoxy with the formation of a female missionary society subtly reveals the orthodox—and therefore benign—nature of woman's work for foreign missions. There can be no taint of woman's rights in an evangelical society dedicated to hearing and telling of "God's gracious work among the nations" if its founder demonstrates such impeccable wifely submission.

Mr. Preston, interrupted while writing a sermon, advises his wife offhandedly to "call a meeting of the ladies and organize." Left to her own resources, Mrs. Preston decides to approach some of the ladies individually to muster support. This was, the writer informs us, "before the time of Presbyterial Societies, and she was too far from Philadelphia or Chicago to seek aid from headquarters."[9] The women Mrs. Preston visits are stock characters, borrowed from sentimental fiction, speaking set pieces. Each in her turn offers a different argument against female missionary societies. Indeed, in this story with virtually no plot, they have virtually no function but to mouth the standard objections to female missionary work and let young Mrs. Preston answer them as she can.

Mrs. Smith receives Mrs. Preston coldly; it is her opinion that "we have plenty of work at our own doors, without going to the ends of the earth to seek it!" Her "elegant toilette" and "the costly trifles that crowded her parlor" testify to Mrs. Smith's ample means, but she cannot be persuaded that it is her duty to deny herself any luxuries in order to save her heathen sisters. Besides, she argues, their own church is in debt, and she is "opposed to giving money away until our debt is paid; I do not think it would be honest."[10] Blind to her own patent selfishness, Mrs. Smith is an object lesson to the readers of *Woman's Work for Woman* who are continually reminded that giving for foreign missions actually strengthens the work at home.

> When, with joy, we "draw water out of the wells of salvation" for the benefit of others, our own souls are watered as never before.... It is a difficult question to answer, whether the partial awakening of the women of the Presbyterian Church to their duty in foreign missions, is of most effect for good at home or abroad.[11]

Timid Mrs. Preston, finding no well of salvation in Mrs. Smith's parched soul, retreats.

Less easily intimidated than the young pastor's wife, the promoters of female missionary work kept up a constant barrage of pleas for sacrificial giving, presenting missionary work as an opportunity for women to practice "that most beautiful Christian grace, *self-sacrifice*." Editorials on "Self-Denial" remind women that gracious giving should not be morbid or gloomy. Nevertheless, Miss

M. E. Andrews of China urged women to give to the point of sacrifice, saying, "You will not offer to your Saviour that which costs you nothing. Not *so* did he redeem you." Women were asked to scrutinize their household budgets, planning new economies that would allow them to give a few pennies more to missions. An editorial titled "Small Gifts Willingly" cites Biblical precedents in the story of the widow's mites and of the cup of cold water given in Christ's name as evidence that small gifts, "if they measure the extent of our ability," are not only acceptable, but spiritually efficacious. Since the burden of missions, if left for the wealthy to shoulder, will not work its gracious blessing in the souls of the poor, women of limited means are admonished to consult their consciences.

> Let us examine ourselves, dear sisters—those of us whose means are so limited that we find difficulty in supplying the real wants of our families—and see if it is not pride, instead of humility, that makes us shrink from bringing forward our little where others can give much....Surely if our hearts are engaged in this work as they should be, we can all do something; and as giving is a means of grace, and an imperative Christian duty, let us be thoroughly awake on the subject, and we can in some way manage to give systematically....If we cannot possibly make it more, let us bring a five, or even a two cent coin.[12]

Their theology told evangelical women that sacrificial giving was both a Christian duty and a means of grace; their definition of woman's nature suggested to them that women were peculiarly capable of practicing the Christian virtue of self-sacrifice. Isabel Hart, an early organizer for the Methodist Woman's Foreign Missionary Society and a frequent contributor to the pages of *Heathen Woman's Friend,* was perhaps the first remotely systematic thinker to examine the movement's theological and historical assumptions. Her "Woman's Place in the Gospel History and Scheme" points, in orthodox fashion, to the crucifixion as the paradigm for Christian self-sacrifice, but then advances the notion that "Christ was the most intensely feminine while he was the most magnificently manly of all beings." Hart defended Christianity as a woman's religion.

There is more truth in the taunt of our enemies than they

know, that *Christianity is a religion of woman, for woman;* but what they hurl as a reproach, we accept as a glory. . . . the salvation of others bound up in the sacrifice of the self.[13]

Women, the Victorians believed, were naturally inclined toward selflessness; illness and poverty, at least by the conventions that governed sentimental novels, reinforced natural inclinations to piety and benevolence. Certainly young Mrs. Preston found the humbler members of her church most receptive to the idea of forming a missionary auxiliary. It was in the "humble home of a dear old Scotch woman" that Mrs. Preston encountered her first supporter, a woman living in relative poverty who nonetheless believed that "God has been gude to us women, and it will be a blessed thing to help tell yon poor heathen souls of His loving kindness." This cliché of the humble immigrant who is spiritually richer than her social superiors allowed the writer to spice her narrative with a hint of dialect before introducing another stock character familiar to readers of sentimental fiction: the sweet, pious invalid. Mrs. Merwin, "long confined to her room by an incurable disease," is interesting to us not as a pathetic figure, but because she is prepared to make the supreme sacrifice called for by the woman's foreign mission movement; Mrs. Merwin is ready to offer her daughter cheerfully "should He call her to give her life to work for Him among heathen women." The gift of a daughter to the mission field was to be compared with "Mary's 'alabaster box of precious ointment' that was not 'wasted.' "[14]

"The Hillerton Auxiliary" drives the point home by contrasting Mrs. Merwin with the well-to-do and presumably healthy Mrs. Brown. When her support for an auxiliary is solicited, Mrs. Brown affects a judicious manner, inquiring minutely into Mrs. Preston's plans, before offering her objections. At first it seems that her principal objection is to the policy of sending single women as missionaries, but her reasoning reveals a basic lack of sympathy for the mission cause and an underlying fear that her own daughter might find such madness tempting.

And so you intend to propose that we support with our money a young lady missionary in China! I must tell you, Mrs. Preston, that I totally disapprove of *single* ladies going out as missionaries. It is very well for *married* women, who have the protection of a home and husband; but I think it highly improper for young girls to go off in a fit of romantic enthusiasm to live among degraded savages, and have their innocent natures sullied by contact with such creatures. I would never permit my daughter Ada to take such an indelicate and improper course.

The retribution that Mrs. Brown suffers for her selfishness is melodramatic: Precious Ada runs away with a "worthless profligate, only to be deserted by him, and to sink lower and lower in sin, until at last she was utterly lost to her heartbroken parents."[15] The moral, of course, is particularly pointed for any mothers in the audience; maternal selfishness could be spiritually ruinous for children.

A decided belief in the mother's responsibility for the salvation of her children led the woman's foreign mission movement to make work with children a primary concern. To instill Christian and missionary ideals in offspring, children's missionary bands were formed—generally with rather more adult supervision than Rebecca and her little friends had in their experiment with home missionary work. The children's departments of the women's missionary magazines contain stories of dying children who leave all their pennies to the mission cause. Interspersed with such pathetic tales are suggestions for raising money. Children are urged to cultivate "missionary gardens." *Life and Light for Heathen Women* printed a plea for children to grow camomile flowers to dry and powder and send to missionaries in Turkey to use as flea powder; larkspur seeds could also be collected to put in alcohol for washing children's heads in missionary schools.[16] Children nurtured in Christian virtues and fed on spicy narratives of missionary adventure would be immune to the temptations of vice, even if they never actually reached the mission field. Poor Mrs. Brown might have saved Ada, if her own heart had been purer.

Mrs. Brown's opposition to sending single women as missionaries, disingenuous as it was, persuaded Mrs. Preston to propose to the next lady on her list that the women of the church support Mrs. L. of Persia. This proposition is far from satisfactory to Mrs. Johnson who opposes any involvement of married women in mission work. Mrs. Johnson considers her own duties as homemaker a full-time occupation and wonders how such duties could be any less for a missionary's wife.

How much can a woman with husband and children do of missionary work, I should like to know? Why absolutely nothing, that is if she does her duty at home. Suppose I should go running about the streets pretending to teach the poor and that sort of thing, what would become of my children and house?[17]

The whole question of missionary wives was a sensitive one for the woman's foreign mission movement. Some denominational societies supported only single women, even demanding the return of passage and outfit money from women who married in the field. Others, as a matter of course, assumed the support of married women by supplying that portion of a married male missionary's salary that exceeded the allotment for a single man. Whatever the financial arrangements, all denominations were plagued by the issue of deciding how deeply a wife had to be involved in the actual work of the mission before being accorded the title of missionary. In the early years, the woman's foreign mission movement tended to count wives as effective missionaries if they did no more than create a model Christian home in an alien culture. In fact, most missionary wives found time for teaching and nursing—and resented any implication that they were not full partners with their husbands in the great task of evangelizing the heathen.[18]

Mrs. Preston's brief for the married woman missionary, with its celebration of the salvific power of a Christian home, is a staple in the rhetoric of the movement during the formative years. Her reproof of Mrs. Johnson for wasting in idle pursuits time that might otherwise be devoted to good works is also standard fare in the journals of the women's missionary societies.

There is no influence so powerful upon the heathen as the wonderful sight (as it is to them) of a happy Christian home, where wife and mother is loved and respected by her husband as his equal, and honored and obeyed by her children. And, dear Mrs. Johnson, pardon me, but do we not spend in useless calls and idle shopping, to say nothing of purposeless strolls and unprofitable books, as much time as would enable us to give an hour or two every day to teaching some ignorant souls about Jesus? We do these things, and yet we do not think we neglect our families.[19]

Clearly, the example of the missionary wife will not only lead benighted heathen to Christ, but will also serve as a reproach to churchwomen whose devotion to duty is less than perfect. At least according to the theory of reflex influence, American women would be inspired to imitate such models of selflessness.

The sacrifice of self that Isabel Hart had argued was the essential—and essentially feminine—lesson embodied in "Gospel History" is, of course, not the only conclusion to be drawn by readers of Scripture. Those who interpreted Biblical admonitions more literally than Hart was wont to do often cited Biblical precedent when opposing female missionary societies. In order to expose the shallowness of such opposition—and implicitly of such Biblical literalism—the author of "The Hillerton Auxiliary" created Mrs. Jones. Mrs. Jones objects to women's societies on principle because "there is always more or less gossip in them." Social groups are exempted from Mrs. Jones's prohibition against women's societies because, for some reason that remains obscure, they seem to her to allow a "true woman to stay in her sphere and look after her family; 'guide the house' as the apostle says." Mrs. Jones, a relentless Pauline prooftexter, cites the apostle again as telling women to be " 'keepers at home' " and challenges Mrs. Preston to "find anything in the Bible about missionary societies." Mrs. Jones is such a patently silly woman, and her reasoning is so confused and inconsistent, that no answer to her objections is even advanced in the story.[20]

The woman's foreign mission movement, however, did not leave such arguments unanswered. Women were ready to fight Biblical precedent with Biblical precedent. An article entitled "Woman as a Christian Factor," published in *Woman's Work for Woman* in 1881, invoked a progressive view of history to support the claim that the time had come to resurrect certain Biblical precepts long ignored.

The question of Mordecai to Esther, "And who knoweth whether thou art come to the kingdom for such a time as this?" is a pertinent one...today. Here and now as never before and in no other land has woman's influence been demonstrated in every department of society, particularly in religious directions. Two generations ago it was far otherwise. In the days of our grandmothers the approved model for woman was Sarah, the wife of Abraham, and the point in her character which evoked peculiar commendation was that meek and quiet spirit with which she adorned herself.

The signs of the times, as interpreted by the leaders of the woman's foreign mission movement, indicated that use of Sarah as a model ought to be discarded in light of a reexamination of the "relation of woman to the New Testament church."

> Our grandfathers dwelt lightly upon that exceeding honor which Christ in assuming human form had cast upon woman. ...Strangely too was it forgotten that Anna, the prophetess, spake of the Babe of Bethlehem to all them that dwelt in Jerusalem, that Mary Magdalene and Joanna and Susanna and many other women, abandoning their homes, followed the weary steps of our Master...and that to the women who labored with Paul in the gospel many of the tenderest of his messages...were addressed. More strangely still was it forgotten that almost the only acts of great self-sacrifice narrated by the evangelists were performed by women; that no man cast all his living into the temple treasury, but a woman and she a widow; only a woman anointed the Saviour with precious ointment, while men disapproved this expression of grateful love; only a woman washed His feet with tears; women were last at the cross and earliest at the sepulchre.[21]

The sarcasm and bitterness of that "strangely" and "more strangely still," combined with the litany of "no man...but a woman," "only a woman," and again "only a woman," reveals the absolute determination of these women to insist upon a new order within the churches. No man, appealing to Biblical precedent or claiming apostolic office, would prevent them from coming into their own— tentative and limited as the work they claimed for their own was in the initial stages of the woman's mission movement.

Like their male colleagues, the leaders of the female missionary societies look back upon their century and saw the providential opening of mission fields. The signs of the times seemed promising indeed to Jennie Fowler Willing.

Russian serfs freed; our own black chattels humanized, enfranchised, even represented in our Senate; the Austrian Concordat repealed; Italy and Spain renovated. In Madagascar, a nation born to the Lord Christ in a single day. China and Japan open to Christian teachers and preachers.... India entreating Christian women to come and teach her degraded daughters.

What these signs meant specifically to Mrs. Willing was that "God is opening mission fields, and fitting American women to enter them."[22] Political developments that opened new fields to evangelization were only half of the providential equation that women saw in the history of the nineteenth century; chance alone could never, to them, account for the coincidence of the opening of mission fields with the dawning of the woman's era. Isabel Hart, in an article replete with images of changing seasons and ripening fruit, traced the pattern of preparation and development preceding the full revelation of Divine intent. "The East," she claimed, "is ready; the soil is prepared for the seed." That divine preparation of foreign soil was, of course, essential; no less crucial, the simultaneous "awakening of Christian women to a sense of power and privilege, duty and obligation;... a deep conviction that much should be rendered, much having been received." The awakening that Hart perceived was one of "women seeking a higher culture, a fuller development." The resulting cultivation of woman's talents was, to Hart, clearly providential because it occurred before any need was apparent.

> Some knocked at the door of medical colleges.... and some of us did not know what all this meant, and why all this was. But soon the cry came from India.... Then we saw the finger of providence, and whither it pointed.[23]

Biblical precedent, as well as a providential reading of history, was used to justify a wider sphere for woman's talents. The author of "Woman As a Christian Factor" rejoiced that "the time has come when Sarah is no longer accepted as the only type of womanhood. Around the cross gather the Marys and Marthas, the Joannas and Susannas, the Phoebes and Priscillas, the Eunices and Loises, the Tryphenas and Tryphosas." And yet these women disclaimed any rejection of femininity; woman's traditional role was not to be abandoned but enlarged.

> While in the home-life woman is expected to be all that Sarah was, in every respect she is expected to be immeasurably more than Sarah could have been.

Isabel Hart, whose claim that Christianity is a feminine religion sounds distinctly unorthodox, used her assertion of Christ's femininity to reassure her readers that the new age would not strip them of their womanliness.

> This is woman's era, not for unwomanly claims and clamor, but for deeper devotion, for fuller consecration, and growing out of these, more earnest and far-reaching activities. It is woman's era to be *more womanly,* in being more like her Lord and Master, Who went about doing good.

The present age was, so far as the leadership of the woman's foreign mission movement was concerned, "the age of sanctified female talent."[24]

Even that rather conservative estimate of woman's role was a more advanced view than the one that prevailed in Hillerton. Recalcitrance among the socially prominent ladies of the church is only the first obstacle set in Mrs. Preston's path. Sanctified female talent is in short supply in Hillerton. Among the few willing to join a missionary society, none is ready to lead in prayer. Mrs. Preston reluctantly performs that office herself at the first meeting. Private efforts to persuade others to pray at subsequent meetings bear little fruit; typically, only the old Scotswoman and Miss Steel, a middle-aged dressmaker, can bring themselves to pray publicly. And since no one can be recruited to prepare missionary papers, the entire responsibility for kindling missionary enthusiasm by laying information before the faithful falls to Mrs. Preston. One might assume that such reticence and reluctance are overdrawn, a failing in the fiction rather than in the reality it is meant to capture; but the issue of praying and speaking publicly is prominently addressed in the pages of women's missionary journals. (Karen Blair notes a similar reluctance among clubwomen in the nineteenth century to speak publicly and to research and write papers for presentation at club meetings.[25])

Contrary to expectations of spiritual revitalization, public prayer and proclamation were the first areas in which the actual reflex influence of foreign missions was made manifest among churchwomen. Mrs. Rufus Anderson, wife of the longtime secretary of the American Board of Commissioners for Foreign Missions and herself one of the charter members of the Woman's Board of Missions (Congregational), wrote an article for *Life and Light for Heathen Women* on the "Reflex Influence of Woman's Missionary Work" in which she spelled out the changes wrought in the first years.

> Four or five years ago, when we first began to hold annual and quarterly meetings, it was almost impossible to find anyone willing to contribute to the usefulness of the meetings, or to assume any responsibility in connection with them.... We rejoice today in the animating change.... Many hearts have been kept warm, many minds bright, in the work of preparing leaflets, writing letters innumerable, talking and planning.

Mrs. Anderson cited the "spiritual benefits," but emphasized the "intellectual resources brought out" and concluded that "God has given to his daughters, as well as to his sons, talents to be used in his service."[26]

Mrs. Anderson was not alone in valuing missionary work for its effect on the workers. Writing in *Woman's Work for Woman*, Mrs. M. N. Blakeslee listed among the reasons "Why We Should Keep Up Our Auxiliaries" the efficacy of the auxiliary in overcoming the "narrowness and reticence" that are "two great evils of the social life of small country towns and villages." Missionary work, she wrote, provides women with food for thought more wholesome than a steady diet of village gossip. Petty personal troubles recede when a woman reflects on the utter degradation of her heathen sisters. Thus missionary work broadens a woman's interior horizons. It can also, according to Mrs. Blakeslee, help her overcome the reticence that conceals her talents.

> We are so afraid we shall get snubbed, or be called enthusiastic or gushing, that we go on locking up within ourselves kindly impulses and generous deeds and loving words.... Village and church life languishes. There is nobody "to go ahead and do things."... We can come out of ourselves about missionary

matters when we might not in something nearer home. . . . Do
not sit in a dumb and dreadful silence. . . . You will be amazed
to see how your powers grow as you use them. One of the surprising things of this last twenty years or less is the way woman's work has brought out quiet, reticent little women. . . who
find themselves good speakers.[27]

To judge from the frequent editorials on "The Casting Out of
Dumb Spirits," "Women's Prayers," and "Women's Voices," the
reluctance to speak and pray publicly that Mrs. Preston encountered
among the ladies of Hillerton was both pervasive and persistent.
More than twenty years after the movement began, *Woman's Work for
Woman* was still fighting the influence of St. Paul's admonition to let
the women keep silence in church, arguing that a correct reading of
the passage would resolve the issue.

> They [those who would use the text to silence women in Ameri-
> can churches in the nineteenth century] do not take into con-
> sideration the context in which the apostle's recommendation
> is said, or they would see that it had special reference to a very
> special condition of things then existing.

Once Biblical injunctions had been swept aside, there remained the
problem of persuading women to overcome ingrained inhibitions.
Specific advice about what to pray for and how to pray stressed the
acceptability of short, informal petitions—even "broken, feeble,
half-articulate prayer"—expressing the "plain urgent wants of
yourself and sisters associated with you in the work for Christ."
Women who "have never yet brought [themselves] to this difficult,
but most blessed duty" were begged to try.[28]

A broken petition was, however, only the first step; women
were expected to hone their skills. Editorials offered advice on the
modulation and projection of the voice in public speaking. The first
imperative for a public speaker was to make herself heard, but
women were promised that they need not in the process make themselves unattractive or unfeminine.

> They must hear what we say, and hear *all* that we say; not here

and there a word or sentence, losing what comes between and completes the sense. To secure this result, it is not necessary to scream, or to pitch our voices on a high, unnatural key, or to fling our words out as if they were pebbles with which we were pelting our audience, or to do anything else but clearly, distinctly, and with proper emphasis, utter the words which bear our thought..., forgetting ourselves.

The implication of this advice is that a woman could—and ought to—be womanly in addressing a missionary meeting. Her voice was in His service; she was the instrument of His kingdom at that moment. "Nor will such use of your voice," readers were assured, "detract from its gentle, womanly quality at other times."[29] The need for such specific instruction and reassurance indicates that the reflex influence of the woman's foreign mission movement might profoundly change the lives of women if it were simply to train women in small towns across the face of America in the art of public speaking. The emphasis placed on retaining femininity in the midst of new work underlines, however, the essentially conservative formulation of woman's role in society that prevailed among the leaders of the woman's mission movement as late as the mid-1880s.

The transformation effected in the ladies of Hillerton, however, occurs mainly on a spiritual rather than a practical plane. In the beginning, unable to resolve their differences over the question of single versus married missionaries, the Hillerton auxiliary

> finally agreed to support a native teacher, the express condition being that she should write every month to the society, and give full and accurate details of each day's work, sending also the names and photographs of all her most interesting converts, with sketches of their history.[30]

The conditions stipulated are so exacting and onerous as to make compliance virtually impossible; the stunted, grasping natures of Mrs. Smith, Mrs. Brown, Mrs. Johnson, and Mrs. Jones lie exposed in the selfish demands they make of that poor, overworked native teacher. The spirit in which they go about ensuring that they get their money's worth out of the teacher offers a stark contrast to the state of their souls after the missionary influence has begun its gracious work.

The key to Hillerton's salvation was held, it turns out, in the frail hands of Mrs. Merwin. She sends her daughter Mary to the mission field in China. Since Mary is one of their own, the Hillerton auxiliary undertakes her support; "through this new and tender tie uniting them to their heathen sisters came a rich blessing upon the women in the home church." The blessing on the church at home as the reflex influence of foreign missionary work provides the moral of this pious tale. What happened to the women of Hillerton can, the author implies, happen anywhere an auxiliary takes root. And precisely what did happen?

> Their hearts were softened, their consciences were quickened, they realized more fully the condition of those who bore alone all the burdens of womankind in a heathen land, unblessed by the knowledge of a burden-bearing Saviour. Then came a sense of their own coldness and ingratitude towards this tender Saviour whom they had always known, and who had encircled all their lives with His loving kindness and tender mercy. There was more heart searching, more secret prayer; and one day the pastor was amazed and overwhelmed with joy to find that his church was in the midst of a gracious and wonderful revival![31]

The revival in Hillerton was wholly feminine in that it occurred without intervention or guidance from the pastor, but it was scarcely feminist. Just as the female mission movement as a whole was formed with no intention of usurping male prerogatives, so the ladies of Hillerton in their reconsecration had no intention of dispensing with the services of Mr. Preston. Instead, they became more active and ardent worshipers in his congregation. The revitalized church in Hillerton must have been a reassuring image to those women—or pastors—who feared that female auxiliaries might convert women to the cause of woman's rights.

The form that the Hillerton revival took is as significant as the fact of the revival. The author describes women offering public prayer as a primary sign of spiritual renewal: "dumb lips opened, and stammering tongues spoke out of the fulness of grateful hearts the wonderful works of God." Women in Hillerton learn to pray, not formally and systematically, but with short petitions for specific objects. They learn to pray as women, not as men pray. Even in prayer the essential womanliness of the female sex sets it apart from the male. Women petition their Maker as wives and mothers on behalf of other wives and mothers.

> For example, at one of these meetings, a letter from Persia was read, which told that death had entered a missionary family, and asked for the bereaved mother the prayers of her Christian sisters. Mrs. Burton's motherly heart melted as she thought of her own little darling, and it was not hard to plead fervently that the Comforter might abide in that stricken home.[32]

Although evangelical women apparently believed that a woman's prayer would differ from a man's, they did not consider a woman's stammering tongue and her broken petition less efficacious than the fluent and formal prayers offered by men. On the contrary, since a woman's heart was naturally more religious than a man's, it followed that a woman's prayer, spoken from the heart, would be more acceptable to God than empty eloquence. A sketch in *Woman's Work for Woman* described two auxiliaries in the same city, one languishing, the other sparkling with life. The secret of the successful society lay in its president's ability to pray a woman's prayer rather than imitate the formal phrases employed by ministers.

> She did not, in her prayer, go all around the universe first, with sweeping generalities of petition. . . . She asked very simply and directly for what *they* needed. . . . It was not a long prayer, it was brief, simple, and from the heart. She did not "make a prayer"—she *prayed*.[33]

Men make prayers; women pray.

The perceived power of female prayer was the motive force driving the woman's foreign mission movement. A paper read at the semiannual meeting of the Woman's Foreign Missionary Society of the Presbyterian Church in 1877 compared the movement with a steam engine on display at the Centennial Exhibition.

> All its parts were in order, the bands in place, the water was in

the boiler, and the fuel in the furnace. But there was no *fire,* and without this it would remain a useless thing, no matter how perfect its construction or how beautiful its finish. And I thought, how like this our missionary work is!

The fire needed to make the machinery of the mission movement work, according to this analogy, was the power of the Holy Spirit— which "can be obtained by united, importunate, persevering prayer." The author added a caveat that suggests that in her opinion women would be particularly successful in calling down this power.

> Of course it must be real prayer; not a mere form of words, or a passing wish, but the firm expression of real desire, offered in firm, unwavering trust in the word and promise of God.[34]

Evangelical women did not, of course, believe that men were incapable of real prayer, only that women were more likely to possess the almost childlike, unwavering trust in which effective prayer was grounded.

The beauty of assigning such importance to prayer was that prayer was a service that any woman might render to the mission effort, thereby playing a vital role in the regeneration of the world. The power of prayer was conceived of as a peculiarly democratic force.

> Let the women in the little churches which are struggling for existence, who are saying "We are too weak to do anything for foreign missions," remember that none are too weak to do what they can, or too poor to pray.

Concerted female prayer was considered so vital to the movement that women were urged to spend a specific hour each week or each day in prayer for foreign missions. The good that might be accomplished by importuning the throne of grace was, these women believed, limitless.

> Suppose on each Sabbath, impressed with this great truth, every woman in our churches, at home and abroad, rich and poor, the learned and the ignorant, the gifted and the simple,

mother and daughter, mistress and maid, should be found each in her closet at that consecrated hour. . . . Who can place a limit to the results? What revivals we should hear of in India, in China, in Japan, in Persia, in Syria, in Africa, and in "the uttermost parts of the earth!"

And last, but not necessarily least, this rhapsodic vision ends with the promise of "new life and growth at home!"[35]

The nature of the new life and growth that the leaders of the woman's foreign mission movement anticipated is given concrete form in the missionary revival that swept through the church in Hillerton. That revival was nurtured in secret prayer and soul-searching stimulated by Mary Merwin's letters from China. Learning to pray publicly was the first fruit of the revival among the ladies, but not its only manifestation. The ladies of Hillerton, we are told, also developed an insatiable appetite for missionary intelligence.

It became delightful. . . to trace through papers and periodicals the steady march of God's hosts. . . . Even the daily papers were laid under contribution and items fresh and suggestive culled to prove that the morning light was breaking, the shadows fleeing, and all things betokening the coming of the King.[36]

The spiritual revival among the ladies of the Hillerton auxiliary typifies the effect that, according to the doctrine of reflex influence, work for foreign missions could be expected to have on Christian womanhood in America. The founders of the female foreign missionary societies did not suspect, although they saw and applauded the temporal skills that work for missions developed in women, that the primary reflex influence of the massive mobilization of Christian womanhood might not be spiritual at all. Combing newspapers and conducting meetings, after all, bear no direct relation to spiritual renewal; both practices could easily be adapted for secular ends, as they were by women of the Progressive era who involved themselves in a broad spectrum of community service and municipal reform projects. The nonspiritual reflex influence of mission work on the leaders of the movement was more immediate and, as we shall see in a subsequent chapter, changed them more radically than it did their constituency in the churches.

The woman's foreign mission movement rapidly developed from its parochial, evangelical beginnings into an essentially modern, international enterprise. That transformation, if unexpected, was not an unwelcome one in the eyes of the movement's leaders. They celebrated the appearance of each new denominational society and moved to coordinate their activities. By the late 1880s, the organizational apparatus of the largest woman's movement of the nineteenth century was in place in all the major Protestant denominations—and in most of the smaller ones. As the denominational societies garnered members and funds, administration of their operation became increasingly complex. The superstructure of Presbyterial societies (and their equivalents in other denominations) and traveling agents attached to regional and national headquarters that had not existed when Mrs. Preston set out to organize the ladies of Hillerton was swiftly hammered together. Full-time, salaried staff positions were created when the societies' business became too complicated and time-consuming for part-time volunteers to manage. Foreign secretaries took charge of the extensive correspondence with missionaries overseas. Home secretaries handled correspondence with regional and local officers—and with candidates for foreign service. Regional officers, particularly in the western part of the country, often became full-time organizers. Those who remained unsalaried had their expenses met by the society, thereby earning what amounted to a subsistence wage. Reflecting the importance attached to the production of missionary literature, the highest salaried employees of any society were usually the editors of the women's missionary magazines. The work done by the officers and agents of the movement offers an instructive contrast to what we have seen as the "task" assigned local auxiliary members.

One of the most successful of the movement's regional officers was Mary Clarke Nind, president of the Western Branch of the Woman's Foreign Missionary Society of the Methodist Episcopal Church. The territory she worked was eventually divided into four separate, and vigorous, branches. Mrs. Nind's job was not an easy one.

Much of her Branch was wilderness. The towns were few and

far apart, the churches weak and struggling.... Her courage
never faltered as by faith she laid the foundations of this great
organization in Minnesota, the Dakotas, Montana, Idaho,
Washington, and Oregon, traveling over the unbroken prairie
and through the wilderness, in wagon, or cart, or sleigh, in
summer and winter, by day and by night, by freight train or
day coach (never in a Pullman, the Lord's money was too precious for such luxuries), compassing as many as 5,000 miles in
a single year.[37]

The incredible Mrs. Nind, hailed on her triumphal tour of mission stations around the world in 1894–96 as "The Little Bishop"
and "Mother Nind," kept to her punishing schedule while raising
four children—two of whom became missionaries.

Since few mothers possessed Mrs. Nind's limitless energy, the
larger societies frequently employed single women as traveling
agents to stir up enthusiasm for the cause and to encourage the local
ladies in small towns everywhere to band together in auxiliaries.
The instructions given one such agent by the executive committee of
the Woman's Foreign Missionary Society of the Presbyterian
Church (North) are typical. Miss S. B. Loring was hired to tour
western Pennsylvania and Ohio, and told to visit "small places off
the Railroad." She received her commission in January 1875; later
that year she reported having "held one hundred ninety meetings,
and assisted in organizing forty-three auxiliary societies, two
Sabbath-school missionary associations, and two [children's]
Bands." She attributed her success not to her own powers of persuasion, but to the fact that she was not "begging" but making "an effort to rouse interest by dispelling the darkness of ignorance."[38] In
common with the leading mission theorists of the age, she believed
that the facts would speak for themselves, that Christian America—
or at least Christian women—would do the right thing if only the
path of righteousness could be made abundantly clear.

Generally more effective than traveling agents in purveying
missionary intelligence were missionaries themselves. Missionaries
on furlough in the States were expected to make speaking tours;
their itineraries were planned by the denominational society's home
secretary in response to requests from local churches. Personal ap-
pearances by missionaries were highly prized in small-town Amer-

ica. Advance notices were placed in local newspapers; ordinarily, an open invitation to attend an evening lecture in the church was issued to the whole community. One such tour, made by Clementina Butler in western New York in 1870, was reported to have "brought about what may be called a 'missionary awakening' among the ladies of that section." The report describes this awakening.

> Passing from town to town, addressing at almost every stopping place some pre-appointed gathering, she has communicated her observations of the degraded and wretched condition of the women in India to hundreds if not thousands of our N.Y. sisters. . . . Many have drunk in her spirit and caught her inspiration. Reports from the auxiliaries formed make frequent mention of. . . her addresses.

Mrs. Butler was something of a celebrity among Methodists; the secretary of one auxiliary observed that "thousands were attracted to hear the wife of the founder of the India mission who would not have been drawn by 'any lady less prominently and personally identified with our missionary work.' "[39] Missionaries with lesser reputations resorted to displaying curiosities (at the sort of parlor meeting described in *Rebecca of Sunnybrook Farm*) to attract an audience. Ettie E. Baldwin returned from China in 1870 bringing "articles illustrative of the life and customs of Chinese people" for just this purpose.

> Among other things I had made a model of the bound foot of a Chinese lady, and I find it interests our friends more than anything else we brought. . . . It was most offensive-looking, and I thanked the Lord that to me was given birth in a Christian land.[40]

Such graphic evidence of the wretched condition of heathen women served the dual purpose of kindling missionary enthusiasm in American women and convincing them that Christianity had indeed blessed and elevated womanhood. It is not surprising that local auxiliaries were organized in the wake of missionary tours.

In the years after the initial formation of auxiliary societies, missionary visits were special occasions that rekindled waning enthusiasm and refilled empty coffers. Other special events sponsored at the local level, such as bazaars and missionary teas, served the same purpose. However, there were never enough returned missionaries to meet the demand for speakers, and—even in theory—the women did not want their cause to depend on momentary interest and occasional generosity. Instead, their goal was to cultivate sustained concern and systematic giving. Toward this end, they employed that favorite tool of nineteenth-century evangelicals, the printing press.[41]

All of the major women's foreign missionary societies began publication of their own magazines almost immediately after they first organized. It is one measure of the popularity of the press among evangelicals that magazines seemed a natural way for those women committed to the missionary cause to approach their evangelical sisters. As a regular and intimate visitor in the home, the missionary magazine did not allow appeals for missions to be limited to a yearly missionary Sunday or the infrequent visits of actual workers home from the foreign field. Jennie Fowler Willing, for one, felt that women needed "continual reminders of responsibility." Auxiliaries, as "associations for the diffusion of missionary intelligence," had a role to play in sustaining interest in missions, but Mrs. Willing believed that the society's journal would be its most effective agent because it could penetrate the home itself.

> Its [the Woman's Foreign Missionary Society's] papers will glide into the homes of the land, as do the Romish Sisters into all places where gentle works have power; not like them, to warp the mind, little by little, toward the Antichrist, but to tone Christian thought up to God's purposes of salvation.[42]

The power of the printed word to work in the heart (like her anti-Catholic sentiments) was an article of faith with Mrs. Willing, as with many evangelicals in mid- and late-nineteenth-century America. In the women's societies, the printed word was regarded as even more effective than the spoken word. Auxiliary members were urged to talk about their cause at every opportunity, not omitting the occasions presented by vacation travel. ("What more fitting theme can there be for a Christian lady anywhere. . . . It is a good thing to talk about on Rye Beach, in the 'Crawford House,' under the porticoes of 'Congress Hall,' on the flying Pullman car, bound for Yosemite.'') But talk needed to be reinforced and buttressed with print; women were asked to solicit subscriptions to mission periodicals from all their friends (''They will not refuse you thirty cents for such a periodical. It will be worth thirty cents to them to see what it is that so much interests you!'') and were reminded ''to have a few copies with you on your summer tour and at camp-meeting.''[43]

The rapid expansion of the evangelical press in the nineteenth century was part of the explosion of print that accompanied the rise of literacy and technological advances in printing. The power of ''special interest'' publications to influence opinion was widely recognized. Writing of the abolitionist press, Catharine Beecher proclaimed, ''There are no men who act more efficiently as the leaders of an enterprise than the editors of the periodicals that advocate and defend it.''[44] Certainly Beecher's claim may be made for the women who editorialized in missionary magazines.

The journals published by the female foreign missionary societies offer a remarkably detailed picture of the movement. They prescribe appropriate activities for auxiliaries and spell out duties for individual members; they report on the progress of the work at home and abroad with great specificity; above all, they communicate to the reader a sense of importance and urgency of the task at hand. The consistency among the journals of the various societies, as well as the frequency with which they reprint each other's articles and report on each other's activities, reinforces the participants' claim that they were not engaged in narrow, denominational work but in one grand movement. This study, therefore, treats the journals collectively as voicing the opinions and attitudes and policies of the leadership of a single, although multifaceted, movement.

This collective voice of the woman's foreign mission movement is distinctively and self-consciously feminine. An editorial in an early number of *Heathen Woman's Friend* announces that the women have designed their magazine to offer an alternative to male-edited church publications that speak to a male but not to a female audience.

Reports in our Church papers and the *Missionary Advocate* are its [the General Missionary Society of the Methodist Episcopal Church (North)'s] principal means of public instruction. Prosy columns of close print, with spiritless rills of statistics oozing through them. Of prime importance to the men who officer the forces, but not attractive to everyday readers; not adapted to create enthusiasm in the homes of the church. . . . One wee Hindoo baby, on its way to the bloody Ganges, would move them more than the new Mission House full of statistics. . . . We mean, by God's help, to send out matter that shall interest the people at home, give them something to talk about, speak to their hearts, bring the heathen to their doors.[45]

By conceiving of their missionary magazines as intimate friends visiting women in their homes, the editors created a personal relationship between auxiliary members and a society's printed voice. The intimate quality of this relationship, fostered in the early years of the movement, resulted in some awkward moments for editors forced by the growth of their operations to adopt a more businesslike approach. The editor of *Heathen Woman's Friend* felt uncomfortable about requiring local auxiliaries to trim lengthy reports and obituaries, but was eventually constrained by space limitations to do so; she was persuaded that no male editor of a secular paper would have felt the same hesitation and compunction.[46]

Intimacy between the constituency of the women's societies and their journals did not exist only in the minds of the editors. That an emotional bond was perceived from the other side is evident in an incident recalled somewhat ruefully by Ellen Parsons when she looked back on twenty-five years as editor of *Woman's Work for Woman*. Shortly after moving to new offices in New York City in 1888, Miss Parsons was visited by "a woman from a country village who had promised herself 'to spend the day with the editor of WOMAN'S WORK' and one forenoon settled herself with her knitting on my window seat.''[47] Parsons's evident dismay suggests that, although touched and flattered, she did not welcome the countrywoman's visit. Her bemused tone is that of the sophisticated professional confronted with uncomprehending naiveté; the distance between editor and knitter is virtually unbridgeable. Parsons, or rather her predecessor, had fostered a relationship no longer either possible or appropriate. The discrepancy between the expectations of editor and knitter are symptomatic of the tensions that developed within the woman's foreign mission movement as the leadership adopted an increasingly professional stance.

The editorial voice of the journals in the early years is not only feminine, but also clearly maternal; it cajoles and instructs, scolds and advises, pleads and praises. Editorial contributors ordinarily assumed that as wives and mothers they shared a common body of experience with their readers. When Mrs. Willing scolded women for setting too rich a table, she included herself among the offenders.

> We make the home, and if we pamper the necessity of devouring thousands every year, to the dire hurt of the body, we are grossly culpable. I am writing for women, else I should have something to say of the *fifty millions* that this *Christian* land pays, yearly, for *tobacco*, chiefly for masculine poisoning, and our annual national *liquor bill of three thousand millions*, with its adjunct taxes, pauperism, thief-catchings, murderer-hangings, etc., which men might vote down if they would.[48]

Mrs. Willing clearly had a message for men (one that she delivered through her work for temperance and for woman's suffrage), but for this audience she felt compelled to limit her remarks to woman's responsibility in that sphere in which her competency would be indisputable.

In later years, editorializers in women's mission magazines did not refrain from commenting on public and political questions outside the realm of the Victorian homemaker; but the housewife as editor was characteristic of the movement in its early phase. It is therefore symbolically appropriate that Harriet Merrick Warren, the editor of *Heathen Woman's Friend* from 1869 until her death in 1893, was the wife of Dr. William F. Warren, the president of Boston University, and the mother of four children.[49] Mrs. Warren, a graduate of Wilbraham Academy in her Massachusetts hometown, pursued her studies in Germany while her husband read theology there; but she never planned to have any career other than that of wife and mother. As the wife of a prominent minister and university president, she gave generously of her time and energy to a number of volunteer causes; she served as a trustee of the New England Conservatory, an officer of the Indian Rights Association, an officer of the American Maternal Association, a member of the Board of Management of the New England Deaconess Home and Training

School, and a member of the Massachusetts Society for University Education for Women—all in addition to her work as editor of a monthly journal. The range and scope of her activities no doubt exceeded that of her average reader; nevertheless, when she wrote editorials it was as a Christian wife and mother that she addressed other wives and mothers.

Mrs. Warren's successor—after a brief interlude when one of her married daughters undertook the editing—was Louise Manning Hodgkins.[50] Miss Hodgkins's appointment reflects the changing mode of the woman's foreign mission movement in the last decade of the century; in choosing Hodgkins the executive committee of the Methodist Episcopal Woman's Foreign Missionary Society abandoned the mother-editor model. Miss Hodgkins came to the editor's desk from a chair in English literature at Wellesley College. She brought to her new job a professional perspective and competence remarkably similar to that with which Ellen Parsons had edited *Woman's Work for Woman* since leaving a teaching post at Mount Holyoke in 1885 in answer to a call from the leadership of the Presbyterian women's societies. But unlike Parsons who had actually served five years under the American Board as a teacher at the American School for Girls in Constantinople, Hodgkins had no missionary credentials either personal or familial; her appointment was apparently made on the basis of professional rather than spiritual gifts, although she was conventionally pious. Her pragmatic approach was immediately evident in her decision to devote two columns of the editorial section each month to "practical suggestions for work."[51] The spiritual admonitions that flowed so regularly from Mrs. Warren's pen were simply not Miss Hodgkins's style.

Nor did Miss Hodgkins confine her editorial comment to issues that fell within a woman's traditional spheres of domesticity and piety. Noting in 1896 that Clara Barton and her Red Cross aides were ready to go to Turkey, she wondered (in print), "Is it possible that the hand of woman, undirected by any self-interest, will untangle this knot so long the embarrassment of the Great Powers?"[52] Like her predecessor, Louise Manning Hodgkins believed that women might be a leavening agent in society, but her conception of their influence extends beyond spiritual to political realms. Compare her words with her predecessor's editorial on bread making which took as its text the passage likening the kingdom of heaven to the leaven "which a woman took and hid in three measures of meal until the whole was leavened."

> Our Lord has honored and dignified and immortalized the bread-making process by likening it to His own divine work in the world, the universal leavening of humanity with truth and holiness. He has in like manner honored and dignified woman by making her the human agent of the work. She is the one who is to take the leaven of His teaching and life, and mix and mingle it with measures of human society until the whole is leavened.[53]

Louise Manning Hodgkins would not have disagreed with these sentiments, but the metaphor of bread making would not have occurred so naturally to her as it did to Harriet Merrick Warren. The difference between the two women is the measure of the change that accompanied growth during the formative years of the woman's foreign mission movement.

The unanticipated emergence of professionalism among the leaders of the movement created tension between the leadership and rank and file members of local auxiliaries; it also encouraged the leaders to formulate anew their vision of woman's appropriate role in the missionary enterprise. The next chapter explores both these aspects of the reflex influence of missions on the women who led the denominational societies.

*Chapter 4*

# The Science of Missions

The symbols of professional authority cultivated by the women who led the woman's foreign mission movement resembled, increasingly in the 1890s, the symbols of male professionalism. No longer satisfied with the use of a room down the corridor from their denomination's general missionary headquarters, the women's societies acquired permanent offices. Such trappings were of sufficient significance that, for example, in July, 1894, some six months after she assumed the editorship of *Heathen Woman's Friend*, Louise Manning Hodgkins illustrated her first annual report on the journal with photographs of the magazine's offices.[1] There are no people in either of the offices shown, only the accoutrements of power and professional expertise: a rolltop desk, flanked by bookcase, chairs, and tables. There are no sentimental feminine touches; the rooms are businesslike. The atmosphere of efficiency is enhanced by the uncluttered desks and general tidiness; strangely, the absence of people in the photos reinforces the sense of work under control, of a well-run operation. And, significantly, without workers at their desks, there is no evidence indicating that these offices belong to women. In this respect the offices serve as a metaphor for the movement itself, which, with the professionalization of its leadership, discarded its special identity as a mission conducted by women, for women and children.

The officers of the women's societies worked closely with their male colleagues in denominational headquarters; when these men, in an attempt to make a "science" of modern missions, instituted more professional methods in mission administration, the women followed suit. Without quite realizing what was happening, they entered a male professional world. Their doing so helped modify the ideal of pious femininity that had shaped evangelical womanhood's role in the Protestant missionary enterprise. Unwilling to accept any longer the constraints that Victorian notions had placed on woman's

93

work for missions, the administrators of the women's foreign missionary societies redefined their task to meet the needs of modern missions. The shift in tone and policy to a more professional mode occurred gradually, although the pace accelerated after 1890 as death thinned the ranks of the original organizers of the movement, and their places were filled by college-educated professionals.

A professionalized woman's foreign mission movement was, however, not simply a carbon copy of the Protestant foreign mission movement, a smudged and fainter version of the denominational societies run by men. For one thing, professionalization did not occur without resistance. The constituency of the women's societies lagged far behind the leadership in embracing new policies and practices. While the men professionalized their operation in part to build a new constituency among businessmen and lay professionals,[2] the officers of the women's societies were responding to a need they perceived for more efficient organization. Since this perception was not shared by the average churchwoman, emerging professionalism brought the leadership of the woman's foreign mission movement into conflict with the rank and file. While their male colleagues concentrated on building an enlarged base of support among laymen, the national officers of the women's societies were seeking to reconcile an extant constituency to new realities. Their compromise with the Victorian ideal of true womanhood was to retain the rhetoric of domesticity while extending the limits of the domestic sphere and to substitute circumstance for nature in explaining the special character of woman.

Actually, the need to reformulate their mission and reeducate their constituency had been apparent to some administrators of women's foreign missionary societies from almost the beginning of their operation. The new note of modern professionalism that characterized the movement after about 1890 can be heard evolving in debates that raged in the pages of women's missionary magazines during the formative years. Three related issues were especially controversial: the practice of assigning "special objects" to particular auxiliaries, the extent to which the function of the local auxiliary ought to be social, and the conflicting expectations concerning correspondence between missionaries and the women supporting them. Looking at each controversy in turn, one finds repeated a pattern of emerging professionalism that brought the leadership of the movement into conflict with the rank and file.

The same assumption that made fiction seem an effective instrument for enlisting women in the mission crusade—that appeals to the emotions would be more effective with women than abstract argumentation—led the women's societies to adopt the practice of assigning special objects to auxiliaries. This method of presenting the need concretely by asking an auxiliary to support a particular missionary, native teacher, or heathen orphan proved extremely popular. Orphan sketches became a regular feature in early issues of *Heathen Woman's Friend;* orphans "adopted" by an auxiliary were renamed, usually for charter members of the auxiliary or for saintly, departed relatives of auxiliary members. Auxiliaries followed the progress of such children through mission school, sent birthday gifts and graduation presents, and often terminated the relationship by packing off a wedding present. (Such ties were frequently terminated less happily, however, when a recalcitrant orphan left school and reverted to "native" life.) Missionaries developed special relationships with supporting auxiliaries and formed friendships through correspondence not unlike the "tender tie" uniting Mary Merwin to the Hillerton Auxiliary. The demand for special objects grew quickly; by 1877, the executive committee of the Woman's Foreign Missionary Society of the Presbyterian Church (North) found it necessary to appoint an extra foreign secretary to deal solely with apportioning special objects among the auxiliaries.[3]

The popularity of special objects among the rank and file did not prevent the leadership from soon perceiving certain disadvantages in cultivating giving with this practice. The first objections voiced, however, came from missionaries in the field. One missionary to India wrote the Baltimore Branch of the Methodist Woman's Foreign Missionary Society in 1872, saying that there were no more unnamed orphans available and urging the women not to overlook hospital and zenana work.[4] A limited supply of orphans, missionaries, and native teachers was not the only drawback to the assignment of special objects. As early as 1873, an editorial in *Woman's Work for Woman* attempted to teach the rank and file "some of the practical lessons taught us by experience during the brief history of our Society."

In the first place, many of our mission bands find it difficult to retain the children they are supporting. They become interested in their protégé, and delight to do and pray for her. A letter comes from the teacher saying she has left school.... The disappointed band must find another child to claim their care. This constant change in the schools adds much to the labor and care of the missionary in charge, also to the Foreign Secretary of the Society. If, however, instead of supporting a particular child, the members of a band pay the same amount for a *scholarship* in the school, their efforts will be more satisfactory.[5]

Further, the editorial recommends that auxiliaries in one locality unite in working for a particular foreign field. These suggestions were, of course, designed to increase the administrative efficiency of the operation from the perspective of the society's headquarters. The practice of giving for special objects was also debated on theoretical as well as practical grounds.

Among Methodist women, the controversy over special objects was touched off by an article written for *Heathen Woman's Friend* by Isabella Thoburn, the first female missionary sent out by the fledgling Woman's Foreign Missionary Society. Appearing in early 1873 under the title "Motives of Benevolence," Thoburn's treatise denounces the complicated and, to her mind, unsatisfactory schemes employed by women's missionary societies to raise money for mission work. Thoburn's attack is double-barreled and, as we shall see, embroiled her in the controversy over the social character of auxiliary meetings as well as the fight over special objects. Thoburn was horrified that American Christians refused to recognize the direct claims of the heathen world and had to be approached through "their selfish side." Charging admission to church sociables and missionary teas made, in her opinion, "a refreshment table . . . the very undignified door of the church treasury." She warns that if one's benevolence becomes selfish it forfeits the blessing promised to self-denial. Similarly, she argues that appeals made in the name of individuals or on the basis of a special relationship between donor and object circumvent the practice of disinterested benevolence. She believed that when a cause is made personal, donors sustain it for their own sakes; the sight of a higher spiritual end is lost, to the detriment of the donors' immortal souls.[6]

Thoburn's criticism apparently stung Jennie Fowler Willing; her reply had to be printed in installments. Thoburn's perspective,

Mrs. Willing suggests, is from the field—half a world away. Willing herself sees things from the perspective of a home worker, familiar with the needs and problems of auxiliaries. She points out that the Methodist Woman's Foreign Missionary Society labors under severe restrictions, with no experienced, salaried secretary and with the prohibition against gathering funds through general collections. She attributes the relatively greater success of the Presbyterian women's societies in fund-raising to their commitment to assigning special objects to every auxiliary. She rejects Thoburn's esoteric, theological objections and adopts a practical approach to the problem.

> Now, with this human unreliability, with the want of confidence in their powers that their training, or rather lack of it, must give, and with the disabilities under which their society works, we cannot expect the women to hold to its work, unless special means are used to keep it constantly before them.[7]

As the clincher to her argument that women are moved to support missions by concrete, tangible appeals, she cites her success in eliciting a contribution from a woman by enclosing a bit of fern from Lucknow in her letter. Objects, she thinks, are like lenses that can focus and intensify woman's diffuse emotional nature. (But even Mrs. Willing, in her defense of special objects, hints that if women did not labor under disabilities the practice of giving for special objects could be dispensed with.)

Thoburn was not silenced by Willing's barrage. In 1875 she wrote again to *Heathen Woman's Friend,* this time taking a practical tack, to point out the problems inherent in a policy of giving for special objects. She reports her observation that utilitarian expenses get cut from mission budgets because it is harder to collect for them. She suggests that missionaries in the field have the best opportunity for judging how and where funds should be allocated; she appeals to women, on the basis of their experience as housekeepers, to grant the validity of her claim.

> All housekeepers know how they sometimes lay their plans, setting aside sums for special household necessities, but how, as the season advances, so many little unthought of things make

demands on the purse that the larger, and in the beginning more desirable, objects must be set aside.[8]

Similarly, she argues, missionaries should be empowered to divert funds contributed for special objects to more immediate and pressing needs.

Missionaries in the field like Thoburn were not the only ones who saw the advisability of wresting the control of funds from local auxiliaries and centralizing allocations in the interest of more efficient management. The executive committee of the Woman's Foreign Missionary Society of the Presbyterian Church (North) made a move toward doing this at their semiannual meeting in 1877 by urging societies with special objects to add a pledge for a percentage of their receipts to go to the general fund.[9] The practice of giving for special objects, while initially effective in soliciting funds and persuading women in a given church to participate actively in auxiliary affairs, rapidly became a hindrance to the work from the perspective of the denominational leadership of the various societies. By the early eighties, an active campaign was underway to educate the rank and file to appreciate the value of systematic giving. Systematic giving had been a part of the ideology of the woman's foreign mission movement from the beginning when dues were typically set at two cents a week on the theory that women had access to only small sums, but that small sums given with regularity by large numbers of women would provide sufficient funding for woman's work for missions. The renewed emphasis on systematic giving in the 1880s focused on the systematic collecting and forwarding of funds; it was part of a campaign to wean women from their attachment to special objects and to put the movement on a more businesslike footing.

The call for systematic giving in this sense was part of a larger call for system in mission work. The need for system in the appropriation of mission funds was, according to an article printed in *Woman's Work for Woman* in 1881, apparent; "common sense business principles" required it. Women were therefore urged to give up any selfish desire "to control the disposition of their own funds" and to allow those in a position to plan wisely to allocate their gifts.

Let us give our money more directly to the Lord, and less directly to this or that specific object, for who can tell whether this or that will prosper? Let us follow it with more prayer and less solicitude about seeing the good it does. Let us have more faith in the judgment of those who make the *whole* work a careful study, and less in our own, which is necessarily based upon partial views.

The trouble with the special object scheme was that "the more interesting and hopeful parts of the work were readily assumed" while equally important but less glamorous aspects of the work were neglected. As the movement expanded it had been possible to count on additional income each year from newly organized auxiliaries to take up slack in the budget, but the leaders realized that the time was rapidly approaching when income from membership dues might level off. They warned that

> the church has been pretty thoroughly canvassed, and societies organized in most places where it is practicable. We cannot much longer depend upon the income from new societies to supply deficiencies.[10]

Weaning women from special objects proved difficult. When Mrs. J. T. Gracey wrote an editorial for *Heathen Woman's Friend* in 1884 urging auxiliaries not to fixate on orphans but to give directly to the treasury for all operations, including mundane expenses, her plea irritated at least one member of a small-town auxiliary. Luthera Whitney of Springfield, Vermont, replied to Mrs. Gracey in a somewhat annoyed and defensive tone.

> Perhaps Mrs. Gracey does not fully recognize the wide space which separates her, with her extensive knowledge of both the home and foreign work of our Society, from the average member of our inland auxiliaries, who seldom hears a missionary lecture or sermon, and where opportunities for hearing returned missionaries or attending the Branch Annual Meetings, or any other missionary rally, are so few as to be landmarks in a lifetime.

The rank and file, the members of the inland auxiliaries, needed the extra fillip that a special object gave their work in order to sustain their interest, Whitney contended.[11] The space separating Mrs. Gracey and Luthera Whitney is analogous to the gap between Ellen Parsons and the country woman knitting on the window seat in Parsons's office; it is the separation between professional and amateur.

The administrative officers of the denominational societies were able to exercise a certain amount of control over local auxiliaries in the matter of giving for special objects. The Woman's Board of Missions (Congregational) simply announced a new policy in 1885 that placed restrictions on special gifts. Alluding to the "dangers to be guarded against" that ranged from placing "too great a tax on the missionaries" to "disappointment at home," they argued that they had been obliged to adopt the following safeguards:

> We do not promise a letter either from or about the native women or girls supported; we do not promise the name of any particular pupil supported, nor of the teacher of a village school; we ask the societies to take *scholarships* in our boarding schools, or *a* pupil, not designating any particular one, and we promise a report of the school shall be sent twice in the year to each one supporting a pupil; we promise to give the names of the Bible-women, also the name of the village in which a school is to be supported, and reports, as in the other work.[12]

Giving for special objects was not entirely eliminated, but such restrictions held it in check. The General Mission Board of the Presbyterian Church (North), in a similar move in 1898, requested that money be designated to classes of work (evangelistic, educational, medical, and miscellaneous) rather than to "one or more objects singled out from those classes."[13]

On the issue of activities appropriate for local auxiliaries to sponsor, administrative officers found it even more difficult to change cherished customs. In fact, even the officers were not entirely in agreement on the question of church sociables, missionary teas, and fund-raising bazaars. Jennie Fowler Willing, for example, admonished auxiliaries to combine "industrial, social, intellectual and religious elements" in their monthly meetings. Mrs. Willing suggested assembling at a fixed hour, say three or three-thirty; sewing or fancywork could occupy the ladies until about five, when the literary committee could present papers, poems, selections, and letters; following this, there should be singing, prayer, business, minutes, dues, subscriptions, and, finally, refreshments. Mrs. Willing's vision of the ideal auxiliary meeting met with opposition from those, like Isabella Thoburn, who felt that serious commitment to missions precluded frivolity. The argument that new members would be drawn to a group because of its sociability did not persuade opponents who felt strongly that missionary societies should be demonstrably different from social clubs.[14]

Mrs. Willing, however, did not expect people—even churchwomen—to operate on the high moral plane that Thoburn described in her treatise on "Motives of Benevolence." In response to Thoburn, she argued,

> We must take people as they are, and not as they ought to be. Church folk are social. . . . What harm can there be in their utilizing their sociality by making it an occasion of giving to a good cause?[15]

Mrs. Willing did not expect the average churchwoman to treat the missionary cause with quite the same high seriousness and businesslike efficiency that those who made mission work a full-time career exhibited. The majority seem to have sided with Mrs. Willing. Some argued that missionary bazaars provided a way for women who could give work but not money to participate.[16] It was as fundraisers that most social functions (other than the serving of refreshments at regular meetings) were justified. The women who worked for missions were ingenious fund-raisers; their missionary magazines promoted schemes that ranged from selling missionary photographs and raising flowers, vegetables, and poultry for profit, to taking up silk culture. (The latter was recommended as a "neat, pleasant, easy avocation, inexpensive to outfit, not difficult to learn, and giving a healthful change from the usual sedentary employments that are left to women."[17]) However, most fund-raising plans involved two essential ingredients: food and entertainment. Missionary teas and pageants were popular; churchwomen were accustomed to selling fancywork and refreshments at bazaars. Such familiar activities were more congenial to most women than writing missionary papers and offering public prayers.

The early leaders of the women's missionary societies considered such activities wholly appropriate; they even dreamed up new
variations on familiar themes. Mary Clarke Nind, offering advice
on raising money in 1884, called attention to a new type of festival
that was gaining popularity in all the branches of the Methodist
Woman's Foreign Missionary Society. She endorsed the use of these
"flag" festivals, which involved

> selling the flag [which would eventually be sent to a mission
> station] in a public assembly stripe by stripe and star by star to
> those present who are specially interested in the State repre-
> sented, each purchaser, if so inclined, giving some interesting
> incident connected with it; this interspersed with singing and
> short addresses, provides a very pleasant and profitable eve-
> ning's entertainment.

Mrs. Nind wished "every auxiliary would have such festivals,"
but warned her readers that the idea of selling the flag was "*a God-
given thought for the Woman's Foreign Missionary Society* and no one has
a right to use it for any other purpose."[18] Such harmless (and finan-
cially rewarding) frivolity continued to complement the more directly religious activities of local auxiliaries despite the objections
of the high-minded. Traditional approaches to fund-raising coex-
isted more or less harmoniously with the efforts of denominational
administrators to employ such new techniques as the printing of
bequest forms in every issue of the society's journal. In fact, the effect of the professionalization of mission administration on auxiliary activities was not pronounced until the early years of this
century when the promotion of systematic mission study transformed auxiliaries from a cross between prayer meetings and social
clubs into study groups.

Inextricably linked to the debate over special objects was the
acrimonious controversy that arose over letter writing. Letters from
an auxiliary's own missionary or orphan were, according to the rationale for assigning special objects, supposed to provide a direct
link between women at home and the work abroad. Indeed, one of
the reasons that Dr. N. G. Clark, secretary of the American Board of
Commissioners for Foreign Missions, gave in urging the women of
Chicago to organize for missions was his expectation that communi-

cation with the board's female missionaries would be improved if
women took over the task of correspondence.

> Ladies will write to each other as they will not write to me, do
> the best I can to win their confidence. They are afraid of ap-
> pearing in the *Herald,* of having their letters placed before a
> grave and dignified committee of gentlemen. The vivacity, the
> touching incidents, the free, hearty expression of their thoughts
> and feelings, joys and sorrows, they reserve for their own sex.[19]

A woman's letters, like her prayers, would be different from a man's
letters—or from letters exchanged between men and women. The
Woman's Board of Missions (Congregational) shared Dr. Clark's
expectations. The first issue of *Life and Light for Heathen Women* announced that the Woman's Board had undertaken the support of
seven missionaries and promised that "from each of these will come
back frank, confiding letters, such as can only be written to mother
and sisters."[20]

Missionary letters and journal entries fill the bulk of the pages
in the early numbers of all the women's magazines. An editorial in
*Heathen Woman's Friend* in 1873 acknowledged the reliance placed on
missionary letters in the work at home.

> The letters our missionary ladies write are worth everything to
> stir the people to interest in this work. . . . If we understand the
> case, no "sensational appeals" that we can make will come
> nearer than noon to midnight in presenting the actual degrada-
> tion and vileness.[21]

Missionary accounts testified to actual conditions encountered in
foreign lands, lending credence to appeals made by organizers at
home. The belief that the cause, presented concretely and objec-
tively, would plead for itself clearly informs the advice offered to foreign correspondents in *Woman's Work for Woman.*

> Give us incidents, facts, descriptions; anything to illustrate the
> work, or photograph the country and people. We need not say,
> avoid sermons and homilies; make your words *few* and *to the
> point.*[22]

Sermons and homilies could safely be left to men. A female audience's attention could be better held by descriptions of people and
exotic customs. Once again, the underlying assumption is that
women respond to personal and particular need, not to abstract discussion of the eschatological implications of world evangelization.

The workers at home wanted letters from missionaries to stir
interest; the missionaries themselves had more immediate and pressing reason for hoping that a frank and confiding, sisterly correspondence would develop: they were homesick. A missionary wrote from
Syria to remind Presbyterian women of the importance of "Mail
Day" to the missionaries, confessing, "I have an awful streak of
homesickness, once in seven days, that lasts about ten minutes by
the town-clock." Her plea to the women at home hints that women
were not always satisfactory correspondents.

> Now don't forget that when you ought to write to "the dear
> missionaries" of this far-off land on Wednesday, and put it off
> till Thursday, you keep "the dear missionaries" on the house-
> top [where they climb to watch for the first glimpse of the mail
> steamer] two weeks longer for your miserable procrastination.[23]

The tendency of the ladies at home to think of the "dear missionaries" with the warmest approbation, but never quite to get around
to writing them, was a sore point with many missionaries.

An indication that the high expectations were being disappointed on both sides appears as early as 1876 in an editorial plea to
the weary missionary to continue to write letters "Christian-ward"
where, after all, the letter reached a wider audience than the teacher's voice could among the heathen.[24] The supporting societies in
America obviously expected, as the theory of reflex influence promised, that their missionaries would supply them as well as the heathen with spiritual blessings. The missionaries, on their side,
considered writing letters to auxiliaries a drain on precious time that
might otherwise be devoted to what they believed to be their real
task; they had not left home and family in order to stir the sluggish
spiritual senses of American women. Missionaries especially resented the expectation that they write regularly to a supporting auxiliary that replied sporadically if at all. They were in God's service,
not the hire of an auxiliary—and they were working women, not,

like most of their supporters at home, simply housewives with ample time for letter writing.

Beginning in the mid-seventies, the journals are filled with editorial admonitions, complaints, and recriminations on all sides. *Woman's Work for Woman* urged workers at home to keep up their end of the correspondence; the point was made through a sampling of comments from "some of our missionaries." One missionary who had received requests from several auxiliaries for students who could be their special objects wrote:

> I always write and can generally give them the names, but then that is the end of the correspondence on their side, and I am expected to keep up the correspondence alone. . . . Is this not a little hard? I see in the last number of *Woman's Work* that this very thing is mentioned, and I was very glad to see it.

Another missionary who felt that "the writing of letters to mission bands, &c., is as much a part of our work as teaching the heathen" did wish that her correspondents would reply more frequently since, she claimed, "no one can estimate the help and comfort which we receive from kind, encouraging letters that our sisters in the homeland send us." Having surveyed the sad experience of the missionaries, *Woman's Work for Woman* made the following plea:

> We beg you, workers for the cause at home, in the name of these noble women on the field, who are laboring for the Master with none of the comforts and advantages which surround you, let not these words of theirs be uttered in vain. They can indeed help *you* much in *your* work, but think what a source of strength and joy it is to them, to be assured of the sympathy, the interest, and the prayers of the band of women who claim them as their own. It is not much of an effort for you to give this to them, but it is very much to them to receive it from you.[25]

Sympathy and interest were perhaps not precisely what most missionaries wanted. When they offered advice to women at home about what to put in a missionary letter, they emphasized news from home—and not just news about church work. One suggested,

Write her warm, friendly letters, not just a few pious plati-
tudes. . . . If you have found a pleasant article in a newspaper or
magazine, mail it to her when you are through with it. Do not
think that because she is a missionary she never wants to read
anything but *The Foreign Missionary* and *Woman's Work*.[26]

Another way of conveying the same messages was through stories that employed the conceit of switched letters. Typically, a letter
to a friend is sent by mistake to a missionary, while the letter intended for the missionary goes to the friend. The letter writer then
receives replies from both. The missionary admits that she could not
help reading the letter, even though she realized it was meant for
someone else, because she so much enjoyed its chatty news; the
friend chides the writer for composing such a dull, dry letter that not
even a missionary would be glad to get it. Such tactics, direct and indirect, were designed to help women establish a close, sisterly correspondence with their missionaries that would fulfill the original
expectations of the movement's founders.

By the mid-eighties, as both the missionaries and the officers of
the societies began to conceive of themselves as professionals, a new
note entered the controversy over letter writing. Auxiliaries were
chastised for demanding information about the work directly from
missionaries rather than relying on information available in published form. The operation had grown too large for a missionary to
respond personally to all the groups that might expect news about
the particular aspect of her work that they supported. Indeed, one of
the reasons that the Woman's Board of Missions put restrictions on
special objects in 1884 was that the correspondence problem threatened to mushroom beyond control. The executive committee explained its reasoning fully to its constituency because the issue was
so sensitive.

With nearly all our missionaries every nerve is strained to accomplish what "must be done" each moment in the day; and,
as has been said, "it comes to be a question as to whether we
shall do our work or write about it. . . ." When a society pledges
the salary of a missionary the correspondence is comparatively
simple. While a missionary is in no sense a beneficiary—she
certainly earns her small salary by unceasing labor—yet it is

pleasant for her to feel that she has been taken to the hearts of a band of Christian women. . . . It is pleasant to receive letters— not merely asking for information, something "stirring," that will rouse the indifferent or "make a meeting interesting. . . ." Answers will come naturally and easily. With the other work . . . correspondence is not so easily established. Very few of the native women and girls can write in English, and the letters must either come from the missionaries, or, what is still more labor, they must see that they are written, translate them, and send them on.[27]

The burden that correspondence placed on busy professionals was not the only objection made. The whole notion that a support- ing auxiliary ought to expect an intimate relationship with a mis- sionary was questioned in *Woman's Work for Woman* in 1885. In contrast to earlier expectations that missionaries would welcome personal, sisterly interest in their lives, this editorial suggests that such interest may constitute an invasion of privacy.

A missionary band or society, in studying the general subject of missions, has become possessed of the idea that it would be a good thing to know more not only of the *work,* but of the indi- vidual workers; and not only of these as connected with mis- sionary life, but of them as *persons,* that is, to know of their private, personal history as one knows it in a biography of one who has gone from earth; and not only to acquire this informa- tion, but to publish the facts, so that all who are interested in the *worker* may be acquainted with the *woman.* . . . Yet because a woman is a *missionary,* does her life become such public prop- erty . . . ?[28]

The distinction made here between woman and worker indicates that the writer of these lines saw missionaries as professionals who had a private life apart from their work. Such a conception was not easy for the rank and file of the woman's foreign mission movement to understand; to them, missionary was not a word describing what a person *did* professionally—like doctor, lawyer, or teacher—but what some women *were,* just as they themselves were wives and mothers. Certainly the missionary hagiography of midcentury catered to their desire for personal detail and had fostered the assumption that they had a right to know such intimate facts as might prove touching and spiritually stimulating.[29]

Just as administrators tried to wean women away from their attachment to special objects, they also attempted to damp the expectations—that they had initially encouraged—of auxiliaries for intimate and regular correspondence with a special missionary. An effort to introduce a compromise, by asking missionaries to write a "half-hour letter" once every three months, did not solve the problem. As late as 1910, an article on "Missionary Correspondence" rehashed the whole issue, quoting accusations on both sides and pleading for mutual cooperation—although, on balance, siding with the missionaries and suggesting that one letter a year was all a missionary could reasonably be expected to send.[30]

In none of the three areas of contention that arose as professionalization gradually separated the leadership from the rank and file were the administrators able to modify entirely the behavior of their constituents. Auxiliaries placidly continued to hold bazaars, complain that they got no letters, and cling, when possible, to special objects. Auxiliaries functioned largely as a cross between female prayer meetings and social clubs. For the members of small-town auxiliaries, the significant reflex influence of mission work was not gradual professionalization but the development of skills in conducting meetings and speaking publicly. Such skills had no immediate professional application for most women, but did equip them to play a more public role in community as well as church affairs. In addition, from "missionary intelligence" they gained a broadened perspective on other cultures that equipped them to be better citizens not only of their own communities, but also of the world. Women were encouraged to study mission fields in ways that must have exercised their mental muscles.

> Bring out your atlas, study up your geography, search histories, delve into the encyclopedia. . . . Try to get access to special books of reference. Thus stored come to your monthly meeting. . . . Let this meeting be not only a love-feast, but a thought-feast. . . . These people afar off, these countries, circumstances, conditions, civilizations, are not myths, but realities; locate them, photograph them, realize them, and you will learn a new answer to the question, "Who is my neighbor?"[31]

More systematic mission study proved, eventually, more effective than editorial admonitions in changing the character of local auxiliaries, but that is a story that belongs to the discussion of the United Study of Foreign Missions in the next chapter. For the moment it is sufficient to note that the woman's foreign mission movement gave ordinary churchwomen a chance to utilize talents that had lain fallow in the home; through their work for missions, women gained confidence in their ability to function competently outside the confines of a narrowly defined domestic sphere. And they were assured that the world needed them.

The most important reflex influence of mission work on the women who ran the denominational societies was their transformation from volunteers into professionals. Even those unsalaried officers who remained technically "volunteers" adopted attitudes toward their work resembling those of their professional male colleagues. Certainly according to the rationale recently advanced by Joan Jacobs Brumberg and Nancy Tomes, these women should be considered professionals.

> Within the nineteenth-century woman's sphere, unpaid work outside the home became a route to self-respect and power oftentimes involving a lifetime commitment to a single organization or cause....Patterns of female persistence in volunteer groups suggest that we consider seriously the notion of a volunteer "career" which embodies some important professional qualities.[32]

As "professionals" the leaders of the women's missionary societies participated in the professionalization of the Protestant missionary enterprise, a development reflected symbolically in the introduction into mission ideology of the phrase "the science of missions." In fact, the "business of missions" might have been a more apt characterization. Following the example of their male counterparts, the women who officered female missionary societies at the end of the nineteenth century prided themselves on their business acumen. As early as 1881 an editorial applauding the use of business method in religion noted that "we have observed with satisfaction for some time past that women are learning financial management in missionary organizations."[33] Agents for the missionary societies urged women to adopt sound business practices at the local level;

Frances J. Baker insisted that the distribution of missionary literature from regional offices should be entrusted to a businesslike woman,

> one who is "always there," with a money-drawer of small coins
> for change, postage stamps, wrapping paper, and string cord,
> who knows what "book post," "third class," and such terms
> mean, and who is ready to mail books and packages by foreign
> or domestic postage.[34]

In 1900, at the Ecumenical Missionary Conference in New York, it was a woman who urged—in a session on "Prayer and Beneficence"—the use of business methods in giving; she argued that "financial matters should always be so conducted as to inspire the confidence of others, pre-eminently so when they are connected with the Lord's business." Yet women apparently felt less than wholly confident of their ability to conduct the Lord's business professionally; it was with some relief that in 1890 the author of a report on the General Missionary Committee Meeting of the Methodist Episcopal Church (North) noticed that men were not always models of efficiency.

> A few crumbs of comfort were picked up, which may be modestly mentioned for the encouragement of many of us who feel our serious lack of business training and experience. We found that the Committee did not always economize time, and that their work occasionally needed reconsideration; that even a corresponding secretary could be mistaken, and make up a report from the wrong figures.[35]

Women embraced business methods with a degree of ambivalence; they wanted to acquire the skills that would make their operation function efficiently, but they did not intend to become businessmen. The becoming modesty of the writer of the report just quoted starts to sound somewhat disingenuous when she proceeds to hint that a business run by women will be conducted on a higher moral plane—or at least with greater civility—than one run by men. Mission secretaries and bishops, she observed, "are not beyond temptation to sharp assertions and sharp retort." She condemns this display of temper by saying that she "privately rejoiced that the work of the women had not yet reached the point where such occurrences are probable." The reader is left to infer that the work of women will, by the grace of God and woman's nature, never be marred by such masculine posturing. Indeed, while women were ready to adopt business methods, neither they nor their male colleagues were prepared to admit that the mission enterprise was simply a business. An editorial in *Heathen Woman's Friend* took issue with precisely that charge when it was made in an article on "Embarrassed Foreign Missions" that appeared in *Nation* in 1895. The reply to *Nation* was a categorical denial that "the period of romance and heroism in missions has entirely given place, as the writer affirms, to 'the prosaic and businesslike.' "[36] But if women were unwilling to substitute business for romance or to renounce entirely their belief in woman's moral superiority, they nevertheless adopted with relish the expanding professional apparatus attached to foreign missions.

One sign of growing professionalism within the foreign mission movement was the phenomenon of the ecumenical conference. At one of the first of these international "professional" conferences, the Centenary Conference on the Protestant Missions of the World held in London in 1888, women played a relatively minor role; only one public session, attended by three hundred people, was devoted to woman's work. Two private sessions on woman's work, at which the only three papers given by women during the entire conference were delivered, drew such crowds—to the surprise of the conference organizers—that these meetings had to be adjourned to a larger hall. It was apparent that in the future the women could not be ignored; the conference appointed Abbie B. Child, home secretary of the Woman's Board of Missions and editor of *Life and Light for Heathen Women,* as chairman of the World's Committee of Women's Missionary Societies and included her as the only female member of the executive committee that planned the next international missionary conference, the Ecumenical Missionary Conference held in New York in 1900. At that conference ten separate sessions were conducted by women.[37]

It is instructive to compare the role women played in these two conferences. In 1888 Miss Child delivered the only paper given by an American woman; her subject was "Woman's Work in the

Mission-field." Her paper followed one read by the Rev. J. N. Murdock, secretary of the American Baptist Missionary Union, that applauded the work of female missionaries but deplored the separation of men's and women's missionary societies. The Rev. Mr. Murdock wanted women's societies to be "always co-operative, but never co-ordinate" with the parent societies. He warned that women "must be careful to recognize the headship of man in ordering the affairs of the kingdom of God."

> We must not allow the major vote of the better sex, nor the ability and efficiency of so many of our female helpers, nor even the exceptional faculty for leadership and organization which some of them have displayed in their work, to discredit the natural and predestined headship of man in Missions, as well as in the Church of God. . . . Woman may not assume, nor may man shirk, the duty of leadership in the great enterprise of bringing the world to the feet of our Immanuel.[38]

Abbie Child, who in 1870 at the age of thirty had assumed the leadership of the Woman's Board of Missions (Congregational), was content to let Murdock's remarks pass without comment. Her own view of woman's special mission to women and children was, in fact, compatible with Murdock's position.

> The aim of this woman's work we conceive to be *in heathen lands*—to be used as an instrument in the hands of our Lord, in bringing the women into His kingdom, in the creation of Christian mothers, and as a consequence Christian homes, and in the providing a Christian education for their daughters. To our fathers and brothers belong the task of opening the way for the Gospel, to make straight in the desert a highway for our God, to strike vigorous blows at the brains of heathendom, to superintend large educational and evangelistic enterprises, to plant the standard of the Cross and win many to its side. To woman belongs the quiet, patient labour in the homes of the people, striving to win the hearts of wives and mothers, to gain the love of the children, first to herself and then for the Master whom she serves. While the men strike heavy blows at the citadel, women try to undermine the stronghold of heathendom.[39]

The paradox that characterizes the rhetoric of woman's special mission lies at the heart of Miss Child's argument: women have a limited mission but one that is ultimately more important than all other work, since the heathen home, controlled by women and accessible only to women, is the final stronghold of heathendom. This paradox allowed Miss Child to maintain a stance of submission that was at odds with her actual role as a mission administrator. Yet it is surely more than coincidence that she chose in her peroration to invoke the image of a professional woman rather than a mother when she made an otherwise conventional plea for dependence upon God's guidance in female mission work. Notice that the woman described here wields a power over the lives of others that the Rev. Mr. Murdock would no doubt have reserved for a man.

> In one of the smaller college observatories in the United States, at nine o'clock on every clear night, there stands a solitary woman, with her eyes fixed on the stars, watching for the crossing of a certain star over the hair lines on a telescopic lens. Through the telegraphic instrument by her side, the mean time, as indicated by the stars, is given to all the time stations within a radius of many miles. The announcement of the correct time is passed from one to another, till it reaches the city time stations, the railways, the shops, the offices, the manufactories, the homes, the schools, the gatherings of people for whatever purpose, in hundreds of places. So it happens that the touch of one woman's hands controls the deeds of thousands of people; not of her own wit or wisdom, but because her eyes are fixed upon the stars. The moment her gaze falters her power is lost. So it is in our Missionary work.[40]

Even if she chose not to challenge Mr. Murdock's remarks directly, Miss Child clearly believed that trained and talented women could and ought to exercise authority—even in arenas ordinarily reserved to men. She had, in following the footsteps of her father, who had served for many years on the Prudential Committee of the American Board of Commissioners for Foreign Missions, made a career for herself in the business of foreign missions. Yet while she behaved like her male colleagues, attending professional conferences and making inspection tours of mission stations around the world, she was content to work closely with the officers of the American Board, carving out a sphere for women in mission work that complemented rather than competed with man's work for missions. Two other women present for Mr. Murdock's speech were less docile. Fanny J. Coppin of the Woman's African Methodist Episcopal Mite Missionary Society had this to say "with reference to what we have heard this morning":

> I think there is nothing, in the law of God's universe, that was made without ample space to move in, without trenching upon its neighbor's domain; and it may very well be said of women that while they are and were created second, they not only were created with a body but they were created with a head, and they are responsible therefore to decide in certain matters and to use their own judgment. It is also very true as I will certainly say, that fools rush in where angels fear to tread; but then I question as to whether all the fools are confined to the feminine gender.[41]

If Mrs. Coppin, speaking for the black women of America, was ready to dismiss with sarcasm the idea that woman needed man's "headship" and was willing to trust the judgment of women in certain unspecified matters, Mary Clarke Nind of the Methodist Episcopal Church (North) was prepared to usurp the priestly functions long denied women. Citing the case of a converted zenana woman who insisted upon being baptized by a missionary lady since she could allow no man but her husband to touch her, Mrs. Nind prophesied that

> the time is not far distant when we shall have to listen to the cry of the women in their Zenanas, that our Christian missionaries and Bible readers will have to administer to these women baptism and communion. . . . I propose to open every door that the Lord sets before me, as a member of the Woman's Christian Temperance Union, or the Woman's Foreign Missionary Society, or belonging to the White Cross Movement, or the King's Daughters, or anything else. Anywhere with Jesus, everywhere with Jesus; and put all my prejudices behind and march on to victory.[42]

The bounds of the domestic sphere were elastic indeed for women like Mrs. Nind who complacently stretched them to encompass every act dictated by her conscience.

The very elasticity of the definition of woman's sphere allowed the rhetoric of home and motherhood and woman's special mission to persist even as the scope of woman's participation in the foreign mission enterprise as a whole widened. Women continued to sing at missionary meetings of making one unbroken household of the nations. At the Ecumenical Conference of 1900, they reiterated the old arguments for woman's work, rehearsing the familiar assumptions on which the appeal they made to American women had long rested. Mrs. Moses Smith, president of the Woman's Board of Missions of the Interior (Congregational) reduced these arguments to "three correlated facts or conditions."

> First: In the Divine economy mothers and home determine the character and condition of any people. This is too evident to need illustration. No people rise higher than mothers.

> Second: In the light of the mother's power the status of woman throughout the world becomes paramount. Barbarism and the ethnic religions combined to degrade womanhood. Among uncivilized people woman is a slave, nude, filthy, her life by a degree above the brute. Only a woman can teach her purity, delicacy, and the divine art of home-making.

> Third:....The present-day problem in missions is to reach the great central power in society, the mothers and home....In all the Orient, and largely in all uncivilized lands, only a woman can break the Bread of life to woman. Logically, it follows that the agency through which this can be done is the most far-reaching and certain force the Church has for the redemption of the race. Thus is demonstrated the value of the Women's Boards of Missions among redemptive forces.

Much of the rhetoric is familiar, but Mrs. Smith's speech reveals a subtle shift in assumptions. Claims made for the ultimate significance of woman's work for woman in the early years were always linked to a formulation of woman's task as a limited mission, subor-

dinate and supplemental to the broader work of denominational
mission efforts. Here, the disclaimer is missing; the submissive note
that Miss Child had injected into her paper in 1888 has no echo in
Mrs. Smith's remarks. An even more striking change is apparent in
the very language Mrs. Smith uses. Her rhetoric—"mothers and
home determine the character and condition of any people," "the
status of woman," "the present-day problem in missions is to reach
the great central power in society"—suggests the influence of the
new science of sociology. Mrs. Smith's language reveals that she has
accepted the categories of what Jackson Lears has labeled a "therapeutic culture" which emphasized the rationalization of society and
the scientific diagnosis and treatment of social ills. Logical argument
has largely displaced emotional appeal in Mrs. Smith's address.[43]

The moral of Mrs. Smith's analysis is that woman's social
function as mother is vital, that civilizations can be redeemed if
women are made (through religion) better mothers. In contrast, the
moral of Miss Child's tale of the female astronomer was that woman's power derived from her connection, through prayer, with the
Divine. Woman's innate religious capacity and her natural ability to
empathize with her heathen sisters, crucial components of the Victorian ideal of womanhood that underlay the initial formation of female foreign missionary societies, are no longer central features in
the justification of woman's work for missions. In Mrs. Smith's
scheme, woman's heart responding to the plight of heathen women
is not (as it was for Ellen Parsons in 1893) the motive force behind
the movement; rather, the task of converting heathen women as-
sumes significance because of their function as mothers. Christian
women have a special responsibility that stems not from the tenderness of their hearts or from any divinely imposed duty, but from
pragmatic considerations of how the Gospel can best be transmitted
to women in non-Western cultures.

These rhetorical changes reflect a shift that occurred at the
turn of the century in the prevailing cultural paradigm of ideal
womanhood. As Sheila Rothman describes it, a "focus on feminine
purity and sensibility" and "virtuous womanhood" that "ultimately defined problems in moral terms and, therefore, focused
ameliorative efforts more on the person than on the system" gave
way to a concern with "educated motherhood."[44] In the context of
the new therapeutic culture, maternal instincts were no longer regarded as sufficient for the vital task of motherhood. Women

needed to be trained, in accordance with scientific theories of child development, for the important social function of rearing children. Within the mission movement, efforts to train female missionaries in kindergarten methods and to introduce kindergartens around the world exemplify the widespread acceptance of this new ideal in evangelical circles.

Continued emphasis on the primacy of motherhood in the lives of women masked the shift in ideological assumptions; it made the older rhetoric of home and motherhood seem compatible with the modern science of missions. Yet clearly the dynamic that Estelle Freedman has pointed to in an article on "female institution building" in nineteenth-century America operated in the woman's foreign mission movement. Women drew upon the ideology of true womanhood with its concept of female moral superiority to create separate female associations that provided them with opportunities to pursue careers not open to them within the churches proper. Ironically, Freedman notes, women who built such separate institutions frequently abandoned the ideology that had empowered them, and as they "entered a public female world, they adopted the more radical stance of feminists."[45] Certainly leaders of the woman's mission movement like Mrs. Smith abandoned the ideology of woman's religious superiority with its concomitant stance of social subordination when they demanded an equal share with men in the administration of missions. No longer persuaded that woman's nature made her especially fit for mission work, these women joined equally and eloquently with men in calling for professional training for missionaries and for business methods in missionary administration. They did not perceive the inherent contradiction between justifying a separate role for women in mission work and demanding equality with men in the missionary enterprise. Eventually, this contradiction would undermine the entire structure of the woman's foreign mission movement, thereby substantially diminishing woman's power base within American Protestantism. In 1900, however, the future of woman's work for foreign missions seemed more promising than ever as the new professionals embarked upon the new century with a widened vision of their mission.

Helen Barrett Montgomery, who would become the principal spokeswoman for the movement in the twentieth century, echoed Mrs. Smith's rhetoric. In the impassioned argument against merging women's societies with denominational mission boards that she made at the Ecumenical Conference, Montgomery called the home "the final citadel of heathenism" and labeled it "a fortress that can be taken by women only." Using the metaphor of the leaven in the loaf that had been so frequently employed during the movement's formative years, she described the woman's work in the mission field as distinctively feminine.

> It seems such slow work, this gathering of children into kinder-gartens, this friendly contact with little groups of mothers, this teaching of needle-work, this living of one's own home-life through long lonely years that seem to count for nothing. It is woman's work, the patient hiding of the leaven in the lump un-til the whole is leavened. And there is no agency which has such power to hasten the triumph of the kingdom of our Lord as this hidden work committed into the hands of women.

Read alone, this statement sounds conventional enough, but it is ac-tually a peroration at the end of an extended plea for the public rec-ognition of the hidden work of women. Her reiteration of the formula that heathen nations will be converted by reaching heathen mothers is something of an anomaly in her speech. The logic she employs in answering objections to separate women's societies is more characteristic of her approach to the issue of woman's place in mission work. She systematically reviews objections raised: the du-plication of administration, the fear that funds would be diverted from denominational boards, and the rejection, on principle, of women's organizations. She then answers each objection by arguing that women's societies have made substantial contributions not to woman's work alone, but to the general missionary effort.

> By their army of unpaid officers and helpers, by their close con-tact with the local church, by their system of minute supervi-sion, by their network of meetings and conferences, by their flood of missionary literature they are the advance agents of missionary prosperity, the John the Baptists preparing the way of the denominational boards. The sowing and cultivating, and I fear, harrowing of the home field, by these indefatigable women's societies is one cause of the harvest of the past twenty years.[46]

It is significant that Montgomery compared women with John the Baptist; her predecessors had preferred to find Biblical metaphors and sanctions for woman's work in the example of the women of the Bible. And, in contrast to her characterization of the work of women on the mission field, there is nothing in the nature of the work of the women's societies at home that makes it peculiarly feminine; acting as the advance agents of missionary prosperity did not require the particular virtues that the Victorian age had assigned to women.

The difference that Montgomery perceived between men and women was not primarily a natural difference, but a circumstantial one. Women were not breadwinners; they had, therefore, time as well as talent that they could afford to offer freely to the church. From a purely pragmatic perspective, Montgomery felt that the church would be remiss if it failed to utilize this potential resource. But it was a resource that, according to Montgomery, was "only to be developed by women's sharing in the burdens of missionary administration." Thus Montgomery's rationale for maintaining separate women's missionary societies rested primarily on practical considerations, not on a belief that women ought to assume a special and subordinate role in the missionary enterprise. Realizing that if the women's societies were merged with denominational mission boards women would no longer exercise the administrative power they wielded in their own organization, Montgomery argued that the talents of women could be most fully utilized if they assumed their share of the "burdens of missionary administration" through the structures of the existing women's societies.[47]

Montgomery had an additional reason for wanting to preserve separate women's missionary societies; she felt that the women's societies had not yet fully accomplished their task of training women to work systematically and efficiently for missions. Women, she feared, had a tendency to sentimentalize and feminize Christianity; through the channels of the women's societies she hoped that women could be persuaded to give up their false and sentimental notions. Without abandoning sex-specific metaphors that placed women in the role of housekeepers, Montgomery called on women to discard Victorian ideas about the nature of domesticity and of feminine piety. She advanced the argument that woman's work, if separate, is nevertheless similar and equal to man's work, not subordinate and complementary. She pointed out that "the kingdom of heaven is likened not only to the shepherd seeking the lost sheep in the wilderness, but also to the woman sweeping the house for the lost coin"; in the eyes of God and of the parable writer, shepherd and housekeeper are on a par. Therefore, Montgomery argued, women's missionary societies had a responsibility to educate women to an "enlarged conception of life."

> And until all Christian women have learned that the cross of Christ is not to be sung about, not wept over, nor smothered in flowers, but set up in our pleasures; that He never commanded us to cling to that cross, but to carry it, the work of the missionary circle will not be done.[48]

Montgomery, with this line of reasoning, added a new dimension to the hoped-for reflex influence of the woman's foreign mission movement. More than a call for spiritual renewal, hers was a call for conceptualizing anew the nature of woman's religious experience and of woman's task in missions. Without abandoning entirely the rhetoric of home and motherhood, Montgomery utterly rejected the image of woman as clinging vine, twining about the limbs of man, the sturdy oak—or about the cross of Christ. She was not certain what shape the future would take, but she sensed that her understanding of the message of Christianity for women had revolutionary implications at home as well as abroad.

> It does not yet appear what we shall be, but is already manifest that the spirit of Jesus . . . is already making a new world; not a man's world, hard, cruel, bitter toward the weak, nor a woman's world, weak, sentimental, tasteless, but a world of humanity in which for the first time the full orb of all the qualities that serve to mark the human shall have free course and be glorified.[49]

If the goal of the Protestant missionary enterprise was the evangelization of the whole world, its reflex influence, according to Montgomery, would be nothing less than radical cultural transformation.

Montgomery was not alone among the professionals leading the woman's foreign mission movement in seeing in the eradication of distinctions between the sexes the fulfillment of the promise of the great task in which they were engaged. Ellen Parsons, editor of *Woman's Work for Woman,* in reporting on the Ecumenical Conference of 1900, expressed her wish that one of the evening sessions given over to women "should have been in charge of men, and that men should have spoken there side by side with women, thus putting our work in its natural relation before the public." For Parsons, the climax of the conference came at the mass meeting for women held one afternoon in Carnegie Hall. Parsons was pleased that the "audience numbered fully 5000," and was especially gratified that "men, while they had been visible at all meetings for women, were now on the floor in such numbers that it would not occur to a casual onlooker that it was a one-sided gathering."[50] Woman's work for woman, as far as Parsons was concerned, had quite rightly become woman's work for men and women. Parsons preferred not to be identified solely with female concerns; in 1905 she announced that the changed role of women in missions had inspired her to change the name of the Presbyterian women's foreign missionary magazine to *Woman's Work.*

> Dropping the last half of the former title had become inevitable, because the term "Woman's Work for Woman," which aptly described the aims of our Presbyterian Societies at the time the first magazine was launched in Philadelphia, April 1871, has with the passage of years become outgrown; it no longer conveys the whole truth. . . . With the present title it is hoped that fewer communications will be sent us upon suffrage, divorce and dairying.[51]

Parsons considered the name change a happy one, the reflection of a development of which she heartily approved. However, as with Montgomery, metaphors drawn from housekeeping coexist in her prose with the new rhetoric of equality in missions; Parsons compared changing her magazine's title with "a little housecleaning [that] freshens up very much."

The process of professionalization that led administrators to redefine the nature of "woman's work" for missions at home produced a parallel development overseas where the presence of professionally trained women missionaries ensured that the definition of evangelism would be broadened to include social service alongside gospel preaching. For local auxiliaries, professionalization meant the introduction of systematic mission study and, more importantly, a changed conception of the part that ordinary church-women could play in the missionary enterprise. The new formulation of woman's work derived by missionary leaders from their experience as "professionals" determined the character of the woman's foreign mission movement at home and abroad during its halcyon years between 1900 and the First World War.

# Chapter 5

# Changing Worlds

The translation of the newly defined conception of woman's work for missions into policy and practice produced startlingly divergent effects at home and abroad. The difference between what professionalization meant on the mission field and what it meant for the members of local auxiliaries, who constituted the home base of the woman's foreign mission movement, offers a tangible illustration of how "the ethos of professionalism...hastened the demise of female culture by widening the distance between career and non-career women."[1] Career missionaries led lives into which ordinary churchwomen could not project themselves imaginatively as they had been able to do when female missionaries' lives appeared to replicate those of the heroines of sentimental fiction. Women who made mission work a career in the new era of modern missions placed greater reliance on their professional competence and less on the prayers of laywomen than had their predecessors. In tracing the development of divergent tendencies in the work overseas and at home, we can see both the part the woman's foreign mission movement played in changing the definition of missionary evangelism and how, in the process of doing so, it sowed the seeds of its own eventual disintegration as a movement.

At midcentury, Dr. John Durbin, the corresponding secretary of the General Missionary Society of the Methodist Episcopal Church who had only reluctantly agreed to countenance the formation of a female missionary society among Methodist women, recognized a need for women to serve overseas. He called for "those Protestant nuns in our society" to work in foreign mission fields as teachers, Bible readers, and physicians. But he warned that "no woman should aspire to serve in Christian missions...who cannot regard such service as a sacrifice unto God, a whole burnt-offering of body, soul, and spirit."[2] Probably few women, even at midcentury, experienced missionary service as such a burnt-offering of the self.

However, the ideal of self-immolation suffuses the early rhetoric of the woman's foreign mission movement. Through a process of professionalization in missionary training that parallels the introduction of business methods into mission administration, this melodramatic ideal yielded to a view of missionary service as a career option akin to teaching, nursing, or social work.

Typical of this new breed of professionally trained missionary is the farmer's daughter from Iowa who took a normal school course and taught in district schools for five years, then spent a six-week summer session in 1896 in training at the Moody Bible Institute in Chicago prior to sailing for India. Once in India, her letters home, far from suggesting any sacrifice of self, report on afternoon teas and tennis matches, picnic breakfasts and croquet games, and even the opportunity of meeting Lord Curzon, Viceroy of India, at a reception. The hardships of missionary life compared favorably with the rigors of teaching school in Iowa; malaria, she told one sister, was preferable to enduring the boarding arrangements made for district schoolteachers. To another sister who had followed in her footsteps as a schoolteacher, she wrote,

> How cold you are all huddled up in a room over a stove, with a walk to school in the snow. While *I* am in a calico dress in a tent. Who wouldn't be a missionary?

Offering advice to a favorite younger sister, she counseled, "Don't stay a *teacher in an intermediate grade. It's dreadful.*" For this young woman, a career in missions was an infinitely preferable alternative to teaching. It afforded a life of travel and adventure beyond the wildest dreams of a district schoolteacher—and supplied an income large enough, meager though missionary salaries were, to help one sister with college expenses and send money home to her parents. Weekly letters to "the folks at home" show how much she relished her new role in life, even while complaining to her parents that "life out here is only enjoyable when one has decent servants." Her work in India began with a stint as an itinerant evangelist designed to acquaint her with the region. But it was not primarily evangelistic work in a narrow sense; when she retired to the states in 1942, she enjoyed a reputation as the most efficient hospital administrator in the Punjab. The photo albums she kept as

a record of her life in India show a picture of missionary life far removed from that envisioned by Dr. Durbin. One photograph of
this farm girl from Iowa on vacation in the hill country of India
sums up the contrast: a handsome, rather stout woman of middle
age, dressed in a well-tailored suit, stands holding a rifle in one
hand and dangling two rabbits from the other.[3] Not at all the picture Dr. Durbin had in mind!

The case of the farmer's daughter is symptomatic of the character that missionary vocations assumed as the definition of what
could be construed as evangelistic work broadened in the era of
modern missions. Providing a variety of social services came to be
seen as an integral part of the missionary task. Female missionaries,
denied ordination, had from the beginning been engaged primarily
in teaching and medical work, but such work had initially been conceived of as a way to establish the contact that would lead to conversion. When social service for its own sake was accepted as a
legitimate part of the Protestant mission enterprise, mission administrators began to review candidates' professional credentials alongside their spiritual ones and to insist upon professional training for
both the evangelistic and service aspects of mission work.

The "Requirements and Conditions for Employment of Missionaries" set out in 1878 by the Woman's Foreign Missionary Society of the Methodist Episcopal Church (North) made a candidate's
belief in her divine calling the first and primary consideration. A
certificate of health and testimonials to her character were required;
experience in teaching and knowledge of medicine were considered
desirable, but not essential.[4] The criteria used in making decisions
about candidates for the foreign field had changed considerably by
1896 when an article entitled "Gleanings from the Portfolio of a
Missionary Candidate Committee" warned that "it is a great mistake to suppose that the glow of warm Christian feeling is *all* that is
required on the foreign field." The article briefly sketches the preparation necessary in each of the *"three paths of service* for single
women." The evangelistic service "requires especially a ready use
of Scripture, a fertility of suggestion, and capacity for quick adaptation to circumstance." Interestingly, it is pointed out that this
branch of service does not "demand such a high degree of book
knowledge" as educational or medical work. Educational work
needs "thorough preparation," while medical missionaries should

acquire "thorough training at a first class medical college, and, if possible, a degree of practical experience."[5]

To provide the professional preparation demanded for work abroad, a number of professional training schools were established in the late nineteenth century. The first and perhaps the most famous of the institutions that offered instruction for women only was the Chicago Training School for City, Home and Foreign Missions opened by Lucy Rider Meyer in 1885.[6] Mrs. Meyer hoped to train a corps of deaconesses along the lines of that produced by the German Lutheran institute at Kaiserwerth. She enlisted the support of Isabella Thoburn who served as housemother for the deaconess home attached to the school in 1887. Thoburn urged young women interested in becoming missionaries to train at the Chicago School; she herself returned to India in 1890 wearing the distinctive costume of a deaconess. The deaconess movement, however, was never widely popular in America. Missionary training schools, without the deaconess component, sprang up on a variety of locations around the country. The Methodist Woman's Foreign Missionary Society took a special interest in the Folts Mission Institute established at Herkimer, New York, in 1893. Methodist candidates for foreign service were advised to take a two-year course—costing $150 per year— following college or seminary. In 1904, the society passed a resolution requiring candidates to attend the Folts Institute for at least one year. Courses offered at Folts ranged from Biblical studies and the history of missions to industrial methods and bookkeeping; the Methodist society chose Folts on the strength of its curriculum and because its "atmosphere [was] electric with missionary enthusiasm." The Congregational journal, *Life and Light for Woman,* favored the Moody Bible Institute for Home and Foreign Missions founded in Chicago in 1889; its practical orientation, requiring students to do field work in city missions, tested the validity of a call to foreign service. A young woman, the editorialist argues, who finds the humdrum and routine of street work unendurable is not fit for missionary service, even if, "attractive and pleasing, she would make a beautiful center in a 'Missionary Farewell.' " A candidate who finds that "climbing shaky stairways, visiting poor homes in dark and filthy alleys, coming in contact with sin-crushed lives, being expected to love unlovely people, brushes away the romance of missions" is better off, from the perspective of the society supporting her and for her own sake, discovering this at home rather than in some mission station overseas.[7]

Presbyterian missionary candidates were advised in 1896 that the Training Home for Christian Workers connected with the New York City Mission Society, as well as the Moody Bible Institute, the Northfield Training School, the School for Christian Workers, the Folts Mission Institute, and the School for Domestic Science and Christian Workers could be recommended for preparatory training. The Woman's Baptist Foreign Missionary Society operated its own training school, Hasseltine House, in conjunction with the Newton Theological School. Hasseltine House, established in 1890, was one of the earliest denominational training schools for women. Two years later the Woman's Board of Foreign Missions of the Methodist Episcopal Church (South) opened in Kansas City the Scarritt Bible and Training School for Missionaries and Other Christian Workers. Other denominations followed suit, often attaching missionary education programs to existing denominational colleges or seminaries. By 1915 the report of a conference on the preparation of women for foreign missionary service held in New York listed twenty-five denominational and ten interdenominational missionary training schools open to women in the United States and Canada.[8]

The women who chose a career in foreign missions, if the rather fragmentary and impressionistic evidence available is to be trusted, fall into two main categories. One group from which a high percentage of female missionaries was recruited during the formative years of the woman's mission movement were women with personal, familial ties to the mission field. Mrs. O. W. Scott concluded from her informal survey on "What Makes Missionaries?" in 1896 that the "daughters or granddaughters of missionaries, *or of those who desired to be missionaries*" had formed the largest contingent among missionaries serving under the women's societies. Daughters of ministers were more likely to become missionaries than the daughters of the laity. Mrs. Scott also noted that some women had been recruited from schools like Mount Holyoke where institutional ties with mission fields had been established. But if the ranks of missionary and ministerial families supplied a disproportionate number of female missionaries in the early years, they were supplemented primarily by a second group of young women from small towns and rural areas whose family economic situation forced them to be self-supporting. Isabella Thoburn observed in 1887 that "most frequently missionaries are called from among the poor; one scarcely knows why." Thoburn considered this unfortunate, not only because it indicated the spiritual bankruptcy of the well-to-do, but also because "the strain of earning money for education often tells" on the health of these volunteers, leading to breakdowns and even untimely deaths on the mission fields.[9]

The advent of the Student Volunteer Movement (SVM) at the end of the 1880s brought larger numbers of college graduates into the candidate pool and increased the percentage of candidates who had no familial ties to the mission field, but there is little indication that it drew from any higher socioeconomic level. The candidate pool seems to have shifted geographically from the East to the Midwest around the turn of the century, but the typical recruit was still from a small town or rural background, ordinarily self-supporting, and past the first blush of youth. A report on "Student Work" in *Woman's Missionary Friend* shows that among the missionaries sent out by the Methodist Woman's Foreign Missionary Society between 1906 and 1910, seventeen were from Iowa, fourteen from Illinois, ten each from Kansas and Pennsylvania, nine each from Ohio, Indiana, and Michigan, seven from New York, six from Minnesota, five each from Nebraska and California, two each from Colorado, Oregon, Washington, and South Dakota, and one each from Georgia, Kentucky, Massachusetts, New Jersey, Rhode Island, Vermont, and Wisconsin.[10] These figures suggest a correlation between the proliferation of denominational colleges (where the SVM enjoyed its greatest popularity) in the Midwest and a disproportionate number of recruits from that region; but such an interpretation must remain speculative since concrete data are fragmentary at best.

Curriculum offerings at the missionary training schools that prepared these self-supporting daughters of the lower middle class for professional missionary service reflected the shifting emphasis in foreign mission work. An article in *Woman's Missionary Friend* (the title that replaced the by-then objectionable label *Heathen Woman's Friend* in 1896) spelled out the nature of modern missions in a survey of training schools proudly titled "Modern 'Schools of the Prophets.' " The approbation given science and specialization in the following passage from that survey indicates that those leading the foreign mission movement were creatures of their culture, ready like most Americans in the late nineteenth century to embrace the notion that a corps of experts could be trained to remedy all manner of social ill.

> The pre-eminently practical spirit of the times has not alone pervaded secular thought, in its new education, its adaptation of science to service, its municipal and humanitarian reforms, but it has entered also the field of Christian effort and declared that if the hand which toils for the food which perisheth must be made skillful by careful and scientific training, far more should the highest form of labor. . . . Specialization, which is a marked feature of the present secular education, is become a necessity as well in preparation for religious work.[11]

The necessity for specialized training had, of course, been long perceived in the area of medical missions. In 1869, Samuel Gregory, M.D., secretary of the Boston Medical College for Women, called for women's missionary societies to search out the right candidates and help them obtain a medical education. He recommended a term of medical lectures for missionary wives as well as for all single women entering missionary service and—lest he be accused of making these recommendations out of self-interest—announced that scholarship aid was available for short-term students.[12]

The rationale for medical missions in 1869 was, however, far from modern; medical missions were justified on narrowly evangelical grounds. One missionary wife, pleading the "Necessity for Female Medical Missionaries," wrote that she found women most vulnerable to evangelical persuasion when they were sick.

> I do not merely look to the bodily good to be done to the native female community. We all know how sickness breaks down prejudice, and prepares the heart to receive impressions for good. It seems to me that the women of this country [India] can be reached by female physicians, both native and foreign, more directly than in any other way, and that they may be influenced in this manner to give attention to religion, education and improvement in every way.[13]

In contrast to the argument that the female physician would be an effective evangelist is the position taken by Grace Kimball, M.D., a missionary to Turkey, in a paper she presented at the Ecumenical Conference in New York in 1900. Dr. Kimball believed that a medical missionary could not be "both an evangelist and a medical person" precisely because "the medical profession is more exacting than any profession that men or women take up." A physician's first duty, according to Kimball, is "to use all the powers of mind or body and soul. . .for the physical benefit. . .of all who require his or her services."[14] From Kimball's perspective, legitimate Christian service on the foreign mission field did not necessarily involve evangelistic work of a traditional sort.

Kimball's position with respect to medical missions is similar to the stance assumed by modern mission theorists regarding educational and industrial missions. Christian social service was deemed compatible with evangelical aims, but not always identical with them. Success on the mission field was no longer measured solely by the number of converts; the relief of famine, the amelioration of social as well as physical ills, and the training of non-Westerners for modern industrial and professional work had become integral parts of the evangelical Protestant missionary crusade by the turn of the century. Missionary training schools equipped prospective overseas workers with the variety of specialized skills required by the growing complexity of mission work.

The broadened definition of evangelism that characterized modern missions has been linked by a contemporary historian to a "considerable interest in the spread of American culture." Charles Forman argues that "often this was implicit rather than explicit."

> The emphasis on efficiency and businesslike methods, for example, was simply assumed in the work the missionaries did, and it necessarily carried influence in the direction of rationalization and modernization of the way of life of other countries. Methods of agricultural work. . .or of medical work. . .had a certain secularized character, which was also assumed and which inevitably had what may be called a secularizing impact. . . . The individualism inherent in the way in which they presented their faith and called for individual conversions also implied a cultural transformation wherever they went.

In certain matters, however, Forman notes that the call for cultural transformation was more explicit; he cites three "cultural advantages that, it was presumed, Americans had to offer."

> An improvement in the position of women was always first and
> foremost.... A Western type of education and Western medical
> science were the other two cultural features that were uni-
> formly recommended by the missions.[15]

The rationale justifying the linkage of evangelism to the spread of at least these features of American culture—and the role played by the woman's foreign mission movement in developing such a rationale—can be seen evolving most clearly in the debate over policy governing educational missions.

At the time when women's foreign missionary societies were being organized in the 1870s, two conflicting views regarding educational work were being aired in mission circles. One group felt that rudimentary education should be offered in the native languages; this group wanted to restrict the goal of evangelical Protestant missions to conversion. They warned against confusing Western civilization and tradition with Christianity. The Rev. J. H. Messmore, writing from Lucknow, claimed that Indian women were happy and contented, that their need was spiritual, not social.

> Our aim is to elevate these women to a higher plane of moral
> and spiritual life, and beyond that we have little desire of effect-
> ing any change in their mode of life.[16]

Dr. Rufus Anderson, longtime secretary of the American Board of Commissioners for Foreign Missions, agreed with Mr. Messmore and consequently was one of the strongest advocates of the view that instruction ought to be offered in native languages rather than in English. Dr. Anderson managed to incorporate his views into official American Board policy at midcentury. It is not surprising therefore that the Woman's Board of Missions associated with the American Board issued the following policy statement in 1870.

> By education, we do not mean placing before them the sci-
> ences, and telling them they must reach up and grasp, neither
> do we mean giving them a new style of dress, and thereby cre-

ate in them a love for outward adorning. They need no more to change their style of dress than their language. Both are adapted to their country and circumstances. We wish to place Christ and him crucified, before them, and teach them to be Christians.[17]

This respect for native culture sounds liberal and modern; however, underlying the policy was a conservative and narrowly evangelical vision of missions. It rested on the assumption that the essence of Christianity could be separated from any particular cultural form, that native populations could be inoculated with the spiritual serum derived from the distillation of Western Christianity into pure Gospel. Proponents of this position separated soul from mind and body.

Proponents of the opposing position considered Christianity and Western civilization inseparable. They favored boarding schools and, generally, instruction in English—at least for talented students being groomed as candidates for higher education and for leadership roles in native churches. Boarding schools, argued Bishop James Thoburn, sent girls back to their villages as "evangelizing and civilizing agents." Although the Methodist Woman's Foreign Missionary Society organized to save the souls of heathen women, not to elevate them physically, mentally, socially, its members were assured by Mrs. E. E. Baldwin that Christianizing women inevitably civilized them, too: "Yes, Christianity does refine, cleanse, and elevate every one that comes under its influence. It makes gentlemen and ladies of them." Indeed, more than one missionary reversed this process and argued that civilizing the heathen was the first step toward converting them. A missionary from India argued that missionary ladies should be "accomplished," since she thought that "anything that tends to cultivate their [Indian women's] tastes, and refine them in any way, tends also to *Christianize* them." Another missionary to India, Mrs. J. T. Gracey, noted in her journal "the rapidity with which these girls and women learn to do fancy work"; she considered it a most promising sign, portending eventual salvation.[18]

As early as 1869 Jennie Fowler Willing advanced an argument for cultural renovation that connected it specifically to the theory that evangelization would only be successful if heathen mothers were Christianized.

When we look at the domestic, civil and religious systems of
Pagandom, we sicken at their rottenness. We feel greatly
moved to give them the blessings of Christian civilization. To
do this economically, *i.e.*, to have the largest results from the
smallest outlay of money, muscle, thought, and spiritual power,
we must get at the fountains of influence. As much as Pagan
men despise their women, they cannot abolish the physical necessity that gives them control of their children, during the
years that most shape the life. To Christianize the women,
would be to capture their stronghold, and insure a better civilization. It would be getting a lever well under their systems of
wrong. With a good fulcrum, and God to apply the power,
there would be a new order of things in those 'habitations of
cruelty,' within a half a century.[19]

Most women's societies, adopting Willing's point of view, came to
regard Western mores and hygiene as part and parcel of evangelization. Women, after all, had a vested interest in educational work, the
greater part of which fell to female missionaries since men went as
preachers, women as teachers.

Protesting against the annual report of a powerful denominational mission board that emphasized preaching rather than teaching as the primary means of evangelization, an editorial published in
*Heathen Woman's Friend* in 1876 tackled directly the issue of strict con-
structionism in defining the missionary imperative of the Christian
message. Noting that the success of women's educational missions
had prompted the board to its discussion of priorities in mission
work, the editorial urged "all like sisterhoods" to determine
"whether we are indeed in such grave danger of overdoing that
branch of the work more especially allotted to us." The editorialist
herself had no hesitation in answering her own question.

In fact, the more we consider the almost infinite variety of social forces and influences of which in every age God has availed
himself for the diffusion of his truth and for the rendering of
that truth savingly effective, the more certain do we feel that
the theory of missions which underlies the [board's] misgivings
is pitifully narrow and practically mischievous.[20]

But if those focused on conventional evangelization through preaching were pitifully narrow, the supporters of educational missions sound (like Jennie Willing) distressingly ethnocentric and imperialistic. Jennie K. McCauley, for example, justified secular education in Presbyterian boarding schools for Japanese girls with the following rationale.

> The shocking immorality that prevails in all heathen countries can only be rooted out by taking girls from their homes and surroundings, collecting them into boarding schools, where, for a period of years, the Christian missionary, day by day, constantly keeps before the mind of her pupil what purity and uprightness mean. In fact, she must instill a conscience and educate a will, as a heathen woman knows none.[21]

McCauley's remarks were made in 1888; by then, the women's societies had discovered that heathen mothers were remarkably resistant to the Christian message. Unable to reach heathen mothers, the woman's foreign mission movement turned to their daughters. Female missionaries and the leaders of the movement at home came to believe that the transformation of the heathen household into a Christian home could best be accomplished by molding the rising generation.

Gradually, education of women in foreign lands became not so much a strategy for evangelization as an instrument for social change. Initially, native women were trained as Bible readers to do evangelistic work in remote villages. Girls were taught the rudiments of housekeeping and Western sanitation in order to make them better wives and mothers; the Christian homes they then established would be models for their neighbors to emulate. Missionaries, however, found it difficult to watch their most talented pupils marry and return to village life. The ablest students were carefully selected for further education. The Methodist Woman's Foreign Missionary Society, for example, brought Chinese women to the United States for medical education before medical colleges for women were opened in the Orient. Missionaries geared high schools and colleges to training women, not for marriage and maternity, but for positions of leadership in their own societies.

For women to assume leadership roles in most countries where Protestant missions operated amounted virtually to cultural revolution—and that was precisely what the woman's foreign mission movement intended to foment. Helen Barrett Montgomery, in her 1910 textbook for the United Study of Foreign Missions, systematically linked the evangelization of women to social change. Montgomery, using the metaphor Willing had applied forty years earlier, saw in mission schools "the mightiest lever for overturning low, contemptuous, and tyrannical ideas and customs concerning women." She understood that the effect of female education was "in fact, a social ferment of the most violent kind," and she applauded.

> These schools, hospitals, clubs, libraries, are developing a new woman in the East, with wants her mother never knew. To meet these expanding desires an expanding ministry will be required. The nurse, the business woman, the musician, the journalist, the dietician, the naturalist, may all find that their contribution is needed to round out this amazing undertaking.

Mission stations, Montgomery claimed, had already become "great social settlements suffused with the religious motive," and she heartily approved of that development. She rejoiced that in the era of modern missions and the social gospel "the old superstitious division between the 'spiritual' and the 'secular'...[when] it was felt to be a waste of precious time and money to send missionaries to deal with anything but the perishing souls of men" was rapidly disappearing.[22]

Montgomery's linkage of the spiritual to the secular and, especially, of Christianity to Western democracy was not simply—or even primarily—a blend of chauvinism and cultural imperialism. Her first mission study text, published in 1906 under the title *Christus Redemptor: An Outline Study of the Island World of the Pacific,* indicates clearly her awareness that Western interest in the Pacific was a result of commercial exploitation and had been less than a blessing to the natives of the islands.

> When the islanders were first discovered by Europeans they were...rude, uncivilized, bewildered by superstition, decimated by wars, and brutalized by cruel customs, but after all

they had their primitive laws and customs. They were free and strong, and life was good to them in their beautiful island home. The first contact with whites was an unmitigated curse, as the contact of commercial civilization, divorced from religion, always is to a weaker race.

Montgomery's text cites instances of the deliberate introduction of disease among island populations and of the conscription of slave laborers. Finally, it indicts the "so-called Christian nations" for "aggressions...conducted without the slightest regard for the welfare of the occupants of the islands."[23]

Deploring the havoc wreaked by Western capitalism as she did, Montgomery remained a realist rather than a romantic. She saw that it was too late to leave the natives alone in their island paradise as some sentimentalists wished to do. Those who opposed foreign missions as the imposition of Western religion on happy natives would, she argued, in removing missionaries, remove from the scene the only friends the native had. The moral solution, in her eyes, was to send more missionaries.

> The strongest reason why the conscience of Europe and America ought to continue and immensely strengthen its missionary forces in the island world is because we owe it to these people to make the largest, most costly and statesmanlike reparation for the ills inflicted on them by unworthy representatives of our race and by our still unchristianized governments.

The benefits she expected the missionaries to bring sound suspiciously like a laundry list of the blessings of Western civilization: schools, hospitals, churches, written languages, and industrial skills. Yet on a conscious level Montgomery opposed cultural imperialism; she noted with approval the policy of Bishop Selwyn in Melanesia to refrain from the "forcing of English methods and ways of life except insofar as they are part of morality and godliness."[24]

Montgomery, however, never entirely divorced Western political and cultural ideals from her understanding of the substantive core of Christianity. She found the characteristic tendencies of the West particularly consonant with the Christian message. On no point was this clearer to her than on the issue of the position of women. She systematically explored the claims made by religious and cultural relativists and rejected them on the basis of her perception of the degradation of women inherent in other religions and cultures. For her, the objective of Christian missions was not, as it had been for the woman's foreign mission movement during its formative years, to Christianize heathendom by converting heathen mothers. Instead, Montgomery wanted to end the oppression of women in other cultures by introducing the Gospel. She labeled the Gospel the "engine of democracy," which is "destined to break in pieces all castes, privileges, and oppressions. Perhaps the last caste to be destroyed will be that of sex." As a suffragist herself, Montgomery was not one to exonerate Western culture of all crimes against women, but she believed that insofar as Western nations were Christian nations their treatment of women was more just than that of non-Christian countries. And with the optimism characteristic of her Progressive generation, she believed that the position of women in America was already evolving toward a desired state of equality.

> Strictly speaking, there is no Christian nation, but only nations in process of becoming Christian. But even so, the steady pressure of Bible ideals, exerted slowly and against tremendous difficulties has already brought a revolution in the position of women.[25]

Montgomery's combined advocacy of social change and cultural sensitivity encouraged women to be less culturally and racially chauvinist even while they remained critical of those facets of other cultures and religions that demeaned humanity by degrading women. Jean Kenyon Mackenzie struck a similar balance between genuine appreciation of non-Western culture and advocacy of cultural transformation in the textbooks she wrote for the United Study of Foreign Missions. Mackenzie's texts reflect the specific influence of her experiences on the mission field in West Africa. In 1904 she went to the Cameroons under the auspices of the Woman's Foreign Missionary Society of the Presbyterian Church. A broadly educated and thoroughly modern young woman, she held tolerant views of the non-Western world that her experiences in Africa tempered somewhat. Her observations of the lives lived by African tribeswomen had the most telling effect on reshaping her perspective. In

1905, she wrote home, "Polygamy is terrible. I had too open a mind about it when I came to Africa—and now I have so many sad thoughts of it." Like most of the new breed of female missionary, she had, although supported by a woman's society, not gone to Africa with any sense of a special mission to women. One soon developed. She informed her family,

> I am coming to be a kind of doctor to the hearts of childless women. . . . To the sorrow of their hearts are added the burdens of superstition and blame heavier than you can imagine. . . . I am glad of the things I believe—for the sake of the women I am more glad than words can tell.

Mackenzie rejoiced that the Gospel freed these women from the burden of cultural oppression; while it may have saved their souls as well, the relief of their anxiety was the visible good that Mackenzie perceived. Describing African women as slaves to "the Bantu triple obsession of goods and sex and fetish," she explained that "to such as these in a very definite sense Christ is a liberator." She reported that "of the women who have come under my hand, many have fastened with a peculiar tenacity on the verses that say for them, 'He has made the captives free.' " The gift that Christianity offered African women was not only the prospect of eternal salvation, but also the validation of their humanity. Mackenzie wrote that the impact of the word of God was to give African women possession of their own souls: "until she [the Bantu woman] heard that word she was never at any time conscious of a self which could not be bought and sold."[26]

Mackenzie's indictment of the treatment of women in Africa is, however, only one aspect of her complicated attitude toward African culture. She saw and attempted to convey to Americans, both through her mission study textbooks and pamphlets and through the letters, stories, and poetry she published in secular magazines, the strength and beauty of tribal culture. But even as her pen sketched the Africa she found, that Africa disappeared. Mackenzie felt greater ambivalence about the impact of the white man on Africa than Montgomery revealed in her simultaneous indictment of Western commerce and celebration of Western mores. Like Montgomery, Mackenzie realized that modernization was inevitable—and in certain respects a blessing—but because she had lived among tribal peoples and cherished the sustaining friendship of cook and lantern-carrier, she appreciated more fully the loss involved. Invalided home in 1913 after nine years among the Bulu of West Africa, Mackenzie embarked on her second career of interpreting Africa for Americans. The emotional color of her attachment to premodern African tribal culture can be seen in her descriptions of "those black maternal hands upon the hair of lonely white women" and of "kind voices at the end of weary journeys that ask, 'What will my child eat tonight?' " The paternalism that so often characterized missionary attitudes is neatly avoided in these scenes that cast Mackenzie as the child of Mother Africa. But if Mackenzie could conceive of a white woman as an adopted child of Africa, she saw the white man in Africa quite differently. She describes him as the irresistible force of modernity, as both a blessing and a curse. In a single passage in her 1917 mission study text, *An African Trail,* images of the white man's rapacious assault on Africa are followed by a list of salutary changes.

> Now, old things are being swept away and new things are being driven into the black man's country. Those roads that cleave the forest are like breaches in an age-old stockade, and through every breach rushes the master of change—the white man, the modifier of thought, of aspect, of manners, of custom—exacting by his very presence new attitudes toward life, toward murder, toward women, toward labor.[27]

Even as Mackenzie devoted her considerable literary talents to describing sympathetically for an American audience the customs, the speech, and the very thought patterns of tribal peoples, she supported the efforts of the colonial government to suppress certain traditional customs. Whimsically, she applauded the government's "curious regard for human life [that] has checked so many of the natural sports of the Bulu. . .until it begins to look as if tomorrow a man must hunt a corner in which to kill his own wife." On a less playful note, Mackenzie reminded Americans that change in Africa was a shock to the black man; the Christian responsibility in this situation, she maintained, was to help Africans make the transition from their primitive culture to a modern, industrial world.

How to meet with honor the new opportunities of cash and commerce, labor and government—this essential education so necessary to a primitive people in this too sudden dawn of a new day—this is the immediate service of the things of God.[28]

From Mackenzie's perspective, the situation in Africa required that industrial and educational missions take precedence over traditional evangelization. (Evangelization had, in fact, been more successful in Africa than in virtually any other large mission field. Mackenzie no doubt anticipated that conversion and adherence to Christianity would accompany industrial and educational work.) Mackenzie noted that in the past—and even in 1917 at a few lonely outposts in the bush—missionaries had to be "all things to all needs"; but she rejoiced and urged her readers to give thanks that "there has been an evolution in mission work." Like Montgomery, she saw room in modern missions for women and men with a variety of professional skills to utilize their expertise in the service of God.

At the heart of every great African mission of every denomination, there is the fact, or the intention, of adequate modern equipment....A man or woman, of whatever degree of skill or training in any one of the essential human crafts, who is at work in one of these modern stations need not lose himself or his craft.[29]

Here is specific assurance that a woman who offered herself for the mission field need not become a burnt-offering, and could even expect to find professional satisfaction in her work.

Mackenzie clearly approved of the specialization and professionalization of mission work that helped it keep pace with the changing political, economic, and social realities of the modern world. How convincing her reasons were to the ordinary churchwoman is, of course, difficult to know. Continued financial support for missions suggests that churchwomen were not questioning decisions made by the professionals on the field and at home. How deeply the sophisticated message contained in the mission study texts written by Mackenzie, Montgomery, and others penetrated is harder to ascertain. Montgomery, apparently, was confident that mission study had had a pronounced effect on the understanding women had of world affairs. She recounted the story of a prominent Washington woman who attributed her knowledge of foreign affairs to mission studies. A foreign diplomat, impressed by her dinner party conversation, inquired if her husband had been in the diplomatic service. He was astonished to learn instead that her interest and familiarity with foreign politics stemmed from mission study classes.

> Then beginning at the beginning Mrs. Baker told the amazed young man how all the women of the Protestant world were united in a joint study of the mission fields of the world; how since 1900 they had used a joint textbook each year, how hundreds of thousands of these books covering every continent and every race had been published, and how she had her own shelf of these textbooks in her house, and when she read any bit of foreign news in the paper she turned to these books.[30]

Probably few women used their textbooks as assiduously as Mrs. Baker claimed to have done, but perhaps exposure to the ideas and information the books contained tempered the provincialism of many ordinary churchwomen and mitigated to some degree the rampant racism and cultural chauvinism of the age. Ultimately, however, the sophisticated ideology of professionalized missions did not maintain the same grip on the imagination of churchwomen that the formulation of woman's special and sacred mission to heathen women had held over an earlier generation. The introduction of systematic mission study did have a definite impact on the character of local auxiliaries that can be linked to the decay of support for the woman's foreign mission movement at home.

The plan for mission study referred to by Mrs. Baker was part of the program for modernizing mission work proposed by the leaders of the woman's mission movement at the Ecumenical Conference of 1900. They hoped it would substitute facts for the sentimental views of mission work cherished by the average auxiliary member. Abbie Child outlined a seven-year course of study modeled along the lines of the then popular International Sunday School lessons. Child's proposal was enthusiastically endorsed by both Helen Montgomery and Ellen Parsons. Anticipating opposition, Parsons argued that old methods were not suitable for the generation of young women being trained in colleges. Her concern is primarily with attracting the New Woman to the missionary cause by presenting the latter as a modern and up-to-date enterprise.

> Now, perhaps, you feel that the ordinary time-honored method of leaflets and little cuttings from our papers, placed upon cards, should not be cast aside....But how about young women accustomed to study? You invite them to your meeting, and you put a little paper in their hand about the women in China, and a little letter about the women in India. The chances are that that young woman, who is accustomed to study thoroughly anything to which she gives her attention, will not come to the next meeting.[31]

Parsons's reasons for wanting to revamp social local auxiliary practice parallel the explanation given by Karen Blair for the post–1890 shift from culture to reform in the woman's club movement, that the New Woman—as a result of expanded educational opportunities for women—had different needs from those of earlier generations.

> Such a woman did not have to undergo the painful lessons in self-assertion in the ways that her mother and grandmother had in culture clubs. Women, in other words, had less need for literary study now. Social and intellectual needs were met in school, jobs, in the world at large. For the New Woman, the old brand of literary club was obsolete.[32]

Women's clubs embarked upon a program of municipal and civic reform that appealed to the New Woman of the Progressive era. Helen Montgomery felt that the introduction of systematic mission study of the sort envisioned by Child would enable women's missionary societies to compete successfully with women's clubs for the time and talent of the new generation. She also hoped that women who were already loyal supporters of missions could be brought through mission study to enlarge their conception of mission work. She deplored a "certain smallness" that, she said, characterized missionary meetings, and she compared them unfavorably with club meetings.

> We have trusted to leaflets, and tracts, and items, and excerpts.

We have done very little original work. We have made very few demands upon the brains of the women in our missionary circles. And as a result, we have been given over to smallness of vision in our missionary life. There is no reason why the State Federation of Women's Clubs should have a higher average of intellectual caliber in the papers that are presented before them than a State meeting of Woman's Missionary Societies.

Montgomery wanted every laywoman "to come to realize that in this cause of foreign missions are included statecraft, and civilization, and geography, and history, and biography, and philosophy, and poetry, and art, and the living history of the living kingdom of the living God."[33] The Ecumenical Conference launched this ambitious educational program by appointing Abbie Child the chairman of a Central Committee on the United Study of Foreign Missions.

The plan to unite all the women's foreign missionary societies of the United States and Canada in the systematic study of missions represented the culmination of discussions begun among the leaders of the various societies at the Woman's Congress of Missions held in conjunction with the Parliament of Religions at the Columbian Exposition in Chicago in 1893. The successful staging of the Woman's Congress of Missions gave women the confidence to inaugurate in 1897 an Interdenominational Conference of Woman's Boards of Foreign Missions of the United States and Canada. The Interdenominational Conferences, similar to those that were held by the general boards after 1893, provide yet another example of the leadership of the women's societies adopting patterns of professional behavior established by men. The women who attended the first Interdenominational Conference in New York were already at least semiprofessional; virtually all of them had made inspection tours of mission stations throughout the world. In the yearly meetings held between 1897 and 1900 they discussed the practical problems of their work at home and abroad. Missionary education was a continuing concern of the women who met at Interdenominational Conferences.[34]

As the administrators of the women's societies themselves grew more aware of the social and political implications of foreign missions and of the importance of professional training for missionaries, they realized the inadequacy of the efforts being made at the local level to lay the missionary cause before churchwomen. They also realized that they were in competition with other organizations for the time and energy of these churchwomen. For a solution they turned to education—the Progressive panacea for all problems. Drawing on the experience of the Student Volunteer Movement in introducing courses of mission study in colleges and universities, they developed their own strategies for systematic mission study. The plan presented by Miss Child to the Ecumenical Conference in 1900 was the fruit of various experiments, ranging from a game called *Pronouncit,* recommended by *Woman's Missionary Friend* to help ladies pronounce foreign names correctly, to the efforts of the Woman's Missionary Social Union in Springfield, Illinois, to place 650 missionary books in the city library and provide 24 missionary periodicals for a special table in the library reading room.[35]

The Central Committee on the United Study of Foreign Missions commissioned Louise Manning Hodgkins to write its first interdenominational textbook. The resulting volume, titled *Via Christi: An Introduction to the Study of Missions,* was published by the Macmillan Company in 1901. (Macmillan published each of the yearly textbooks until 1910, when the Central Committee took over publication, complaining that "from the first year when the Macmillan Company would risk only five thousand, and twenty thousand were actually sold, this lack of faith hampered the work of the Committee."[36]) Hodgkins's text is a comprehensive overview of the history of missions from St. Paul to Adoniram Judson. Hodgkins managed to compress an enormous wealth of detail into 250 pages, heading each chapter with chronological tables listing great events, great names, and great productions. Suggestions for discussion and further research follow each chapter. The volume, in the context of the proposed course of mission study, is remedial in intent; it sketches general background for subsequent volumes treating the history of missions in particular countries through the nineteenth century to the present. The content of Hodgkins's text is, however, not elementary; she presents the complexities of Christian history with remarkable deftness—and a fair-mindedness unusual in rabidly anti-Catholic evangelical circles.[37]

The textbooks produced annually for the Central Committee proved to be best-sellers; cumulative sales figures indicate that by 1905 nearly fifty thousand copies of each text had been distributed.

The popularity of the textbooks generated columns of advice in the women's missionary magazines on how to use the new materials. *Woman's Missionary Friend* suggested that each member of a local auxiliary be made responsible for "the gist of one paragraph in *Via Christi.*" Where once the magazines had offered detailed instructions on offering prayer and researching and writing missionary papers to be read at meetings, they now attempted to tell women how to use professional teaching aids and methods. "Charts as Missionary Accessories" were recommended as a way to make statistics more palatable; muslin a yard square was deemed adequate for use in small rooms and for local societies, while double width muslin was desirable for a chart to be hung in a "large audience room." Large colored maps were available at cost from society headquarters. Special feature articles and stories in the magazines were keyed to the chapter for the month from the current textbook.[38]

The application of professional pedagogical techniques to mission study was expanded and institutionalized by the decision made at the Sixth Interdenominational Conference of Woman's Boards in 1904 to establish summer conferences for missionary workers. Such conferences were already well-established features of the millennialist, evangelical subculture in England and America. In Britain, the Keswick conventions were an influential force. The Student Volunteer Movement, born at Dwight L. Moody's first summer school for college students at Mount Hermon in 1886, relied heavily on such summer gatherings. Borrowing from these and other familiar models—the camp meeting, Chautauqua, and summer county institutes for schoolteachers—the leaders of the woman's mission movement set about training a corps of "professional" teachers to take charge of mission study in local churches.[39] The decision to institute summer schools of missions in scattered locations around the country was made by a handful of women who considered themselves mission experts. Clementina Butler, daughter of the founders of Methodist missions in India and secretary-treasurer of the Central Committee on the United Study of Foreign Missions, expressed satisfaction, in her report on the Interdenominational Conference, that amateurs had been excluded. She described the conference as "an event of real importance to the missionary world."

Not because of the size of the audience,—in fact no announcement had been made of the meetings as it was desired to restrict attendance to experts, in order that the discussions might have the greater value,—but because of the gathering of Boards, Baptist, Congregational, Episcopalian, Lutheran, Presbyterian, and Methodist Episcopal, all intent on discovering and carrying forward the best plans.

The officers of these boards discussed "Special Work, Problems and Methods, United Effort on other lines than Study, Christian Stewardship, 'Should we require a College Education for Candidates?,' 'Is Apportionment an Advantage?,' and How to interest more Church Women"; but the most significant action taken was to name a committee to plan summer schools.[40]

The first summer school for missions, held at Northfield, Massachusetts, in 1904, drew 235 delegates. Helen Montgomery and Louise Manning Hodgkins taught women how to conduct mission classes in their home churches. Dr. T. H. P. Sailer was imported to discuss pedagogical techniques. He condemned three methods: the lecture, the paper—which he criticized as "the weakness of women"—and recitation. In place of these outdated methods he recommended roundtable discussions.[41] Summer schools proliferated and proved popular. In 1915 there were 916 delegates registered for the twelfth annual Summer School for Foreign Missions at Northfield. Denominational rallies were held, presided over by officers of the various societies; returned missionaries addressed meetings and led classes. A general Bible study class each morning included visitors as well as registered participants. In addition, delegates attended three Bible study and three mission study classes plus "methods hours for women and children's societies" and "a new class this year which proved to be of great benefit. . . on methods for young women's work." Evenings were devoted to missionary addresses and devotional services led by, among others, Helen Montgomery, who was teaching a daily class that summer on the textbook she herself had written. The week, ordinarily capped with a Field Day, climaxed in the summer of 1915 with a festival celebrating the "Spirit of Northfield."

[A pageant] represented Desire—the churches at home—being led by Hope to see the real spirit of Northfield. Each camp acted out in its own way one of the six attributes which go to make up the Spirit—Faith, Humility, Truth, Love, Joy, Service.[42]

The production of such a pageant suggests that Montgomery had not entirely succeeded in eradicating the sentimentality with which women were wont to surround the cross. The tears have been wiped away, but there is a certain narcissism in this adoration of the spirit of Northfield that is perhaps less admirable spiritually than weeping over missionary martyrs. The complacency that came with the apparent success of the summer schools kept the leaders from noticing that the very fabric of the movement in the churches at home was weakening.

The Northfield Summer School may have been the oldest of these annual summer sessions, but it was not, in 1915, the only or even the largest one. The ninth Minnesota Summer School drew 1,300; the School of Missions for Oklahoma and the Southwest enrolled 404 in its fourth year of operation. California boasted both the Mount Hermon Federate School of Missions and a Woman's Congress of Missions at San Francisco in the summer of 1915. All reports indicate that women returned from a week of emotional and concentrated attention to missions with renewed enthusiasm for mission study at home; young girls frequently offered themselves for the foreign field at emotionally charged consecration services on the final night of a conference.[43]

The textbooks, and the summer schools planned in conjunction with them, changed the character of missionary meetings in local churches. That, of course, had been the intention of the experts; Lucy Waterbury, a prominent Baptist missionary society leader and chairman of the Central Committee on the United Study of Foreign Missions (after Abbie Child's untimely death), saw a clear need for summer schools to train women to lead mission study classes.

> Would not hundreds of women, young and old, leaders of study classes and missionary societies, welcome the opportunity to attend normal classes where all the work of the year would be thoroughly presented by inspirational leaders?

Comparing these summer sessions with normal school courses as she does indicates the "professional" terms in which Mrs. Waterbury conceived of training mission study leaders. She dismissed the reservations expressed by some women about the effect that such new approaches to mission work at home would have. She claimed,

> Few will share in the feeling expressed by one dear old sister, who says she feels concerned about all this study of missions. She thinks it is a mistake, and is leading us away from the study of the Bible. She does not approve of these sensational methods. Another fears that we may lose the tenderness and prayer which should characterize our meetings.[44]

Mrs. Waterbury's dismissal of the dear old sisters' objections reflected her assumption that the new, more systematic study of missions would not displace prayer and Bible study. The scientific study of missions was intended, by the women who promoted it, to supplement rather than replace the piety that had characterized mission work by women. However, Mrs. Waterbury should perhaps have paid more heed to the dear old sisters; the actual transformation wrought in auxiliary meetings by the introduction of textbooks was a dilution of their religious, prayer-meeting atmosphere. One leader of a local auxiliary reported proudly that since they had begun using textbooks their "missionary meetings [were] almost as popular as any club meeting, and no matter what the weather is a goodly number attend." As modern, "up-to-date" women, the leaders of the woman's foreign mission movement applauded rather than regretted change. In 1909, Mrs. M. H. Lichliter reviewed the effect of textbooks on auxiliary meetings and concluded that "the rise of the missionary textbook marked the dawn of a new era of modern missions." Local auxiliaries, she reported happily, need no longer rely on the visit of an occasional missionary or on leaflets for scraps of information—"a paucity of facts and a multiplicity of pathetic incidents." Instead, Mrs. Lichliter rejoiced that with the introduction of textbooks "the church began to learn facts."[45]

Learning facts, making a science of missions, was consistent with the temper of the times. Science was in the ascendancy in America at the turn of the century; "scientific" methods were recommended for solving every conceivable problem. In an age of increasing specialization, laymen and women turned to experts for answers—and leadership. This was so within the foreign mission movement at large as well as among the women's societies. For women, however, the adaptation of scientific pedagogical principles to mission study created special difficulties since—or so the leadership believed—women were not in the habit of studying. Mrs. Lichliter suggested that it would be necessary to find a woman with pedagogical training to lead an auxiliary's mission study. She blithely assumed that every auxiliary would have some member who had taught school before marriage or one who, remaining single, had made teaching her career. The woman's foreign mission movement would have to depend on such women to provide the expertise needed for mission study. Asserting the need for professional skill in conducting mission studies challenged the competence, so heavily stressed in the formative years, of each auxiliary member to pray and speak publicly. That this was not the intended effect of the introduction of the textbook method is apparent in Mrs. Lichliter's expressed hope that "accurate knowledge" would enable women "to pray more definitely." There is, however, little indication that her hope was realized. Textbook sales grew steadily (at least until 1916 when, for the first time, the Central Committee lost rather than made money on its textbook); but in 1907 the Woman's Foreign Missionary Society of the Methodist Episcopal Church (North)— the largest of all the denominational women's societies—announced that it would not publish a prayer calendar for the coming year because the demand for one had fallen so low.[46]

The use of textbooks did not cause a decline in the faithful exercise of pious duties, but the introduction of systematic mission study was accompanied by a significant change of emphasis in women's missionary magazines: women were not so frequently urged to pray as to inform themselves; the rhetoric of woman's special responsibility, the suggestion that the blood of the souls of her heathen sisters would be upon her skirts unless she ceaselessly importuned the throne of grace, disappeared in the era of modern missions. The decline in personal piety was no doubt due more to the rising tide of secularism in American culture than to the absence in women's missionary magazines of admonitions to pray, but by tacitly acquiescing the magazines did nothing to stem the tide. With the advantage of hindsight, Helen Montgomery recognized their mistake in 1924 when she wrote *Prayer and Missions* as the Central Committee's textbook for that year.

The displacement of prayer in a movement that had, as we saw earlier, located in prayer a source of power available to the humblest seamstress, encouraged the stratification of the movement into a hierarchy based on knowledge and expertise, a hierarchy engendered by the mission study movement's call for trained leaders. Woman's instinctual gifts, her natural religious impulses, were now not so highly valued as cultivated gifts of intellect and managerial or pedagogical skill. The distance separating leaders from the rank and file, already apparent in the debate over giving for special objects, widened as experience and training initiated certain women into the inner mysteries of missions and made the rest of them dependent upon instruction from the initiates. A division was created not only between ordinary churchwomen and national or regional leaders, but also between members of local auxiliaries on the basis of who had and who had not attended a summer school or a regional or national missionary conference.

Missionary magazines, conceived of as intimate visitors in the homes of all churchwomen, communicating missionary intelligence as mother to daughter or sister to sister, became professional journals, aiding and supplementing the work of trained leaders. Both the new hierarchy of knowledge and the new role played by the missionary magazine are illustrated in the response made in *Woman's Work* to a woman from Kansas who requested help in pronouncing proper names mentioned in missionary literature. Note the impersonal and professional tone in the opening phrase; the language used emphasizes how far the editor feels herself removed in place and circumstance from the women of Kansas.

> The management of WOMAN'S WORK keenly sympathizes with the desire to pronounce correctly, and with those societies which are located at such a distance from Board centers, that they are comparatively deprived of assistance along this line. Women living in the suburbs of New York, Philadelphia, Chicago, etc., have only to attend the regular monthly meeting at Board Headquarters and, in the course of a year, they will hear the majority of important places in the missions named by those who know how to pronounce the names. The case is very different with our friends in Allen County, Kansas.[47]

For the benefit of women without access to experts, *Woman's Work,* the editor promises, "will offer some aid to pronunciation for some months to come." However, in what seems almost a display of superior erudition, she adds a caveat: "Pronunciation of many Asiatic proper nouns requires guttural sounds, aspiration, or variation of pitch, for which there are neither signs in the English language nor type in the printing office." So while the magazine will try to help the women in Kansas, the best way to learn correct pronunciation is "to consult every missionary we meet, go to every missionary meeting we can, especially where representatives from the field or the Board make addresses, and to keep our ears open." This must have made it clear to women in small-town auxiliaries that they would have to rely on information fed to them by the delegates they sent to county, state, and regional meetings and to summer schools. What they could hope to learn directly from the magazine was limited and inferior to the knowledge possessed by inititates.

Actual leadership at the local as well as the denominational level had no doubt always been exercised by a handful of women. On a theoretical plane, however, the distinctions between the duties of leaders and of the rank and file were minimal when prayer and communication of missionary intelligence had been linked with sacrificial giving as the principal duties of all members of female missionary societies. Women had been encouraged to feel a direct, personal responsibility and to take an active rather than a passive interest in missions; they were reminded that proof of the discharge of their duty to their heathen sisters would be required of them at the last judgment. With the introduction of systematic mission study, the role assigned the rank and file was vastly diminished. The work continued to depend, of course, upon their interest and their gifts; but the journals no longer reiterated that missions were sustained by their prayers and their letters to particular laborers on the field. They were no longer called upon to prepare missionary papers and deliver them in turn at auxiliary meetings. Instead, their function, according to an article in *Woman's Work* in 1909 on "Duties of the Rank and File of the Missionary Societies," was to be an audience. Regretting the tendency to place the burden of responsibility on the officers of the society, the author of this article reminds members of *their* responsibility to be a receptive audience.

Many members who are regular in their contributions and
faithful in reading their magazines are uncertain in the matter
of attendance at regular meetings, unless they chance to have a
part in the programme of the day. It does not seem to occur to
them that it is decidedly chilling for the presiding officer, and
for participants in the meeting to face practically empty chairs.
I venture to say that one-half of all good speaking is due to an
interested, appreciative and sympathetic audience.... To the
rank and file, then, belongs the duty of inspiring speakers of
the monthly meeting by their presence, their kindly interest
and sympathy.[48]

The transformation of auxiliary meetings from prayer groups into
mission study classes led by trained leaders and officers reduced the
rank and file from vital participants whose spiritual force worked
wonders on the mission field to auditors whose bodies filled otherwise empty chairs. The focus of the article is on making the meeting
successful; no indication is given as to how successful meetings further the cause of foreign missions. The sense of a larger purpose that
permeated the literature of the woman's foreign mission movement
during the formative years is oddly lacking in this discussion of the
duties of the rank and file. Even the measure of the movement's success at home has shifted from the focus of the author of "The Hillerton Auxiliary" on spiritual renewal to the empirical evidence of
filled chairs.

Perhaps unintentionally, the message conveyed in women's
missionary journals concerning the anticipated reflex influence of
woman's work for foreign missions had changed dramatically between the publication of "The Hillerton Auxiliary" in 1880 and the
appearance of a much better piece of fiction in *Woman's Missionary
Friend* in the spring of 1910. The didactic content of "The Hillerton
Auxiliary" is clearly focused on the spiritual regeneration that will
change the lives of women who embrace the missionary cause. In
contrast, "Mrs. Farley's Substitute" is primarily a secular rather
than a religious romance; the didactic purpose of this piece of fiction, if it has one, is decidedly less apparent. Its function seems to be
mainly to entertain rather than instruct. The inclusion of such pieces
of fiction in serial form in missionary magazines was prompted by
the desire to entice readers into opening the magazine when it ar-

rived in the mail each month. Even without explicit didactic content, however, "Mrs. Farley's Substitute" teaches its readers lessons about the nature of woman's work for missions that are quite different from those so thinly disguised in fictional form in "The Hillerton Auxiliary."

"Mrs. Farley's Substitute" tells the story of a "timid little dressmaker" named Sarah Elizabeth Bond. Sarah Elizabeth, a loyal member of the Woman's Foreign Missionary Society of the First Church of New Bedford, endures the misfortune of having included among the names of those women she must solicit for contributions for a missionary box to be sent to China that of the wealthy and selfish Mrs. Maria Farley. Gentle Sarah Elizabeth encounters the formidable Mrs. Farley at her worst, and is treated to a display of rudeness, extravagance, and waste; she retreats, shutting the garden gate with a bang. In the next episode, Sarah Elizabeth wraps her own contributions for the mission box, inserting a card with her name and a "sentiment" in each gift, "according to the agreement to send a personal message."[49] The reader is free to assume, since it is the pious dressmaker who considers a card with a brief "sentiment" an adequate personal message, that the sisterly correspondence between missionaries and auxiliary members idealized during the movement's formative years is no longer expected of even the most conscientious auxiliary woman.

Only when all her own packages are done up does Sarah Elizabeth recall that, since Mrs. Farley refused to contribute, a gift must be supplied in her name, according to the agreement made among the members of the New Bedford Society when they planned the missionary box project. For Sarah Elizabeth, whose means are quite limited, the necessity of providing an extra gift threatens to work a real hardship. Having given already all her hoarded treasures—a white apron, two hem-stitched handkerchiefs, a pair of black lace stockings and a "dainty pincushion...fashioned from pretty scraps"—and with only two dollars in savings to meet any emergency, Sarah Elizabeth despairs. Providentially, a ball of white silk rolls out of her thread box. "The very thing! She would crochet one of those pretty four-in-hand neckties that she learned to make while visiting in Philadelphia last spring."[50] For the reader, there are several lessons implicit in this bit of the story. First, the necessity of doing any actual work for missions falls primarily to those who lack the means to make monetary gifts. Second, sacrificial giving is no longer being urged. The writer never hints that Sarah Elizabeth ought, like the widow with the two mites, give all she had, depending upon God to provide for her in an emergency. The pragmatism of the modern age, replacing the more romantic religiosity of the Victorian era, dictated that young women who had to earn their own living should save for a rainy day. Finally, Sarah Elizabeth's sense that the latest fashions would be acceptable on the mission field conveys to the reader, in a frivolous way, the message that missionaries are modern, up-to-date women.

Sarah Elizabeth muses sentimentally while she crochets, imagining hospital and school scenes in China.

> With every stitch her mind was in Hing Kiang. She saw in her imagination the hospital with each little iron bed, and its occupant's suffering appealed to her. The girls at school, at play and at work, were her company in the quiet hour.

Sarah Elizabeth decides that it would "be fun some day to sail away, away over the ocean and enter the work, if only to be a seamstress!" She knows, of course, that she lacks the professional skills required for modern mission work, but she wonders if perhaps she could sew for the missionaries and teach the girls to sew. She has, however, no real expectation that her dream will ever be realized; instead, she resigns herself to doing all she can do: finish crocheting a silk tie and pray for the success of the mission at Hing Kiang.[51] The relegation of prayer to such an insignificant place in both the story and the work of the New Bedford auxiliary is a marked contrast to the importance assigned prayer in the tale of "The Hillerton Auxiliary."

When the ladies of New Bedford's First Church gather to pack the missionary box, the occasion is purely social. They gossip and tease one another, speculating particularly on the contents of the small package labeled "Mrs. Maria Farley." After the box has been carted off to the express office, Sarah Elizabeth and Edith Smith remain behind the others to restore order in the church basement. As they go about their task, Mrs. Farley's hired man rushes in with a bundle wrapped in newspaper. Sarah Elizabeth breaks the string on the package and "out rolled an old white tarlatan dress covered with gilt stars." Mrs. Smith collapses in laughter.

"Well, did you ever!" exclaimed Edith. "Why, that is the old tarlatan dress that one of the Farleys has worn to every masquerade party for the last forty years, more or less." And she sat down on a chair and laughed until the tears came.[52]

When she has recovered her equilibrium, Mrs. Smith insists upon being let in on the secret of the small package supplied in Mrs. Farley's name. Sarah Elizabeth swears her to secrecy and admits the truth.

At this point in the narrative, the scene shifts to China to follow the fate of Sarah Elizabeth's substitute gift. The missionaries are portrayed as delighted with the contents of the box, although somewhat puzzled over the tie. Pouring over the old issues of *Ladies' Home Journal* thoughtfully tucked in the box, they discover that ties worn with tailored waists are all the rage in the States. Nevertheless, they decide to give the tie to Dr. Buxton, who "is so lonely since his wife died." It is, after all, the only item in the box remotely suitable for a man. In a not-so-subtle message telling readers who pack missionary boxes that they no longer ought to think only of women, Dr. Mary Winters muses, "And isn't it strange that the tie is the only thing in this box that a man could possibly use? I suppose they took 'girls' school' in its literal sense."[53] The underlying lesson for readers is not simply to remember the men when they send missionary boxes, but to enlarge their conception of the work for which they feel responsible to include the whole enterprise—not just girls' schools and women doctors.

The denouement of this story, of course, involves the bringing together of Dr. Buxton, on furlough in the States and wearing his treasured silk tie, and Sarah Elizabeth. This happens at a reception given for him at the New Bedford Church. Mrs. Smith narrates the story for the benefit of her husband who has been away on business. She clearly relished her own role in the drama, which came when Dr. Buxton attempted to thank Maria Farley for the tie. Mrs. Smith pushed Sarah Elizabeth forward as the true maker of the tie. As she tells it,

I stopped out of breath and no doubt triumphant. There was a look of gentle surprise on Dr. Buxton's face, one of angry annoyance on Maria's and poor little Sarah Elizabeth was blushing like a sixteen-year-old girl.

Mrs. Smith immediately scented a budding romance and, apparently having nothing better to do with her time, waits with watchful eyes for further developments. Her vigil is rewarded; as she tells her husband,

> This afternoon it was raining and I saw him come up the street with Sarah Elizabeth under his umbrella—and George, she had hold of his arm in the most confidential manner! I ran to the north window to see where they stopped and I saw them go into Maria Farley's house.

Not content with what she has learned from spying out of her windows, Mrs. Smith shamelessly pumps her servants for information.

> I went right down to the kitchen and asked Katie if Mrs. Farley's folks were going to have company to dinner. She said yes, that Manda had been over in the morning to borrow our cake pans and she said that they had invited the missionary to dinner and some young lady who had decided to go back to China with him. Now, you mark my words, George Smith. If Sarah Elizabeth goes to China, she will go in double harness, and what's more, Maria Farley will claim that she made the match![54]

The romance of missions has become an ordinary romance in this tale. The tie uniting the auxiliary in New Bedford with the mission field is not the spiritual and personal "tender tie" that Mary Merwin's letters to the Hillerton Auxiliary knit, but the white silk tie crocheted by Sarah Elizabeth. For her, this leads, however improbably, to a matrimonial bond that draws her to the mission field in China—at a time when a single woman who was only a seamstress would never have been appointed as a missionary by one of the women's societies. For the New Bedford auxiliary, Sarah Elizabeth's romance is entertaining but not transforming. There is no hint in the story that this new link with missions will lead to a revival at the First Church in New Bedford. Mrs. Farley has not learned the error of her ways; unlike selfish Mrs. Brown of Hillerton, her daughters are not ruined by profligate young men. Neither do her daughters become missionaries; life at a mission station in China constitutes a happy ending for Sarah Elizabeth, who is, after all, only a seamstress; but Mrs. Farley's daughters have more promising futures at home. While her invitation to dinner at the Farleys' home shows that Sarah Elizabeth has risen in social status through her association with Dr. Buxton (there would have been no invitations to dinner for a mere seamstress), "Mrs. Farley's Substitute" never suggests—as did "The Hillerton Auxiliary"—that the ladies of New Bedford ought to offer their own daughters for the mission field. The picture that the reader is left with in "Mrs. Farley's Substitute" is of missionary auxiliary work as suitable and entertaining employment for the leisure hours of the female members of the very best families. The story makes no implicit plea for readers to sacrifice for a noble purpose, nor does it promise that such self-sacrifice will lead to spiritual renewal; it suggests no important way in which work for foreign missions differs from any nonreligious charitable cause. The publication of such frivolous fiction in a woman's missionary magazine displays the despiritualization of rhetoric that accompanied professionalization of the woman's foreign mission movement (and secularization of the whole Protestant mission enterprise). But perhaps more significantly it reveals that the supposed benefits of systematic mission study apparently did not penetrate to the local congregational level; there is not the slightest hint that the ladies of New Bedford devoted any time to thorough and sophisticated study of the Protestant missionary enterprise throughout the world.

Early reports that systematic mission study had revitalized auxiliaries and made them competitive with women's clubs and civic clubs were, beginning around 1910, replaced with comments indicating that auxiliaries were losing the competition. Noting that "the development of any organization depends upon its recruiting power" and that "the successful lodge and wide-awake club are the ones that are always out on a campaign for new members," Carrie M. Wheeler of Nebraska offered the following advice on strategy for winning new members:

It makes a wide wide difference how we put the question. "How will you have your egg this morning?" said a hostess to her guest. He answered, "Soft-boiled, if you please," and turning to another said, "...If she had said, 'Will you have an egg this morning?' I should have said, 'No, thank you,' but when she said, 'How will you have it?' what could I say but soft-boiled?"[55]

The very metaphor she uses is probably more appealing to the True Woman than to the New Woman. In any case, instruction in the fine art of not eliciting negative responses did not solve the underlying problem; club work simply seemed to offer women greater opportunities for active service than did the women's missionary auxiliaries. A report on "Missionary Societies vs. Women's Clubs," published in *Woman's Work* in 1915, spells out the contrast.

Attendance upon the Women's Club Federation meetings frequently held in any of our cities will awaken in one feelings of interest...over the keen alertness of mind and body of the women present and regret because of the comparison that instantly flashes into mind between this meeting and that of a presbyterial or synodical missionary organization. The missionary gatherings usually suffer by comparison in numbers as well as in the general atmosphere of absorbing interest and knowledge of the work and all it involves. Club members are well versed in all departments of their ever-widening work, and delight to put their wits and minds to work to devise new methods in civic improvement, sanitation, plans for advancement of artistic and literary studies, etc.[56]

To the writer of this report it seemed strange that "women in missionary societies can not locate accurately such splendid schools [as the society supported in various fields,], tell others...something of the lives of men and women who are making these schools stand for something,...name at least six of the famous hospitals in various Asiatic countries, tell the story of their establishment, and of their equipment in men and appliances and the people whom they serve." She wanted the women and girls of the churches to feel their individual responsibility for the work and to recognize the need for united effort. She found it difficult to understand their failure to rally to the cause, yet her own description lays bare the contrast between club work and missionary society work that explains the greater appeal of club work. Women in missionary auxiliaries were expected to take a vicarious interest in work directed and carried out by others; women in clubs were involved actively in work and policy making that made a visible difference in their own communities. (Home missionary societies, particularly in the South after the turn of the century, functioned much like women's clubs in undertaking active reform work. This perhaps explains the greater appeal that home missions seemed to have for Southern churchwomen in this period.)[57]

Women in missionary auxiliaries were no longer being told that the success of the work abroad depended as much on their active service—their prayers and their letters—as it did on their financial support. They had become—to borrow a metaphor from business, as missionary administrators were fond of doing—simply small stockholders in a large corporation. They were furnished with investment prospectuses and shareholders' reports, but they actually exercised little influence on the board of directors and company officials.

Modern missions, particularly educational missions, played a crucial role in the cultural transformations that accompanied modernization in the non-Western world, perhaps most markedly in changing the status of women in the non-Western world. The very nature of modern missions, the commitment to social service as a legitimate means of evangelization, would, however, ultimately subject the whole Protestant missionary enterprise to fundamentalist attack in the 1920s. And even though the liberals defeated the fundamentalists within the mainstream Protestant denominations, the liberals themselves, chastened by the horrifying spectacle of Christian nations at war, were moving toward a cultural and religious relativism that eventually led them to abandon the business of worldwide evangelization to more orthodox evangelicals.

Within the woman's foreign mission movement a similar dynamic was at work. The new formulation of woman's work that grew out of the "science" of modern missions led the movement to abandon its adherence to the Victorian ideology that had initially made its appeal to women so enormously successful. In contributing to a new set of cultural attitudes regarding the nature of woman, the administrators and theoreticians of the movement helped smooth the way for woman's entry into the secular world in a variety of professional and civic capacities. And by abandoning the notion that women are inherently religious, they unwittingly encouraged the secularization of the home itself. Ironically, as we shall see in the final chapter, the woman's foreign mission movement had, by triumphantly embracing modern missions, helped undermine its very existence as a mass movement among American women.

*Chapter 6*

# Other Times, Other Ways

The hoopla surrounding the woman's missionary Jubilee of 1910–11 obscured the first disturbing signs that the woman's foreign mission movement was deteriorating at the auxiliary level. The idea of mounting a nationwide, ecumenical Jubilee extravaganza was conceived of by Helen Barrett Montgomery's close friend and fellow officer of the Woman's Baptist Foreign Missionary Society, Lucy Waterbury Peabody. In her capacity as chairman of the Central Committee on the United Study of Foreign Missions, Mrs. Peabody commissioned Helen Montgomery to write a history of woman's work for missions as the interdenominational textbook for 1910. Study of *Western Women in Eastern Lands* in local churches across the country served as a prelude to the Jubilee which began in October, 1910, in Oakland, California, and wound up in New York City the following April. During the course of the winter two-day meetings were held in forty-eight major cities; many smaller towns and cities staged one-day celebrations. Helen Montgomery led the troupe of Jubilee speakers that toured the country, appearing at the Jubilee meetings scheduled successively across the continent. A great deal of publicity in the secular press attended these events; newspaper coverage was solicited in advance at luncheons given for selected reporters in each city. As a result, Montgomery became one of the most quoted women in America.[1]

An enormous amount of time and energy was expended on advance preparation to ensure the success of each city's celebration. A pamphlet written by Abby Gunn Baker on "The Story of the Washington Celebration of the Woman's National Foreign Missionary Jubilee" records that the women of Washington began work in November for their February meetings. A committee of carefully chosen society women and wives of prominent ministers planned the program. Washington merchants offered their help, loaning the committee a desk and typewriter and contributing carbon paper and blotters. Careful preparation paid off; the Washington Jubilee was a triumph, beginning with an informal afternoon reception at the White House, hosted by the Tafts. A separate evening meeting "for colored women, with fully two thousand in attendance was held at the Metropolitan American Methodist Episcopal Church. . . . A young colored woman, Miss Nannie Burroughs, admirably presided." A mass meeting "for busy women" was held from 5:00 to 5:45 in the afternoon. The heart of the celebration, however, was a luncheon on the second day that featured speeches by Mrs. Montgomery, Mrs. Peabody, and Dr. Mary Riggs Noble. Mrs. Montgomery, described as "our peerless woman leader, a missionary speaker pre-eminently, and yet more widely known in a dozen different fields than any other woman in America today," was the star of the show.[2] Newspaper accounts of the Washington Jubilee, carefully pasted into a scrapbook by Mrs. Wallace Radcliffe, wife of the pastor of the New York Avenue Presbyterian Church, focus on Mrs. Montgomery's words and presence. Publicity in the *Star* and the *Post* included biographical sketches, supplied by the organizing committee, that labeled Montgomery as "probably the best known church and club woman in the country today."[3]

The message that Montgomery delivered in her Jubilee speeches is consistent with the views contained in her mission study textbooks, but the subtlety of her thought is missing from newspaper accounts of her words. The stress on Christianity as a progressive and transforming force in non-Western cultures remains, but she apparently voiced none of her more critical comments on the state of Western civilization. Only when she argues that Christianity enables women in foreign lands to throw off their shackles, making it possible for them to think and act for themselves as Western women do, does Montgomery even hint that women in the West were once enchained.

> Once the eastern nations become thoroughly Christianized they will no longer lag behind modern nations. They are steadily becoming more progressive as they adopt Christianity. The Christian woman of the east is the same as the Christian woman of the west. She will not consent to stay behind closed doors and be treated like a child. She thinks.[4]

As a thinking woman herself, Montgomery knew that progress remained to be made regarding the status of women in the West if the ideal of equality she felt was implicit in Christianity were to be fully realized. But perhaps it is not surprising that in the midst of the buoyant optimism that characterized the Jubilee, her public pronouncements made it sound as if the battle in the West had already been won. Certainly the fight to establish women's missionary societies in the churches had been won. In an article entitled "The Trend of Things: Then and Now," Montgomery claimed with obvious satisfaction that it was now "hard to realize that there ever was a time when there were none of the active and ubiquitous women's missionary societies that seem so much a part of the structure of church life."[5]

The Jubilee had been planned as a demonstration of the strength of the woman's foreign mission movement, of the extent to which it had become a powerful force in the churches. This demonstration was inspired in part, one Jubilee flyer suggests, by jealousy over the publicity generated by the new Laymen's Missionary Movement. The Jubilee planners adopted the methods employed in the Laymen's Missionary Campaign of the previous year, the flyer acknowledged, but were "celebrating fifty years of work rather than inaugurating a new work." *Woman's Missionary Friend,* reporting on the success of the Jubilee, concluded that its record compared favorably with that of the Laymen's campaign and attributed the fact that the Jubilee had "accomplished its work more quickly" to "the more perfect organization of the Women's Boards."[6]

Printed in Jubilee literature among the prayers to be offered for the Jubilee was one asking "that the Jubilee may glorify God, and nowhere degenerate into mere glorification of woman's work."[7] Despite the implicit warning in that prayer, the Jubilee did glorify woman's work; at its worst it degenerated into an orgy of self-congratulation. The New York *Observer* reported luncheons at noon in three hotels during the final Jubilee session. Speakers were whisked from place to place by auto. The menu was the last word in elegance, although in deference to the temperance women among them, the six thousand diners refrained from toasting their success with champagne—a wise decision since even maraschino cherries raised some eyebrows.

The first course at the Astor was "Pamplemousse au Maras-
quin." Some of the women hesitated when it came to maraschino, but with the exception of wearers of white ribbons most
of them enjoyed the cherries and all.[8]

The six thousand women at lunch on that day were proud to be
part of the movement that, they were told, had "not only changed the
type and scope of missionary labor," but also contributed to "the fundamental changes taking place in Christless nations."[9] The approach
used by Jubilee organizers with women who considered themselves
modern and progressive struck a responsive chord in these women;
the Jubilee's Progressive agenda was apparently their agenda.

> Woman's work in Foreign Missions should appeal to every
> broad-minded Christian woman who is interested in educa-
> tion, civics, sanitation, social settlements, hospitals, good liter-
> ature, the emancipation of children, the right of women to
> health, home and protection; and the coming of the Kingdom
> of our Lord.[10]

The basis of the appeal made here is radically different from the
multifaceted appeal, made in the movement's formative years, that
emphasized woman's spiritual kinship to her heathen sisters and her
special responsibility for their salvation. (The founders of the woman's foreign mission movement would never have listed the coming of
the Kingdom last.) Here the dominant evangelical culture seems to be
embracing the very reform agenda that, according to Jackson Lears,
embodied the ideal of facilitating full development of human potential
*in this world* that characterized the new therapeutic culture.[11] The shift
away from the older emphasis on self-denial and otherworldly salvation was accompanied by a new conception of women's spiritual—
and monetary—capital. The force of female prayer was less often
discussed than the need for active service by women. And the pennies
amassed through countless small acts of self-denial were superseded
by dollars collected through modern fund-raising strategies. Ironically, liberal evangelical Protestantism shifted theological ground to
accommodate itself to the very forces of modernization that were
gradually secularizing American culture. In theory and in practice,
the woman's foreign mission movement followed suit.

The Jubilee itself was not aimed so much at spiritual renewal among Protestant women in America as it was at galvanizing women into action. However impressive the spectacle of the Jubilee had been, Helen Montgomery pointed out, if the spirit it aroused did not move women to action, the progress of the Kingdom would suffer. She cited William James as her authority for this prediction.

> Professor James has told us that the chief use of an emotion is to arouse the will to action; that to indulge an emotion without allowing it to eventuate in its appropriate action is to be a sentimentalist.

The Progressive agenda proposed for ushering in the Kingdom of God required professional expertise rather than feminine sentimentality to implement it. Montgomery herself was no sentimentalist, and she did not propose to let other women luxuriate in sentiment and nostalgia when there was work to be done. She chided women for not adopting modern methods.

> Ruth has been a-field gleaning handfuls of purpose; but no steam reapers have been covering the whole field with the hum of their activity. Why sickles, oxcarts and tallow candles in the Lord's work, and mowing machines, automobiles and electric lights for business?[12]

Tallow candles might provide a romantic glow, and sickles and oxcarts were picturesque, but modern missions needed the latest in equipment and techniques in order to function efficiently.

Montgomery expected the women of America to provide for the future on a larger scale than they had imagined in the past.

> We have timidly asked for pennies so long that hundreds of women have been unconsciously trained to include foreign missions among their minor charities. The same women who go buoyantly into a campaign to raise fifty thousand dollars for a local children's hospital ask and gratefully receive five-dollar gifts for foreign missions, the most tremendous, the most needy and the most significant enterprise of the twentieth century. ...Today is the era of women with check books as well as

women with small change. To ask only for littles. . . is to belittle
our cause.[13]

In the decade following the Jubilee, the woman's foreign mission
movement did what Montgomery demanded of it; it launched the
great ecumenical venture that would be its lasting monument in the
twentieth century: the establishment of seven Christian colleges for
women scattered throughout the Far East. Montgomery and her
friend Lucy Peabody were instrumental in transforming the loose
Interdenominational Conference of Woman's Boards of Foreign
Missions into the Federation of Woman's Boards of Missions that
sponsored the college-building enterprise. The two friends settled on
higher education as their priority during a tour of mission stations
around the world that they made in 1913–14 as official representatives of the federation. They returned home persuaded that the education of women would be the transforming force that Montgomery
felt religion must be in the modern era. In arguing that the funding
of colleges for women was a religious task, Montgomery told members of women's missionary societies that their "conception of religion as a precious personal consolation must give way to that of
religion as the great transforming force of life."[14] Whether or not
women were willing to forego the personal consolation that religion
traditionally offered, they were willing to support the interdenominational ventures that their leaders proposed. Yet Montgomery's appeal for large gifts gives one pause; increasing reliance on substantial
gifts from a handful of donors made the maintenance of a broad base
of support among churchwomen less crucial. We have already seen
that popular support among women for foreign missions was being
eroded at the auxiliary level; here is yet another message to the average churchwoman that her interest in missions is not vital to their
success. Such indications that the movement was in deep trouble
went unnoticed in the midst of Jubilee euphoria; the ability to meet
and surpass goals set in fund-raising drives was taken as a visible
sign of the movement's glowing health. The momentum built up in
the prewar years carried through to completion in the early twenties
the great joint project of establishing colleges for women in the Orient; but significantly, that consummation was achieved through a
substantial contribution from the Laura Spelman Rockefeller Foundation rather than through small gifts from millions of women. By

the time the project was finished, a vast interdenominational woman's foreign mission movement could, properly speaking, no longer be said to exist. Several of its major denominational components had been merged out of existence; others had been restructured so that foreign missions were no longer their principal concern. But the woman's foreign mission movement was not simply phased out of existence institutionally, it also lost its visibility in American culture. No publicity in the secular press attended its demise—and even the majority of churchwomen were indifferent to its fate.

Helen Montgomery had argued eloquently against the proposed merger of women's societies with denominational mission boards at the Ecumenical Conference of 1900, with apparent success. But pressure for such mergers mounted as the women's societies wielded ever greater financial and administrative influence. At the World Missionary Conference in Edinburgh in 1910 several denominational board leaders announced that the time had come for merger; the issue was thereafter contested, denomination by denomination.[15] The Methodist Episcopal Church (South) merged its societies in 1910. In 1922, the Presbyterian General Assembly, without prior consultation of the bodies involved, merged the woman's board with the general board. In 1924, the National Council of Congregational Churches ordered a similar merger of its women's boards with the American Board. Baptist women resisted merger successfully until 1955, but then their society had never enjoyed the same degree of autonomy that several other major women's boards exercised. Methodist women maintained a separate Woman's Division within their denomination after the union of the Methodist Episcopal Church (North) with the Methodist Protestant Church and the Methodist Episcopal Church (South) in 1939, but this division was not concerned solely—or even primarily—with foreign missions.

Such mergers inevitably diluted the power formerly wielded by women in foreign missions. Women members were usually in a minority on merged boards and rarely held the top executive posts. When they retired, they were generally replaced by men.[16] Women administrators of reorganized umbrella associations of churchwomen, forced to combine home missions and Christian education with foreign missions, found their energies and loyalties divided—and denominationally rather than ecumenically focused. Consequently, it is not surprising that the officers of the women's foreign missionary societies, who had made careers in the field of foreign mission administration, resisted mergers. Having renounced a special and limited mission to women, however, and having proclaimed their equality with men in missions, they had no justification for maintaining autonomy aside from the desire to retain legitimate power. They realized that power brought influence, that it had finally made men take them seriously. Clementina Butler, for example, was gratified that twenty years after the Foreign Mission Conference of North America was organized it finally invited women's societies to send delegates in 1913, but she saw very clearly that this was a recognition of the power of women and not of their rights.

> Note the fact that women are now members of this conference, not because they are interested in missions, but because they are officers of Boards that raise and administer funds—some of them as much as any of the General Boards save five or six of the largest.[17]

Miss Butler herself felt that such participation was a right; "that officers of such organizations should have a voice in the policy that shall govern the work on the field is only reasonable." But while having a voice in policy matters may have been only reasonable, the reluctance with which women had been allowed a voice made it prudent to suppose that the privilege would be withdrawn if women surrendered the power they held. And so, having renounced the rationale on which the woman's foreign mission movement had been founded, the administrators of women's societies tried to hold on to the power they had gained and consolidated through forming separate female societies. They argued that only in such separate female institutions could woman's talents be fully utilized. They warned that if women with talent were not able to exercise their abilities within the church, the church would lose them altogether.

> Any plan that would tend to lessen the sense of responsibility in the hands of the womanhood of the church [must be opposed]. The cultural effect of this work in the hearts of women, their own in which to succeed or fail, cannot be underestimated. Talents have been given, and education to develop these gifts;

shall outside organizations, excellent though they may be, offer stronger inducement for the administrative ability and organizing power than the church, which needs its daughters within its fold?[18]

Competition with secular pursuits for the talents of their daughters was, as we shall see, a battle that the woman's foreign mission movement had already begun to lose before the women's societies surrendered their autonomy. Apparently few members of the younger generation wanted to use their talents as administrators of women's missionary societies. Nor is there any evidence that ordinary laywomen shared the concerns of those who opposed mergers. For if the officers of the women's societies were reluctant to give up the power they had become accustomed to wielding, one must remember that the very policies they instituted as the operation of missions was professionalized and secularized had tended to reduce the power of local auxiliary members who had very little to lose through merger. Mission study textbooks continued to be issued annually through the thirties; local auxiliaries could, it they wished, continue to function without change. Some did. Especially in congregations that had maintained close personal connections with particular missionaries or projects and had habitually sent delegates to summer mission conferences, women's auxiliaries operated much as they had during the halcyon days between the Ecumenical Conference of 1900 and the Jubilee. The evidence suggests, however, that such auxiliaries constituted a small remnant of the faithful. Women remained the backbone of local, congregational support for missions, as they did of all church work; but foreign missions no longer particularly gripped the imagination of large numbers of laywomen in postwar America. Among the women, as in the mainstream Protestant denominations in general, missions no longer occupied a position of preeminence. With the expansion in the teens and twenties of the numbers of professional religious educators, young women who wanted careers as religious professionals chose this new field. Even before the war, women's foreign missionary societies had experienced difficulties in recruiting young women to join the ranks of mission administrators.

In the 1890s, in an attempt to coordinate their efforts with those of the Student Volunteer Movement, the women's societies had made concerted efforts to enlist college girls. Most of the women's journals featured a special section on student work or had a young woman's department. Fiction designed to appeal to college girls appeared frequently. One story in *Heathen Woman's Friend* in 1891 used a touch of humor to break down prejudices that girls might have against missions. In a dorm room, one of the more flippant girls involved in a discussion of the SVM announces, " 'Better call it Spinsters' Voluntary Martyrdom, and done with it!' " Then, true to the conventions governing missionary magazine fiction, this lighthearted, carefree girl is the one who ends up on the mission field. Others made more serious appeals to college women. Isabel Hart, in one of the last editorials before her death in 1891, talked of the ties between colleges and missions; she felt that "one of the most significant features of the age is the missionary revival among college students." By the mid-nineties discussions of the connection between colleges and missions had become commonplace. A single issue of *Heathen Woman's Friend* in 1895 contained one article by Professor Ellen R. Martin on "Ohio Wesleyan: A Missionary University" and another by Professor Sarah Whiting of Wellesley College on "The Missionary Movement and Colleges for Women." Beginning in 1901, Louise Manning Hodgkins published a series of sketches of college graduates who had chosen the mission field. By listing women college graduates who had married missionaries, she reassured girls who feared that a career in missions might preclude marriage. Such attempts to enlist college women for foreign service seem to have been successful—although the Student Volunteer Movement rather than the women's societies may well deserve the credit. At any rate, by 1910, Student Volunteers constituted practically one-third of the entire missionary force; and the actual number of Student Volunteers did not begin to decline until the 1920s.[19]

The record of the women's societies in recruiting young women to staff their home base operations was significantly less impressive. In the emotionally charged atmosphere of Student Volunteer meetings, students were pressed to offer themselves for overseas service. It was hard to generate the same emotion for a commitment to full-time service as a field secretary or traveling agent for a woman's missionary society. The obituary of Grace Todd, who died in 1910 while itinerating for the New York Branch of the Methodist Episcopal Woman's Foreign Missionary Society, hints at the problem the woman's foreign mission movement was having in finding enough young talent to sustain its work. Miss Todd, forced by health problems to return from China after two years, had worked as a field secretary, as first secretary of the general office, and as a public speaker traveling for the society in many states. According to her obituary, she "belonged to the group of younger workers, still far too small to give absolute assurance on the human side for the future of our Society, who are just beginning to shoulder the real burdens of the work of the home base." The plea for home base workers implicit in Todd's obituary was made explicit later that year in a "letter" printed in *Woman's Missionary Friend* addressed to a "girl graduate," urging her to consider the need at home. An article on "Our Young People" pointed out that the future of the movement depended upon recruiting new workers.

> The success of the Woman's Foreign Missionary Society depends upon the success it meets in winning the young women who must so soon take the places of the older women. . . . While many of them will be needed in the foreign field, many more will be needed in the home side of the work. They must prepare to take the places of those now growing old.[20]

Calls for home base workers apparently fell upon deaf ears. By 1913, a letter to the editor of *Woman's Missionary Friend* proposed that consideration be given to salarying home officers at competitive levels; that, the writer pointed out, would make it possible to recruit college girls who had to support themselves and contribute to their families' finances. Unwilling or unable to offer competitive salaries, the woman's foreign mission movement continued to mourn "the unoccupied places of leadership in our missionary work."[21]

It was not simply in full-time staff positions that the movement found itself losing the competition for the energies of talented women. "Inert presidents and vice-presidents" of local auxiliaries were blamed for the growing apathy among churchwomen toward foreign missions, but it was difficult to persuade natural leaders to accept office in missionary societies when there were so many other demands for their talents. One regional officer in New York recognized the difficulties but was convinced that "perseverance, tact and prayer can accomplish wonders." She urged renewed efforts to en-

list in the missionary cause the active, vital  women who were increasingly being drawn into club work and the professional world.

> This is a day of very general activity among women. We know
> of women who are doing splendid work in nearly all the profes-
> sions, and filling efficiently all sorts of business positions. . . .
> But since activity is the watchword of the day, since women are
> working along all lines, since every woman's club has a waiting
> list of would-be members, why should we who are longing for
> the coming of God's Kingdom even to the uttermost parts of
> the earth, be contented to allow the missionary society to strug-
> gle along while so many efficient women of our churches are
> outside its membership?

If only those "efficient women" could be persuaded to take charge
of the auxiliaries, Mrs. Finley cherished the hope that "the rank and
file" would "follow as the well-trained army follows its general and
his lieutenants."[22]

Mrs. Finley's fond hopes were not realized. World war drew
women into war work, leaving little spare energy for mission work;
but even after the war, at the Interdenominational Conference of
Woman's Boards in 1919, recruitment in all its aspects was a major
concern. Alice M. Davison delivered a paper on "The Demobilizing
Woman" in which she urged that Red Cross nurses and canteen
workers be met at the dock with a "definite proposition": the need for
medical workers in foreign lands. Mrs. J. A. Cushman of the national
board of the Young Women's Christian Association reminded the delegates that employed women about to be displaced from their jobs by
demobilized soldiers would be a fertile field for recruiting home base
staff personnel. And Helen Montgomery, addressing herself to the
difficulties being encountered at the auxiliary level, urged in a paper
titled "The Professional Woman" that auxiliary meeting times be
changed to mesh with the schedules of working women.[23] Ingenious as
these solutions were, they were doomed to failure because they did
not attack the basic problem, a loss of interest among middle-class
American women in the whole foreign mission enterprise.

What accounts for this loss of interest? Why did the woman's
foreign mission movement experience such difficulty in maintaining
a broad home base of support among women in the years after the

Jubilee? Declining interest in foreign missions cannot be simply attributed to the secularization of the culture. That may explain the movement's loss of cultural visibility, but not its loss of viability as a self-conscious movement among active churchwomen. It seems evident that recruiting women for careers in missions, as workers on the field and especially as administrators at home, would inevitably become more difficult as career opportunities for educated, single women multiplied; but why did the movement flounder at the auxiliary level? There is, of course, no single answer, but the professionalization and secularization of the mission movement did transform it from an especially congenial cause for women, in which they invested themselves emotionally and spiritually, to one that asked them to invest only their intellect and a bit of their spare time and cash. And modern missions did not seem to require a self-consciously female movement.

The rhetoric employed by the professional administrators of the women's missionary societies in the modern era did not suggest to American women that their role in mission work was essentially different from the role of churchmen. That marks a change in rhetoric that reflects the change in assumptions about the nature of woman; it also reflects the reality of the situation in most mission fields in the twentieth century. It was simply no longer true in the non-Western cultures, where the efforts of modern missions were focused, that only women could reach women. Leaving aside the Moslem cultures that had proved particularly resistant to both Christianization and Westernization, the Protestant mission movement had, with regard to the status of women, largely succeeded in effecting the cultural transformation called for by the leaders of the women's societies. Certainly the most dramatic abuses of women had been curtailed. It was, for the most part, cultural transformation without Christianization; nevertheless, success on this score eliminated one of the most powerful grounds on which a special appeal to American women had rested.

Perceptive as the leaders of the woman's foreign mission movement were about the nature of cultural change and its effect on the lives of women in the non-Western world, the transformation of woman's role in American society caught them by surprise. When they happily discarded Victorian notions about woman's nature and her sphere, they never suspected that women's religious impulses might in part have been culturally induced, firmly rooted in Victorian socialization. They assumed an inherent religious impulse in women and men alike that could be cultivated and channeled in directions prescribed by modern sociology and liberal theology. They embraced the new paradigm of womanhood that Sheila Rothman has labeled "educated motherhood" and wholeheartedly endorsed the reforms associated with this ideal: protective legislation for women and children employed in industry, publicly supported preventive health programs for mothers and infants, and the introduction in the public schools of new curricula designed to incorporate the insights of new "scientific" theories of child development. They found this new (and basically secular) ideal of womanhood compatible with the mission they had defined for themselves as they stretched the bounds of the Victorian domestic sphere to its outermost limits. The paradigm of educated motherhood, like the older ideal, stressed the value of woman's maternal role; both offered women a justification for stepping outside the domestic sphere into the public arena, one in her character as moral guardian and the other as an advocate of social legislation necessary to buttress her function as mother. But these Progressive women were not prepared for yet another shift in the paradigm of ideal womanhood that Rothman tells us occurred in the 1920s.

With the popularization of Freudian theory, a new ideal emerged: "women as 'wife-companion.' "[24] The wife-companion model had no public dimension to parallel the public functions associated with both of the older ideals. It encouraged a turning away from involvement in a corporate, public life. The domestic sphere, to which most middle-class women were still confined after marriage, was reprivatized. The abdication by women of public responsibilities was not anticipated by the leaders of the woman's foreign mission movement any more than the dissolution of Progressive reform had been imagined in the prewar climate of optimism. Like other mass women's movements of the nineteenth century, the woman's foreign mission movement barely survived the First World War. The impact of the new ideal of womanhood, reinforced by widespread disillusion regarding social reform in the postwar period, made any mass movement among American women improbable in the twenties. The secularization of the dominant culture following the war made it doubly unlikely that any religious woman's movement would have wide appeal. Far too many young women of the middle and upper classes in postwar America found, like Ellen Glasgow's heroine Dorinda, that "religion did not satisfy."

The growing indifference of nominally Protestant women to religion was not something foreseen by those who officered the female missionary societies. Nor had they anticipated the backlash of fundamentalism within their churches and isolationism in their society that challenged their vision of missions as a transforming cultural force in the non-Western world. Under the circumstances, the disintegration of the woman's foreign mission movement as a self-conscious movement in mainstream Protestantism—and in American culture—was perhaps inevitable. America's was no longer a Protestant culture; but these women, accustomed to cultural dominance, found it impossible to abandon their goal of renovating society according to Christian precepts. And unwilling to sacrifice their theological liberalism, they made no concerted effort to forge an alliance with the fundamentalists in their own churches or the women of other, smaller evangelical groups who advocated a more conservative brand of evangelism. (Even had such an alliance been formed, there is no assurance that a self-consciously female mission coalition would have resulted; these groups had neither a strong tradition of, nor a rationale for, female *leadership* in mission work.) The leaders of the woman's foreign mission movement ultimately discovered that they lacked the power to preserve their own position in their churches (and in their culture) or to prevent the mainstream Protestant denominations from gradually disengaging from involvement in foreign missions.

The irony and the poignancy of the fate of the woman's foreign mission movement in the twenties is perhaps best illustrated in the careers of two of its most perceptive and articulate leaders. When Jean Kenyon Mackenzie and Helen Barrett Montgomery called on evangelical Christians to participate in the modernization of other cultures and to adapt the techniques of business management to the science of missions, they borrowed their rhetoric from the forces of science and business that would eventually secularize American culture and undermine the woman's foreign mission movement. Mackenzie and Montgomery had assumed that the social implications of the Gospel and the apparatus of professional administration could be successfully grafted onto the conventional evangelical piety that informed their own personal devotional practice. Their vision integrated the sacred and the secular; they were unprepared for the radical separation of sacred from secular, of religion from politics, that came to characterize American culture in the decade after the First World War.

In the buoyant years before the Great War, when an evangelical hegemony controlled the cultural and political life of the nation, it had seemed possible and plausible to both women that the arts and the sciences could function harmoniously in the service of evangelical religion. After the war, as the forces of secularism and materialism threatened, and the tide of gradual Christianization in Western culture receded, these women struggled to hold together the component parts of their vision, to keep focused on missions the attention of the massive audience of women that had applauded them during the Jubilee. Mackenzie's message, embedded in prose and poetry of more than ordinary literary talent, remained unchanged in the face of a dwindling audience. Montgomery, too, retained faith in her vision of a social gospel that would redress the wrongs of women the world over; but the emphasis in her writing was inverted in the twenties in an effort to reestablish the base of evangelical piety on which she had so blithely assumed she was building before the war. Montgomery's case, then, is perhaps more interesting than Mackenzie's because she fought the forces of evil arrayed against her vision. Without abandoning her liberal theology, she issued a call for spiritual renewal that echoed somewhat hollowly in the emptying mainline churches. Sketching the careers of these two women, the one an artist and a consultant on Africa to mission boards, and the other a scholar and an administrator of missions, produces a pattern of diminishment that mirrors the disintegration of the women's foreign mission movement in the twenties.

Jean Kenyon Mackenzie's correspondence with her editors at Houghton Mifflin in the mid-twenties charts the collapse of a promising literary career. As a Presbyterian missionary in Africa from 1904 to 1913, Mackenzie's letters home had, as a matter of course, been printed in *Woman's Work*. Recognizing their literary merit, and presumably their appeal to a wider and not specifically religious audience, the editor of the *Atlantic Monthly* reprinted several of the letters and encouraged Mackenzie to offer them to the public in book form. The resulting volume, *Black Sheep*, was brought out by

Houghton Mifflin in 1916. The critical acclaim it received reached beyond missionary circles. Ellen Parsons noted that it was "being eagerly read...by a class of people who care nothing for missions."[25] The popularity of *Black Sheep* inspired the Central Committee on the United Study of Foreign Missions to invite Mackenzie to write its 1917 textbook. Not only was *An African Trail* a best-seller in the missionary auxiliaries where over 130,000 copies were distributed, its last two chapters were also featured as essays in the November and December issues of the *Atlantic* in 1916.

The style and substance of Mackenzie's prose appear to have been equally acceptable to religious and literary audiences. Indeed, those audiences were not entirely separate at the time Ellery Sedgwick, editor of the *Atlantic,* promoted Mackenzie as a literary prodigy. Mackenzie's articles—more prose poems than fiction—and her poems continued to be placed apparently indifferently in religious and secular magazines in the years immediately following the war. "Exile and Postman," first published in the *Atlantic* in 1917, was considered something of a masterpiece, worth reprinting in the second series of Atlantic Classics. In 1922, another story based on her African adventures, "The Silver Cup," graced the pages of the *Atlantic. Forum* and *McClure's,* as well as the *International Review of Missions,* accepted her contributions in the early twenties. So it was with some confidence that Mackenzie assembled a volume of essays for publication by Houghton Mifflin in 1924 under the title *African Clearings.* It was an offering that she felt would be appreciated by both her audiences, the religious and the literary. A letter to her editor at Houghton Mifflin, suggesting strategies for publicizing the new book, describes her "two publics."

> One I have made with the help of the *Atlantic Monthly* and in speaking to colleges and secular clubs. The other is a large Christian public who read my work believing that I tell them the truth about things in which they have a particular interest. To a degree which is perfectly ridiculous I represent their African interest to these people.[26]

In this and in a succession of subsequent letters, Mackenzie offers her publishers advice on how to reach her religious audience. She points out that "April is the month set aside in our church calendars for the study of Africa—and it is the occasion of the semiannual union meetings of the women of our societies throughout the country."

> These semi-annuals are called the Presbyterials—I cannot think you know much about Presbyterials—but they represent an opportunity for our book as there are secretaries of literature at all Presbyterials—who are familiar with my writings and who will be glad to push *African Clearings*.[27]

Mackenzie also wanted Houghton Mifflin to distribute circulars at the Presbyterian General Assembly, and she reminded her editor that "the Northfield summer conferences are another of my markets."[28]

Despite the dismantling of the women's boards, enough of the apparatus of missions remained in place in the churches to encourage Mackenzie to advertise her book through familiar channels; yet sales in the religious market which she confidently considered her own were disappointing. A favorable review in the *New York Times* in May made her hope that her literary public would be aroused, but the response there, too, was disheartening. She urged her editors once again to take advantage of the offer of the Presbyterian secretary for publicity "to circularize the book through her correspondence with the women of the church throughout the country," because she felt it would be "the widest appeal that can be made."[29] However, by midsummer of 1924, her optimism about reaching either of her publics was sadly diminished. She feared, she wrote her editor, that *African Clearings* "falls between two stools."[30] He agreed with her assessment, replying that

> the so-called missionary public shy off from it as a book of prose poetry not tending entirely toward "edifications"; while on the other hand, the unregenerate literary public shy off from it for the contrary reason.[31]

The style and substance of Mackenzie's prose had not changed; indeed, in *African Clearings* she once again mined the rich vein of African memories that had made her literary reputation in the first place. What had changed dramatically was the temper of her audiences. The two stools, once so close together as to form a solid foundation for her literary career, had been pushed apart. The distance separating the religious and the literary publics is apparent in the very tone of her editor's comments; his obvious scorn for the narrowness of the "so-called missionary public" places him squarely in the camp of the unregenerate literary audience. His only regret was that the unregenerate could not transcend the religious substance in Mackenzie's prose and celebrate its style. Mackenzie, perhaps because the material she drew on was located in her past rather than in the present, made no effort to accommodate herself to a religious audience made suspicious by fundamentalist controversies of innovative and experimental approaches to missions. And her unwavering if somewhat mystical commitment to evangelical Christianity made it impossible for her to write for a secular literary audience that rejected her religious premises.

Mackenzie's allegiance to Presbyterian missions lasted until her death in 1936. She served as a consultant on African affairs to the Board of Missions and continued to write pamphlets aimed at arousing support for missions among churchwomen. In 1928 she edited and in large part wrote the Central Committee's study text, *Friends of Africa*. She expressed to her editor at Houghton Mifflin the rather forlorn hope that the textbook would once again bring her name before the missionary public, causing sales of *African Clearings* to pick up; but her confidence in its ever reaching an appreciable and appreciative audience had clearly waned.

> Hoping for a better return from *African Clearings* this year when Africa is studied by the women of the churches. It has had a lot of publicity in the reading lists and the bibliographies in the study books. But it isn't, after all and as you once told me— either fish or fowl.[32]

The women of the churches, who had once formed Mackenzie's largest audience, were apparently no longer avid readers of missionary adventures in Africa. In that they differed from Mackenzie herself who believed that missionary biographies would "be read more rather than less with time"; they differed as well from their mothers and grandmothers who, Mackenzie told them, had "read about Africa what was current to be read" and were "a tribe of women truly interested in African needs and in their duty toward those needs." Mackenzie believed that it was "the history of African change" that Christian women needed to learn in order to understand their responsibility for assisting Africa in the traumatic transition to the modern world, and she emphasized the social dimensions of modernization in *Friends of Africa;* but as an artist she remained enthralled by missionary adventures that she knew could have only "a nostalgic fascination in a fully explored world."[33]

There is the suggestion in Mackenzie's work that she felt herself neither fish nor fowl, that she was an alien and an exile living in postwar Manhattan. She confessed that she often went to the "maproom in the public library" and asked "for the Southern Cameroon." Preserving on paper the Cameroon that she had known helped her to preserve her distance from the culture that had changed around her. In a revealing passage she wrote,

> Many a time, when I am in the subway, I remember the ineffable stillness of the forest. I wonder to find myself where I am— so savagely circumstanced—so pressed upon by alien bodies—so smitten by noise. Traveling like this, in white man's fashion, you are certainly safe from the snakes and leopards and the cannibal tribes of that other world where you traveled in other fashions. Now that you are shut up so safely in the guts of Manhattan, your friends feel at ease about you—surely the sun shall not smite you by day nor the moon by night.
>
> And yet, perversely, in this perfect safety, you are intimidated. Suddenly passive after your desperate adventures with traffic, you feel the hidden things of memory rise and flood your heart; you dream. You remember other times of day than the manufactured night of the subway, and other ways of travel. And suddenly, in the indestructible silence that is the core of that incessant clamor, you hear a bugle calling in a forest clearing that is halfway round the world.[34]

Jean Kenyon Mackenzie escaped the manufactured night of the twenties by living, through imagination, in her memories. Imaginative escape is an artist's prerogative. Helen Montgomery, prominent administrator and author of enormously popular mission study texts, had to face the postwar realities of her church and her culture head on. Before the war Montgomery had celebrated "the political revolutions by which the greater portion of the world is brought under the hegemony of Christian nations" as indications that the nineteenth century had brought the world to the threshhold of a new age. Although aware of some of the darker aspects of political and economic imperialism, she nevertheless considered the legacy of colonial rule, particularly British rule, in some respects a blessing. Ultimately she advanced the argument that European and American imperialism was in partnership with the evangelical churches in the great enterprise of ushering in the Kingdom.

> And are not these empire-builders also builders of the King's Highway? Is it not profoundly true that all the great accomplishments of civilization by which anarchy is put down, property rendered safe, communications opened up, education made possible, are John the Baptists crying in the wilderness: "The Kingdom of Heaven is at hand"?[35]

For Montgomery, as for many progressives of her generation, that partnership between religion and politics was dissolved in the Great War and the climate of disillusion that was its aftermath. Always aware that America and other Western nations were not fully Christian, Montgomery had nevertheless believed that the characteristic tendencies of Western culture were consonant with Christianity. Her confidence in the progressive Christianization of America was severely shaken in the decade after the war. The apocalyptic reading of history that had led her to see, in the successive opening of widely dispersed mission fields, the rapid approach of the Kingdom of God was displaced in her thinking in the twenties by a cyclical view of history. In 1917 she had posed rhetorical questions designed to persuade her readers to share her apocalyptic sense of urgency.

> The hour has struck for the most momentous advance of Christianity since Paul crossed into Macedonia. Will the Church, by prayer and gifts of men and money, rise equal to the opportunity? Or will Christ once more weep over the cities of rich America as he did over Jerusalem?[36]

Montgomery's questions assumed that the church could rise to its

supreme opportunity. In the twenties, it must have seemed instead
that Christ wept over Boston and New York.

When Montgomery wrote the 1920 textbook for the United
Study of Foreign Missions, *The Bible and Missions,* she emphasized
the repeated tragedies of Judeo-Christian history. No longer convinced that Christian history could be read as a linear evolution toward the Kingdom of God, she warned that the church might fail in
the historical moment, although the Gospel would ultimately triumph. Despite her new pessimism, Montgomery still conceived of
the triumph of the Gospel as the Christianization of nations and cultures. She compared the Protestant churches of America with Israel
which, she said, had failed "to discern the meaning of God's election
of his Servant Nation." Israel, she claimed, had monopolized God's
gracious blessing rather than sharing it with the world. Her description of Israel's failure bears a remarkable resemblance to her perception of the Protestant churches which were threatened by the
pervasive materialism of postwar America and wracked by internal
dissension between liberals and conservatives.

> But the mind of the nation stuck on privilege and its eyes were
> jealously bent earthward or haughtily averted from other na-
> tions. The election to service was transmuted into a charter of
> privilege.... The nation turned from the worldwide vision of
> the prophets to the disputations of warring sects, and, though
> custodians of the ideal of a Kingdom of God on earth, failed to
> recognize the King when he came.

The Jews were not, Montgomery argued, "the only instance of a
nation richly dowered for service that failed God." She cited both
the Greeks and Romans as peoples who had failed to realize their
ideals, and then demanded, "Will the Christian Church prove another tragic instance of a thwarted purpose of God?"[37] *The Bible and
Missions* represents Montgomery's effort to avert such a tragedy; it
asserts the primacy of the missionary message in Scripture and calls
on conservative and radical alike to unite behind a cause that transcends petty differences and distinctions.

Montgomery feared that the missionary nature of Christianity
would be ignored in a church embroiled in a controversy between
fundamentalists and liberals. Therefore, she charted a careful course
through the dangerous crosscurrents of fundamentalism and liberal-

ism by defining the fundamental nature of Biblical Christianity as missionary and calling upon the church to recapture the sense of mission that lay at the core of its existence. Taking the same tack that she would employ as president of the Northern Baptist Convention when dissension nearly split that denomination in 1921, Montgomery diplomatically sought to avoid open conflict. Finding herself, in *The Bible and Missions,* "on one of the battlegrounds of interpretation," she claimed that "questions of Biblical criticism are outside the purpose of this brief study." The Bible's missionary message, she argued, had been "quite overlooked" while "men have gaped at the whale." The story of Jonah, she said, teaches the same lesson "whether we belong among the severe literalists, or to the company of those who understand the prophet to be making use of a parable or allegory to enforce the truth committed to him."[38] Montgomery belonged to the latter company, but did not intend to alienate those who differed over what she considered a minor matter.

On disagreements between liberals and conservatives over questions of mission policy, Montgomery made her own position quite clear. Deeply influenced by the liberal theologies of Walter Rauschenbusch and Borden Parker Bowne, she rejected the conservative call for a return to narrow evangelism. She took as her text the great missionary commission in Matthew to go and make disciples of all nations, baptizing them and teaching them, and argued that "those who would reduce missions to purely evangelical proclamation of the Good News find here an equally binding command to teach." Yet she also warned that "those who would make missions only social settlements and agencies for the blessings and benefits of modern civilization" were failing to fulfill the church's mission. She agreed with conservatives that "no missionary should be sent forth who goes to take a question, none who has not in his soul a personal experience of Christ's grace and redemption." Her position on this point was not a concession to conservatives; it simply made explicit the nature of the religious commitment in which she had assumed the social revolution she called for in 1910 would be grounded. She continued to claim in 1920 that "in its social passion the Bible stands forth supreme." Echoing Rauschenbusch she argued that the Bible teaches that social reform is a Christian duty.

In ages when the serf and the slave had no spokesman, the Old Testament gave the laws from a God who cared. When women and children were still considered as *"impedimenta"* in the pilgrimage of the race, in the Bible a tender concern, a growing respect were visible. The prophets thundered for the poor in messages that are today tracts for the times, and in the New Testament the flowers of brotherhood bloomed in the world's darkness. No other sacred book even approaches the Bible in this concern for social values and social obligations. The outstanding illustration of this social point of view is found in the thought of the Kingdom of Heaven that runs through the prophets. . . . They are social reformers with a vengeance.[39]

From Rauschenbusch, Montgomery borrowed a vision of the Kingdom of God that demanded participation in struggles for social justice. In the personalism preached by Bowne she found a "theistic conception of the universe" that offered "Christianity's final challenge to blank materialism."[40] Personalism as an ideology had social implications, but its implications for a privatistic formulation of Christian piety dominated her thought in the mid-twenties.

From Montgomery's perspective, the spiritual life of America had sadly deteriorated by 1924 when *Prayer and Missions* was published by the Central Committee on the United Study of Foreign Missions. Her catalog of the symptoms of decay moves, as she had moved in her own thinking, from a consideration of broad social problems to the private practice of piety.

The testimony of the Christian nations of the West is marred by injustice, race prejudice, covetousness and immorality. More than a million children, in this richest nation of the world, are denied opportunities for education, and sacrificed on the altar of greed. Prohibitory laws, the outstanding manifestation of America's idealism, are meeting such a widespread and determined opposition in their enforcement as to make of our country a byword and hissing among nations. Our churches are tainted with worldliness and hypocrisy. . . . Family religion is at a low ebb. Family worship, the daily reading of the Scriptures, the family singing of hymns, have almost disappeared. Disrespect of the Sabbath is widespread; and attendance upon the church services and upon the weekly prayer meeting are in most churches not half the membership of the church. All these and a hundred other threatening symptoms call loudly for some remedy, some fresh stimulus to spiritual living.

The remedy Montgomery recommends is prayer. She attributes the neglect of prayer to "the swift and only half-digested progress of scientific knowledge, the sudden accumulation of material gains, the failure to maintain habits of church-going and Bible reading; the decay of family religion." In urging the church to return to its knees, Montgomery was not abandoning the struggle for social justice; the call to prayer was a call for Christian evangelicals to regroup for the battle. Montgomery had always anticipated that "as we come to put the Kingdom of God, Christ's supremest passion, in the center and forefront of our lives, our prayer life will deepen and expand." As evidence mounted that prayer, even among the members of missionary auxiliaries, was being neglected, she felt compelled to address the issue directly.[41]

Montgomery's sense that the mission movement needed to be reminded that its cause had been "planted and has germinated in the hearts of believing, praying disciples" emerges clearly in the pages of *Prayer and Missions*.

> Absorbed in the raising of money, the administrating of great trusts, the solving of perplexing problems, it seems as if the missionary enterprise depended upon us. We need to be called back again and again to the fact that through prayer we get the charter of our forward movements and their direction and success.

The woman's missionary movement, she recalled, was "born and nurtured in prayer," but she feared that it had abandoned the "mightiest weapon in every reform that helps the progress of the Kingdom of God."

> A missionary society ought to be first of all a society for prayer. Is it? Are there not societies where they repeat the Lord's Prayer unless the minister's wife is present to lead? Are there not societies so nearly dead in spiritual power that no one will pray?

It would seem that women needed to learn again to pray publicly, a skill assiduously cultivated during the movement's formative years but one that had fallen into disuse in the era of modern missions. As she watched the "vast enterprise of winning the world for Christ halt and falter" in the early twenties, Montgomery placed the blame on the decline in evangelical piety in America. Without ever recognizing her own complicity in undercutting the prayer life of the woman's missionary movement, she urged women "to put the devotional service first and central" in missionary auxiliary meetings and to "cultivate the individual prayer life of the members" by assigning each woman a "prayer partner" among the missionaries.[42]

In returning to the practice of the founders of the woman's mission movement regarding prayer, Montgomery did not display their optimism in anticipating spiritual renewal as the reflex influence of work for foreign missions. Instead, she added a new twist to the doctrine of reflex influence that reflected her belief that the Western temperament was preeminently practical while the East possessed the gift of prayer. Her hope for the spiritual renewal of America lay not in the effect that working for missions would have on the workers, but in the enlarged vision of Christianity that would be revealed to the West when "its glories are reflected back from the redeemed nations of the East."

> Over against the practicality and literalness of our western tempers, living always in the life of active service, lies this Oriental temper of mysticism of meditation. The richest treasure of the Eastern soul is prayer. . . . To our gift of service may they not add their gift of prayer; to our will to power may they not add their spirit of meditation?

In the midst of her dismay at the decline of Christianity in American culture, Montgomery—like her male as well as female colleagues—took comfort in the promise for the future that she discerned in the young churches of the East. She found new confirmation for her faith and new incentive for her practice in studying "the wondrous story of the praying Christians of the Orient."[43]

Montgomery remained faithful to the vision of the women who had instituted the United Study of Foreign Missions; with them, she believed that knowledge would move people to action—and to informed prayer that could channel the blessing of God in the world. She urged women to study "the story of the twenty-ninth chapter of the Acts that is being written today in a hundred fields of mission activity." She chided women for their "languid interest in the cause of Christ," and informed them that failure to "read the annals of his far-flung enterprise" would produce "sterility and deadness in prayer."[44] And though *Prayer and Missions* had no noticeable effect in reversing the trends it deplored—the apathy of churchwomen, the steady decline in volunteers for the mission field, and the relative decline in receipts for missions in contributions to the churches—Montgomery wrote yet another textbook for the Central Committee's United Study series in 1929. In the new text she moved away from the privatistic concerns of *Prayer and Missions* and returned to the themes of social Christianity and the role of women in religion that had been her emphasis in the halcyon days before the war.

*From Jerusalem to Jerusalem* reviews the history of Christian missions from Pentecost to the International Missionary Council held in Jerusalem in 1928. Throughout, it highlights the role of women in missions. Montgomery attributed the rapid spread of Christianity in the first century in part to "the use it made of the talents and services of women." Reiterating the conclusions she had drawn in *Western Women in Eastern Lands* in 1910, she compared Christianity to the world's other great religions on the issue of the treatment of women.

> Jesus alone of all the great religious teachers of the world made no sex bar in his religion. . . . Confucius regarded women as essentially subordinate in intellect and spirit to man. Buddha gave her only the hope of being reborn a man in some future incarnation. . . . The great Hindu law giver, Manu, condemned her as the source of moral corruption, and enjoined upon her the worship of her husband. Mohammed fixed upon her the yoke of polygamy, and in his picturing of a sensual heaven revealed the deep corruption that has always dogged the steps of Islam.

Women, Montgomery claimed, had been admitted to "a democracy of the spirit" in the early church; it was only in the second and third centuries "as ecclesiastics gained control in the Church" that the "position of women declined."

In the centuries that followed women were limited, forbidden to preach, forbidden to testify, discriminated against by man-made laws, until the clear witness of the gospel was obscured, and women, some of them, came to feel that Christianity discriminated against them.

The great missionary movement of the late nineteenth century, Montgomery argued, had allowed women to regain "their true place." But she warned that the organized church must now grant women full equality if it hoped "to avail itself of the talents of women."

> And while the Church hesitates and mumbles over old formularies, business and society and politics are freely opening to women new doors of opportunity. It behooves those who long to have every grace and gift used in the service of Jesus to study the story of expanding Christianity and learn what its message to women was. In the words of its divine leader in the dusk of the Eastern morning it was, "Go! Tell!"[45]

As Montgomery surveyed her world in 1928, it seemed to her crucial that the talents of women be employed in missions. With "wickedness and crime...rampant, bitterness and cynicism widespread, the pall of unbelief and hopelessness darkens the sky"; the church would need all its resources to meet the menace of materialism. But the response to her plea to women was disappointing.

This last book, despite its return to the themes of her more popular texts, did not find a wide audience even among churchwomen. Lucy Peabody, chairman of the Central Committee on the United Study of Foreign Missions throughout the twenties as she had been for most of the two previous decades, failed to mention *From Jerusalem to Jerusalem* in her tribute to Montgomery. Instead, Peabody's brief memoir lingers lovingly on the sales figures from the period of prewar triumphs. And so, while Montgomery found much to celebrate in the history of missions, it was perhaps fortunate that she had developed, in *Prayer and Missions,* a rationale for locating her hopes for the future of Christianity in the younger churches of the East; for she concluded, when she turned from the past to the "unfinished task," that "the unchristliness of the West" was the "greatest obstacle to the Christianizing of the East." As evidence for this assertion she pointed to five areas in which she found the West in general and America in particular far from Christian. She called for the elimination of war, an end to racial prejudice, the Christianization of business, an end to imperialism, and the abolition of the liquor trade. In an unqualified endorsement of social Christianity, she told her fellow evangelicals that they "must not be satisfied until Christ is crowned lord of the nation's conscience." She spelled out what she meant.

> The duty to register, to vote, to struggle with might and main, is laid upon us all. As Christians we must care about the great reform causes that demand our suffrages. For whenever the spirit of Jesus triumphs in a law that protects the weak, or enlarges the life of a submerged tenth, that spirit is glorified among the nations.[46]

Unhappily, Montgomery uncovered little evidence suggesting that evangelical Christians in America were living up to what she saw as their responsibility to control their culture.

In *From Jerusalem to Jerusalem* Montgomery abandoned the effort at reconciliation with conservatives that marked both *The Bible and Missions* and *Prayer and Missions*. She returned to the resounding endorsement of liberal theology, with its call for cultural renovation, that characterized her prewar pronouncements. Ironically, she discovered that in the intervening years, some liberals had moved on to new territory. The direction they were taking was one in which she was unwilling to follow. She reported with alarm that an American scholar had recommended at the Jerusalem Conference that "the missionary to a Buddhist people enter into partnership with them in a great spiritual quest for truth." Having entered the missionary enterprise through the woman's mission movement, Montgomery was naturally inclined to view the question of the relativity of religious truth from a woman's perspective. Her own analysis had persuaded her of the systematic degradation of women in non-Christian religions; the testimony at the Jerusalem Conference of the female delegates from the Eastern churches confirmed her in the opinion that Christianity was not simply one version of a universal truth in which all religions participated.

It was, in fact, while the discussion was going on in regard to the relative position of the great religions of the world, when each woman rose, one after another, and told with telling effect what Christ had meant to her and to the women of her country, that the measureless difference between Christianity and other faiths was most clearly seen.[47]

At the very moment when it seemed to Montgomery that the specific goal of the woman's foreign mission movement in the modern era had been largely accomplished, that legislative and educational revolutions—products of the combined influence of evangelization and Westernization—had transformed the lives of women in non-Western cultures, she found herself betrayed by religious liberals ready to value abstract quests for spiritual truth above the concrete realities of the lives of women.

Montgomery suffered a series of strokes in the early thirties that forced her retirement from active mission work. Thus, when the report of the systematic survey of world missions conducted by the liberal Laymen's Foreign Missions Inquiry was made public in 1932, her reaction was not recorded. Her antipathy to its proposal that collaboration replace an emphasis on conversion as the goal of missions and that Christianity renounce any claims to the possession of absolute truth can, however, be inferred from the warnings on the dangers of syncretism that she issued after the Jerusalem Conference.

> This subtle danger of compromise confronts the church today. Syncretism has ever proved a foe to real power and spirituality. It is not less so today. When we find that the missionaries of this ancient "Church on Fire" [the Nestorian church] lost their power to convert through compromise with other faiths, let us be warned in time. Let us refuse to send out missionaries who have no clear message of the Cross.[48]

It was then with an embattled defense of her vision, rather than a ringing affirmation of the social and political as well as spiritual benefits that Christianity bestowed upon women, that Montgomery ended her career.

Rather like Jean Kenyon Mackenzie who discovered in the

twenties that her work was no longer acceptable to either of her publics, Helen Barrett Montgomery lived out the final years of her long career of service to missions in relative obscurity, no longer "our peerless leader...more widely known...than any other woman in America today."[49] Despite her conventional views on evangelical piety, her commitment to social Christianity made her vision unacceptable to conservatives. Her special concern for the welfare of women caused her final break with religious liberals. Her own zeal for reform, as well as her demand for full equality for women in mission work, contributed to the woman's foreign mission movement's loss of a special identity and, consequently, its reduced power within the missionary enterprise of the evangelical churches of America. The massive audience of women that had applauded her Jubilee speeches and studied her early textbooks was sadly diminished by the end of the twenties. Like Mackenzie, Montgomery was steadfast in her vision; they suffered the same fate—the loss of an audience.

The history of the woman's foreign mission movement parallels the course of the careers of Mackenzie and Montgomery. The large measure of success that it enjoyed before the First World War did not secure for it a broad, enduring constituency. The remnant that remained faithful to the vision of uniting the nations in one unbroken household under Christ's dominion were largely ignored in the secular and increasingly isolationist climate of postwar America. The dramatic abuses of women in other cultures—child marriage, suttee, and foot binding—that had gripped the imagination of Victorian women had been largely eliminated. The less melodramatic rationale for modern foreign missions, however persuasively presented by advocates like Montgomery and Mackenzie, exercised less power over the female imagination and engaged relatively few young women in the mainline denominations after the war. In 1920 when Montgomery, in an oblique attack on the so-called five points of fundamentalism, compared the "plan of salvation" to an architect's blueprints she used a metaphor that appealed to the women of her generation: "We do not exhibit the working drawings of our house; we show our friends through the home."[50] It was a graceful argument for social service rather than narrow evangelism in mission work, but the daughters of bourgeois America felt they had better things to do than play the role of gracious hostesses in the Kingdom.

# Notes

*Introduction*

1. Charles W. Forman, "II. The Americans," *International Bulletin of Missionary Research,* April 1982, 54.

2. Kenneth Scott Latourette, *A History of the Expansion of Christianity* (New York: Harper and Brothers, 1938–45), vol. 4, *The Great Century in Europe and the United States of America, A.D. 1800–A.D. 1914* (1941), 48. More recent studies have also pointed to the importance of laymen's and student movements. In his article on "Motives in Protestant Missions, 1890–1917," *Church History* 23 (1954): 68–82, Paul Varg links these movements specifically and the missionary revival generally to the spread of Moody-style revivalism. Valentin Rabe's study of *The Home Base of American China Missions, 1880–1920* (Cambridge: Harvard University Press, 1978) focuses almost exclusively on the Laymen's Missionary Movement; two paragraphs are devoted to women's societies (20, 143–44) despite the fact that a prominent mission administrator is quoted as saying in 1900 that it sometimes seemed that without the woman's work nothing would be left. In his 1974 Ph.D. dissertation (Washington University) on "The American Board of Commissioners for Foreign Missions and the London Missionary Society in the Nineteenth Century: A Study of Ideas," Alan Frederick Perry observes that student and lay movements "do not explain everything" and spends two pages sketching the work of women with the American Board as an example of the emergence of women's societies in the 1870s that "accounts for a good deal of the missionary revival" (502–3).

3. Latourette, *The Great Century,* 49.

4. Forman, "The Americans," 54. For the most thorough analysis of parallels between business styles and mission strategies see Rabe's *Home Base;* the central thesis of this study is that the promoters of the late-nineteenth-century missionary revival optimistically assumed that they could effectively "substitute businesslike planning, organization, and promotion to achieve the same objectives [as could the "spontaneous enthusiasm and spiritual dynamism" that were "lacking"]" (4–5).

5. Latourette, *The Great Century,* 49–50; Forman, "The Americans," 55. Denominational historians in general have paid more attention to the role

women played in missions than have secular historians of religion in America; Methodist historians in particular have produced in the last fifteen years a rash of articles that explore various aspects of the history of women in Methodist churches, including their work for foreign missions. But to view woman's work for missions from a denominational perspective is usually to lose sight of the broader questions raised by the phenomenon of a movement among women that crossed denominational boundaries. The only historian whose breadth of vision encompasses the larger picture is R. Pierce Beaver. His *All Loves Excelling: American Protestant Women in World Mission* (Grand Rapids: Eerdmans, 1968) surveys the history of women's involvement in American Protestant mission efforts from 1802 through 1968. Written from the perspective of a committed liberal evangelical, its tone is celebratory; it is, nevertheless, a scholarly tour de force in its untangling of the complicated web of institutions and agencies through which women worked for missions and in its marshalling of a vast number of facts and mission statistics into an engaging narrative. The revised edition, issued in 1980 under the title *American Protestant Women in World Mission: History of the First Feminist Movement in North America,* contains a new chapter on "The Decade of the Seventies" that—like the new title—reveals some of the interpretive flaws in Beaver's evaluation of the woman's foreign mission movement. From the perspective of women's history, it is inaccurate to label woman's work for missions as the first feminist movement; I would hesitate to call it a feminist movement at all. More significant is what I see as Beaver's failure to comprehend the cultural gulf that separates our own time from that which spawned the woman's foreign mission movement. Beaver's final chapter is a lament that the Woman's Liberation Movement did not "spur churchwomen to a determined effort to recover their place of leadership in the Protestant world mission" (p. 213) and that the "still urgent need for unmarried women in world mission [who]...are more often ready [than husbands and wives] to live simply and to adjust to the standard of living of national colleagues" (p. 218) is not being met. His final plea for a renewal of "female voluntaryism" ignores the radical changes in patterns of female participation in the labor force in this century and especially in the decade of the seventies.

6. The changing cultural paradigms of ideal womanhood discussed in this study are those developed by Sheila M. Rothman in *Woman's Proper Place: A History of Changing Ideals and Practices, 1870 to the Present* (New York: Basic Books, 1978). The shifts she describes from "virtuous womanhood" to "educated motherhood" to "wife-companion" parallel, in the first two instances, significant changes in the formulation of woman's role in mission work; the wife-companion ideal that prevailed during the period in which the woman's foreign mission movement disintegrated helps to explain the movement's loss of appeal for women.

On the transformation of American culture from Protestant to secular in its dominant orientation, see Jackson Lears, *No Place of Grace: Antimodernism and the Transformation of American Culture, 1880–1920* (New York: Pantheon, 1981). I have found his characterization of the new secular culture as "therapeutic," with its emphasis on personal adjustment and fulfillment, particularly relevant to the social service aspects of missionary work which assumed such prominence in the era of "modern" missions.

*Chapter 1*

1. The 3,000,000 figure is quoted in *Woman's Work* (Philadelphia and New York: Woman's Foreign Missionary Society of the Presbyterian Church) 30 (June 1915): 138. Ruth Bordin's recent *Woman and Temperance* (Philadelphia: Temple University Press, 1981) claims that the WCTU was the largest woman's organization in America until the General Federation of Women's Clubs surpassed it sometime after 1900, but Bordin gives a figure of nearly 150,000 members in 1892—larger than the Women's Clubs' 20,000 or the National American Woman's Suffrage Association's (NAWSA) 13,000 in 1893, but no larger than the Woman's Foreign Missionary Society of the Methodist Episcopal Church (North) alone which had 151,000 members in 1895. A petition presented jointly by fourteen denominational female missionary societies to President Cleveland in 1896 claimed to represent over 500,000 women. However, in reporting on the petition to her readers, the editor of *Woman's Work for Woman* noted that membership figures in annual reports were inaccurate and that 600,000 members would be closer to the truth. At the time of the woman's foreign missionary Jubilee in 1910, Helen Barrett Montgomery placed the movement's total membership at 2,000,000 in her history titled *Western Women in Eastern Lands* (New York: Macmillan, 1910), 243. Karen Blair, in *The Clubwoman as Feminist* (New York: Holmes and Meier, 1980), 142n.22, gives a figure of 1,600,000 women associated through the General Federation in 1914, up from 800,000 in 1908 and 1,000,000 in 1912. Statistics for the suffrage movement are fragmentary at best, but Aileen Kraditor offers in *The Ideas of the Woman Suffrage Movement* (New York: Doubleday, 1965) figures indicating that NAWSA had grown to 75,000 by 1910, 100,000 in 1915, and 2,000,000 in 1917. Membership rolls alone are not a sufficient measure of a movement's importance, of course. But the other claims that Bordin makes for the WCTU must be modified in light of the existence of another organization controlled by women and exclusively female in membership that surpassed the WCTU in size and breadth and depth of local organization.

2. Frank Luther Mott, *Golden Multitudes* (New York: Macmillan, 1947), 136–37. Further biographical data on Southworth is derived from Beatrice K. Hofstadter's article in *Notable American Women*, ed. Edward T. James et al., 3 vols. (Cambridge: Harvard University Press, 1971), 3:327–28. Bio-

graphical data on Wiggin and Glasgow are derived from the entries on each (by Doyce B. Nunis, Jr. and by Marjorie R. Kaufman) in *Notable American Women* (3:605–7; 2:44–49) and from their respective autobiographies, *My Garden of Memory* (Boston: Houghton Mifflin, 1923) and *The Woman Within* (New York: Harcourt, Brace and Company, 1954).

3. Emma D. E. N. Southworth, *Fair Play; or, The Test of the Lone Isle* (Philadelphia: T. B. Peterson and Brothers, 1868), 125. All further references to this work *(FP)* appear in the text.

4. Kate Douglas Wiggin, *New Chronicles of Rebecca* (New York: Grosset and Dunlap, 1907), 273. All further references to this work *(NCR)* appear in the text.

5. See Barbara Welter, "The Feminization of American Religion: 1800–1860," in *Problems and Issues in American Social History,* ed. Wm. O'Neill (Minneapolis: Burgess Publishing, 1974), reprinted in *Clio's Consciousness Raised,* ed. Mary Hartman and Lois W. Banner (New York: Harper and Row, 1974), 137–57; and Ann Douglas, *The Feminization of American Culture* (New York: Knopf, 1977). For speculation on what opening the mission field to women as a professional arena meant, see Welter's "She Hath Done What She Could: Protestant Women's Missionary Careers in Nineteenth-Century America," in *Women in American Religion,* ed. Janet James (Philadelphia: University of Pennsylvania Press, 1980), 111–25.

6. Kate Douglas Wiggin, *Rebecca of Sunnybrook Farm* (New York: Grosset and Dunlap, 1903), 181–82. All further references to this work *(RSF)* appear in the text.

7. Ellen Glasgow, *Barren Ground* (Garden City: Doubleday, Page and Co., 1925), 42. All further references to this work *(BG)* appear in the text.

*Chapter 2*

1. Standard denominational histories that mention the ladies include Robert G. Torbet's *A Venture of Faith* (Philadelphia: Judson, 1955); Wade Crawford Barclay's monumental *History of Methodist Missions,* vol. 3 (New York: The Board of Foreign Missions of the Methodist Church, 1957); and Arthur Judson Brown's *One Hundred Years: A History of the Foreign Missionary Work of the Presbyterian Church in the U.S.A.* (New York: Fleming H. Revell, 1936).

From the perspective of women's history, the importance of the missionary movement has been pointed to by Page Smith in a brief chapter titled "Raising Up the Heathen" in his *Daughters of the Promised Land* (Boston: Little, Brown and Co., 1970) and by Barbara Welter in her article, "She Hath Done What She Could." For data on the comparative size of nineteenth-century woman's movements, see chap. 1 n.1 supra. An instructive comparison can also be made between the woman's foreign mission movement and the Laymen's Missionary Movement (LMM) in both size and scope. See Valentin H. Rabe, *The Home Base of American China Missions, 1880–1920* (Cambridge: Harvard University Press, 1978), 158–71, for evidence that the LMM never engaged the numbers of laymen in active mission work (or even encouraged participation beyond simple stewardship of funds) that the woman's movement enrolled in its program.

2. Alexis de Tocqueville, *Democracy in America*, vol. 2 (New York: Vintage, 1945), 114.

3. Nancy Cott, *The Bonds of Womanhood* (New Haven: Yale University Press, 1977), 132–33.

4. Kathryn Kish Sklar, "The Founding of Mount Holyoke College," in *Women of America: A History*, ed. Carol Berkin and Mary Beth Norton (Boston: Houghton Mifflin, 1979), 187.

5. Carroll Smith-Rosenberg, "Beauty, the Beast, and the Militant Woman: A Case Study in Sex Roles and Social Stress in Jacksonian America," *American Quarterly* 23 (1971): 562–84; Ruth Bordin, *Woman and Temperance* (Philadelphia: Temple University Press, 1981); and Karen Blair, *The Clubwoman as Feminist* (New York: Holmes and Meier, 1980). See also Estelle Freedman's important theoretical analysis in "Separatism as Strategy: Female Institution Building and American Feminism, 1870–1930," *Feminist Studies* 5 (1979): 512–29.

6. A number of historians have sketched the contours of what Barbara Welter labeled "The Cult of True Womanhood" in her influential article under that title in *American Quarterly* 18 (1966): 151–74. Barbara J. Harris has done an admirable job of summarizing subsequent scholarship on the subject in *Beyond Her Sphere: Women and the Professions in American History*, Contributions in Women's Studies, No. 4 (Westport, Conn.: Greenwood Press, 1978). My own thinking has been particularly influenced by Ronald Hogeland, "The Female Appendage: Feminine Life Styles in America, 1820–1860," *Civil War History* 17 (June 1971): 101–14; and Ann D. Gordon and Mari Jo Buhle, "Sex and Class in Colonial and Nineteenth-Century America," in *Liberating Women's History*, ed. Berenice Carroll (Chicago: University of Illinois Press, 1976), 278–300.

7. Gerald R. Moran, " 'Sisters' in Christ: Women and the Church in Seventeenth-Century New England," in *Women in American Religion*, ed. Janet Wilson James (Philadelphia: University of Pennsylvania Press, 1980), 47–65. I am indebted to Amanda Porterfield for pointing out the significance of the marriage analogy in Puritan theology in her study of *Feminine Spirituality in America* (Philadelphia: Temple University Press, 1980).

8. Among others in the late eighteenth century, Mary Wollstonecraft

took the *philosophes* to task for their views on women in *A Vindication of the Right of Woman,* written in 1791.

9. See Barbara Epstein's comparison of conversion accounts in the two Awakenings in *The Politics of Domesticity* (Middletown, Conn.: Wesleyan University Press, 1981).

10. Linda Kerber, *Women of the Republic* (Chapel Hill: University of North Carolina Press, 1980).

11. See Keith Melder's discussion of Beecher and Hale in *Beginnings of Sisterhood* (New York: Schocken Books, 1977), 129–33.

12. Catherine Beecher, *A Treatise on Domestic Economy* (New York: Schocken Books, 1977), 158, 161–65. (Beecher's biographers consistently spell her name Catharine, but her publishers apparently preferred Catherine.)

13. Ibid., 166–67.

14. Ibid., 9.

15. "Pastoral Letter of the General Association of Massachusetts (Orthodox) to the Churches under Their Care," *The Liberator* (Boston), August 11, 1837; reprinted in *Up from the Pedestal,* ed. Aileen S. Kraditor (Chicago: Quadrangle Books, 1968), 50–52.

16. Catherine Beecher, *Essay on Slavery and Abolitionism* (Boston: Perkins and Marvin, 1837), 46, 97–98.

17. Ibid., 100–102.

18. Ibid., 102, 104.

19. Ibid., 107–9.

20. Ibid., 136–37.

21. *Angelina Grimké,* Letters to Catherine Beecher (Boston: Isaac Knapp, 1838), 30–31.

22. Ibid., 104, 108.

23. *Woman's Work for Woman* 1 (April 1871): 24–26.

24. George M. Frederickson, *The Inner Civil War* (New York: Harper and Row, 1965), 98. See also Mary Elizabeth Massey, *Bonnet Brigades* (New York: Alfred A. Knopf, 1966) and Eleanor Flexner, *Century of Struggle* (New York: Atheneum, 1973) for evaluations of the effect of the Civil War on American women.

25. *Heathen Woman's Friend* 1 (May 1869): 2.

26. *Heathen Woman's Friend* 11 (September 1879): 60.

27. Daniel Scott Smith, "Family Limitation, Sexual Control, and Domestic Feminism in Victorian America," in *Clio's Consciousness Raised,* ed. Mary Hartman and Lois W. Banner (New York: Harper and Row, 1974), 122.

28. Flexner, *Century of Struggle,* 179.

29. For an evaluation of the enormous interest shown in the Ann Jud-

son story see Joan Jacobs Brumberg's *Mission for Life* (New York: The Free Press, 1980), chaps. 1, 2, and 4, and her article, "The Case of Ann Hasseltine Judson: Missionary Hagiography and Female Popular Culture, 1815–1850," in *Women in New Worlds, Volume II,* ed. Rosemary Skinner Keller, Louise L. Queen, and Hilah F. Thomas (Nashville: Abingdon, 1982), 234–48. The phrase *harrowing of the home field* is Helen Barrett Montgomery's in a speech published in *Report of the Ecumenical Conference on Foreign Missions,* 2 vols. (New York: American Tract Society, 1900), 1:217.

The linkage of missions and imperialism has become a commonplace. Stephen Neill titles his chapter on 1858–1914 in *A History of Christian Missions* (Harmondsworth, Eng.: Penguin, 1964) "The Heyday of Colonialism." John K. Fairbank chose to conclude *The Missionary Enterprise in China and America* (Cambridge: Harvard University Press, 1974) with an essay by Arthur Schlesinger, Jr., on "The Missionary Enterprise and Theories of Imperialism." More recent interpretations focus on imperialism of a cultural sort. Here a consideration of women is beginning to emerge, not as promoters of missionary enthusiasm in the United States, but as cultural imperialists *par excellence.* Charles Forman has perceptively argued, in "The Americans" (*International Bulletin of Missionary Research,* April 1982, 54–56) that an important item on the agenda of missionary imperialism (for men and women alike) was an improvement in the status of women. Somewhat less persuasively, Adrian A. Bennet alleges that "female missionaries were more culturally imperialistic than their male counterparts" ("Doing More Than They Intended," in *Women in New Worlds, Volume II,* 249–67).

30. Beecher, *A Treatise on Domestic Economy,* 2, 12, 13.

31. *Heathen Woman's Friend* 1 (May 1869): 1.

32. Mary Lyon, "To the Friends of Christian Education, 1835," and "Letter from Mary Lyon, 1836," reprinted in *Women of America,* 199–200.

33. Literacy patterns cited in Sklar, "The Founding of Mount Holyoke College," 179–80.

34. For details of Hale's life and career I have drawn on Ruth E. Finley's dated but fascinating biography, *The Lady of Godey's* (Philadelphia: J. P. Lippincott, 1931); Isabelle Webb Entrikin's *Sarah Josepha Hale and Godey's Lady's Book* (Philadelphia: University of Pennsylvania Press, 1946); and Paul S. Boyer's entry on Hale in *Notable American Women,* 2:110–14.

35. Quoted in *Missionary Crumbs* 1 (January 1863): 14.

36. *The Missionary Link* 1 (July 1865): 21.

37. Biographical data on Doremus is drawn from a lengthy eulogy in *The Missionary Link* 7 (January 1877): 2–21; and from Mary S. Benson's entry on Doremus in *Notable American Women,* 1:500–501.

38. *The Missionary Link* 7 (January 1877): 9, 13, 17.

39. *Missionary Crumbs* 1 (January 1861): 19.

40. Isabel Hart, *Historical Sketches of Woman's Missionary Societies in America and England* (Boston: Mrs. L. H. Daggett, 1879), 48.

41. Beaver, *All Loves Excelling,* 91.

42. *Life and Light for Heathen Women* 1 (March 1869): 1; 1 (June 1869): 46; 1 (September 1869): 95.

43. The standard contemporary history is Frances J. Baker, *The Story of the Woman's Foreign Missionary Society of the Methodist Episcopal Church* (New York: Eaton and Mains, 1898). Barclay's *History of Methodist Missions* contains the most thorough scholarly account.

44. Ruth Bordin claims that Willard's comprehensive strategy for organizing at the local level throughout the country was "the factor that made the WCTU unique among nineteenth-century organizations" (Bordin, *Woman and Temperance,* 90). But, in fact, the Methodist society had already set the pattern that Willard copied after she became president of the WCTU in 1879. Information on Willard's Methodist connections is drawn from Mary Earhart Dillon's entry on Willard in *Notable American Women,* 3:613-19.

45. Membership statistics are taken from the Annual Reports of the Woman's Foreign Missionary Society of the Methodist Episcopal Church. The study cited is Mrs. George Isham, "Our Organization and Task," in *Our Work for the World,* comp. Mrs. Wm. McDowell (Boston: Woman's Foreign Missionary Society, Methodist Episcopal Church, 1913), 20-22.

46. Isham, "Our Organization and Task," 5, 6.

47. *Heathen Woman's Friend* 1 (June 1870): 100.

48. *Heathen Woman's Friend* 1 (May 1869): 3.

49. Woman's Foreign Missionary Society of the Presbyterian Church, Minutes of the Executive Committee Meetings, vol. 1 (1870-78), meeting of September 5, 1871. (Handwritten.)

50. "From Miss Loring," *Woman's Work for Woman* 5 (July 1875): 120.

51. H., "And She Left Her Waterpot," *Woman's Work for Woman* 5 (September 1875): 159.

52. Quoted in *Woman's Work for Woman* 8 (July 1878): 199.

53. Jennie Fowler Willing, "Our Prayer," *Heathen Woman's Friend* 6 (January 1875): 782. For information on Willing's career, see Theodore L. Agnew's entry on her in *Notable American Women,* 3:623-25; and Bordin, *Woman and Temperance.*

54. Jessie W. Radcliffe, "Ask Somebody Else," *Woman's Work* 13 (July 1898): 188.

55. Blair, *The Clubwoman as Feminist,* 63-64.

56. "Shall We Combine the Home and Foreign Missionary Work?" Issued as a leaflet by the Woman's Board of Missions of the Interior (Congregational) and reprinted in *Woman's Work for Woman* 8 (January 1878): 12.

57. Ellen C. Parsons, "History of Women's Organized Missionary Work as Promoted by American Women," in *Woman in Missions: Papers and Addresses presented at The Woman's Congress of Missions,* comp. E. M. Wherry (New York: American Tract Society, 1894), 107–8.

58. "Here—And There," *Woman's Work for Woman* 3 (May 1873): 66.

59. Parsons, "History," 89–90.

60. Stanza quoted in Hart, *Historical Sketches of Woman's Missionary Societies,* 51.

*Chapter 3*

1. *Woman's Work for Woman* 1 (April 1871): 23.

2. *Heathen Woman's Friend* 17 (October 1885): 82, 84.

3. *Heathen Woman's Friend* 3 (September 1871): 182.

4. Jennie Fowler Willing, "A Word to Western Women," *Heathen Woman's Friend* 1 (July 1869): 13.

5. Mrs. S. J. Rhea, *Woman's Work for Woman* 1 (April 1871): 19.

6. *Heathen Woman's Friend* 1 (June 1869): 2.

7. See the discussion of the relationship of evangelicals to fiction in Joan Jacobs Brumberg, *Mission For Life* (New York: The Free Press, 1980), especially chaps. 3 and 5; and Ann Douglas, *The Feminization of American Culture* (New York: Knopf, 1977) on the intersection between sentimental fiction and religious culture.

8. "The Hillerton Auxiliary," *Woman's Work for Woman* 10 (January 1880): 18.

9. Ibid.

10. Ibid., 19.

11. H., "And She Left Her Waterpot," *Woman's Work for Woman* 5 (September 1875): 158.

12. *Heathen Woman's Friend* 1 (December 1869): 54; 3 (September 1871): 180; M. E. Andrews, "An Appeal to Christian Women," *Life and Light for Heathen Women* 5 (January 1875): 14; J. G. J., "Small Gifts Willingly Offered," *Woman's Work for Woman* 5 (March 1875): 31–32.

13. Isabel Hart, "Woman's Place in the Gospel History and Scheme," *Heathen Woman's Friend* 3 (August 1871): 287.

14. "The Hillerton Auxiliary," *Woman's Work for Woman* 10 (January 1880): 20, 21; *Woman's Work for Woman* 4 (January 1875): 293–96; 2 (July 1872): 164.

15. "The Hillerton Auxiliary," *Woman's Work for Woman* 10 (January 1880): 19–20; 10 (February 1880): 54.

16. *Life and Light for Heathen Women* 5 (June 1875): 182.

17. "The Hillerton Auxiliary," *Woman's Work for Woman* 10 (January 1880): 21.

18. See, for example, "An Open Letter," *Woman's Work for Woman* 5 (March 1890): 59.

19. "The Hillerton Auxiliary," *Woman's Work for Woman* 10 (January 1880): 21.

20. Ibid., 19.

21. S. W., "Woman As a Christian Factor," *Woman's Work for Woman* 11 (December 1881): 417-18.

22. Jennie Fowler Willing, "The Better Time," *Heathen Woman's Friend* 2 (July 1870): 8.

23. Isabel Hart, "Our Work and Our Age," *Heathen Woman's Friend* 4 (March 1873): 429.

24. S. W., "Woman As a Christian Factor," 418; Hart, "Our Work and Our Age," 429; *Life and Light for Heathen Women* 1 (December 1870): 274.

25. Blair, *The Clubwoman as Feminist*, 66-68.

26. Mrs. Rufus Anderson, "Reflex Influence of Woman's Missionary Work," *Life and Light for Heathen Women* 5 (April 1875): 107-8.

27. Mrs. M. N. Blakeslee, "Why We Should Keep Up Our Auxiliaries," *Woman's Work for Woman* 14 (July 1884): 236, 237-38.

28. "The Casting Out of Dumb Spirits," *Woman's Work for Woman* 7 (March 1877): 29-30; "Women's Prayers," *Woman's Work for Woman,* 13 (March 1883): 91-93; "Women's Voices," *Woman's Work for Woman* 12 (October 1882): 351-52. (The quotations given are from "Women's Prayers," 91 and 93.)

29. "Women's Voices," 351-52.

30. "The Hillerton Auxiliary," *Woman's Work for Woman* 10 (February 1880): 52.

31. Ibid., 54-55.

32. Ibid., 55.

33. "What Was the Matter?" *Woman's Work for Woman* 10 (September 1880): 300-301.

34. H. M. Merrick, "The Secret of Power in Woman's Work for Woman," *Woman's Work for Woman* 8 (March 1878): 75, 77.

35. Ibid., 79-80.

36. "The Hillerton Auxiliary," *Woman's Work for Woman* 10 (February 1880): 55.

37. C. S. Winchell, "Mary Clarke Nind," *Woman's Missionary Friend* 37 (November 1905): 382-83.

38. Woman's Foreign Missionary Society of the Presbyterian Church, Minutes of the Executive Committee Meetings, vol. 1 (1870-78), p. 141, meeting of January 5, 1875. (Handwritten.); "From Miss Loring," *Woman's Work for Woman* 5 (July 1875): 120, 121.

39. *Heathen Woman's Friend* 2 (August 1870): 20.

40. *Heathen Woman's Friend* 2 (November 1870): 49–50.

41. See Brumberg, *Mission for Life,* for an extended discussion of the evangelical love affair with the printing press.

42. Jennie Fowler Willing, "A Word to Western Women," *Heathen Woman's Friend* 1 (July 1869): 12, 13.

43. "The Work of the Month," *Heathen Woman's Friend* 2 (August 1870): 18, 19.

44. Catherine Beecher, *Essay on Slavery and Abolitionism* (Boston: Perkins and Marvin, 1837), 22.

45. Jennie Fowler Willing, *Heathen Woman's Friend* 1 (September 1869): 30.

46. *Heathen Woman's Friend* 17 (August 1885): 31.

47. Ellen Parsons, "Twenty-five Years," *Woman's Work* 27 (February 1912): 28.

48. Jennie Fowler Willing, "A Word to Western Women," *Heathen Woman's Friend* 1 (July 1869): 13.

49. Biographical data on Harriet Merrick Warren is taken from her obituary: Mrs. J. T. Gracey, "Our Translated Leader," *Heathen Woman's Friend* 24 (March 1893): 212–15.

50. *Heathen Woman's Friend* 25 (December 1893): 160.

51. Ibid., 166.

52. *Woman's Missionary Friend* 27 (February 1896): 217.

53. *Heathen Woman's Friend* 2 (November 1870): 55.

*Chapter 4*

1. *Heathen Woman's Friend* 26 (July 1894): 7–8.

2. For a thorough discussion of the most important effort to build a mission constituency among businessmen, see Valentin Rabe's study of the Laymen's Missionary Movement, *The Home Base of American China Missions, 1880–1920* (Cambridge: Harvard University Press, 1978).

3. Woman's Foreign Missionary Society of the Presbyterian Church, Minutes of the Executive Committee Meetings, vol. 1 (1870–78), p. 240, meeting of September 25, 1877. (Handwritten.)

4. Mrs. Thomas, Letter, *Heathen Woman's Friend* 3 (February 1872): 238.

5. "All for Christ," *Woman's Work for Woman* 3 (September 1873): 166.

6. Isabella Thoburn, "Motives of Benevolence," *Heathen Woman's Friend* 4 (April 1873): 441.

7. Jennie Fowler Willing, "Missionary Sociables," *Heathen Woman's Friend* 5 (August 1873): 508–9, and "Definite Work for Our Auxiliaries," *Heathen Woman's Friend* 5 (October 1873): 540–41.

8. Isabella Thoburn, *Heathen Woman's Friend* 6 (April 1875): 824.

9. Woman's Foreign Missionary Society of the Presbyterian Church,

204     *Notes to Pages 99-109*

Minutes of the Executive Committee Meetings, vol. 1 (1870-78), p. 245, meeting of October 10, 1877. (Handwritten.)

10. Mrs. S. M. Henderson, "The Necessity for System in Our Work," *Woman's Work for Woman* 11 (August 1881): 274, 277, 275.

11. *Heathen Woman's Friend* 15 (June 1884): 278-79; Luthera Whitney, Letter, *Heathen Woman's Friend* 16 (September 1884): 57.

12. "Special Appropriations," *Life and Light for Woman* 14 (December 1884): 455-56, reprinted as "Special Objects," *Woman's Work for Woman* 15 (April 1885): 135.

13. Mary Pinneo Dennis, "The Broader Outlook in Special Objects," *Woman's Work for Woman* 13 (November 1898): 307.

14. Jennie Fowler Willing, *Heathen Woman's Friend* 4 (August 1872): 318-19.

15. Willing, "Missionary Sociables," *Heathen Woman's Friend* 5 (August 1873): 508.

16. *Heathen Woman's Friend* 8 (November 1876): 110-11.

17. *Heathen Woman's Friend* 15 (September 1883): 60.

18. Mary Clarke Nind, *Heathen Woman's Friend* 16 (November 1884): 107.

19. Quoted in Grace T. Davis, *Neighbors in Christ: Fifty-Eight Years of World Service by the Woman's Board of Missions of the Interior* (Chicago: Woman's Board of Missions of the Interior, 1926), 9.

20. *Life and Light for Heathen Women* 1 (March 1869): 6.

21. *Heathen Woman's Friend* 5 (October 1873): 541.

22. *Woman's Work for Woman* 1 (April 1871): 22.

23. Ibid., 4, 5.

24. *Heathen Woman's Friend* 7 (March 1876): 204.

25. "A Little Hard," *Woman's Work for Woman* 4 (September 1874): 169-70.

26. "Married Missionary Ladies," *Woman's Work for Woman* 8 (January 1878): 8.

27. "Special Appropriations," *Life and Light for Woman* 14 (December 1884): 456.

28. "Look at Both Sides," *Woman's Work for Woman* 15 (September 1885): 319-20.

29. See, for example, the discussion of a hagiographical halo surrounding Ann Hasseltine Judson in Brumberg, *Mission For Life,* chaps. 1-4.

30. "Letter Writing On the Field," *Woman's Work for Woman* 5 (September 1890): 250; "Missionary Correspondence," *Woman's Work* 25 (November 1910): 258-59.

31. Isabel Hart, "Uniform Readings," *Heathen Woman's Friend* 11 (August 1879): 38.

32. Joan Jacobs Brumberg and Nancy Tomes, "Women in the Profes-

sions: A Research Agenda for American Historians," *Reviews in American History* 10 (June 1982): 285.

33. *Heathen Woman's Friend* 12 (January 1881): 156.

34. *Woman's Missionary Friend* 29 (October 1897): 104.

35. Paper delivered by Miss M. D. Wingate, secretary of the Woman's Board of Missions of the Interior (Congregational), on April 24, 1900. Published in *Report of the Ecumenical Conference on Foreign Missions,* 2 vols. (New York: American Tract Society, 1900), 1:191; *Heathen Woman's Friend* 22 (January 1891): 163–64.

36. *Heathen Woman's Friend* 27 (July 1895): 5.

37. *Report of the Centenary Conference on the Protestant Missions of the World,* 2 vols. (London: James Nisbet and Co., 1888), 1:397–417, 2:140–83; *Report of the Ecumenical Conference,* 2:353–84.

38. *Report of the Centenary Conference,* 2:165, 167.

39. Ibid., 2:169.

40. Ibid., 2:173–74.

41. Ibid., 2:175.

42. Ibid., 2:181.

43. *Report of the Ecumenical Conference,* 1:219. For Jackson Lears's description of the shift from a Protestant to a therapeutic culture, see his *No Place of Grace* (New York: Pantheon, 1981), xiii–xviii, 4–26.

44. Sheila M. Rothman, *Woman's Proper Place* (New York: Basic Books, 1978), 4–5, 63–64.

45. Estelle Freedman, "Separatism as Strategy: Female Institution Building and American Feminism, 1870–1930," *Feminist Studies* 5 (1979): 512–29, 521.

46. *Report of the Ecumenical Conference,* 1:215–17.

47. Ibid., 1:216.

48. Ibid., 1:217.

49. Helen Barrett Montgomery, *Western Women in Eastern Lands* (New York: Macmillan, 1910), 73–74.

50. Ellen C. Parsons, "The Ecumenical Conference—Past," *Woman's Work for Woman* 15 (June 1900): 156–60.

51. *Woman's Work* 20 (January 1905): 1.


*Chapter 5*

1. Joan Jacobs Brumberg and Nancy Tomes, "Women in the Professions," *Reviews in American History* 10 (June 1982): 286.

2. *Heathen Woman's Friend* 1 (May 1869): 7.

3. Kate Alexander Hill, Letters to family members, MSS, and photo albums, Kate Alexander Hill Papers, Presbyterian Historical Society, Philadelphia.

4. "Requirements and Conditions for Employment of Missionaries," *Heathen Woman's Friend* 9 (June 1878): 274.

5. Mary Pinneo Dennis, "Gleanings from the Portfolio of a Missionary Candidate Committee," *Woman's Work for Woman* 11 (November 1896): 309-11.

6. For an evaluation of three Methodist training schools, including the Chicago school, see Virginia Lieson Brereton, "Preparing Women for the Lord's Work," in *Women in New Worlds,* ed. Hilah F. Thomas and Rosemary Skinner Keller (Nashville, Tenn.: Abingdon, 1981), 178-99.

7. Robert Moats Miller, "Lucy Jane Rider Meyer," in *Notable American Women,* 3:534-36; Isabella Thoburn, "About Missionary Candidates," *Heathen Woman's Friend* 19 (October 1887): 89; and Lucy Rider Meyer, "Duty of the W.F.M.S. to the Deaconess Movement," *Heathen Woman's Friend* 22 (February 1891): 184-85, give a perspective on the relationship of the deaconess movement to missionary training. Mrs. E. E. Baldwin promoted the Folts Institute in *Heathen Woman's Friend* 27 (August 1895): 41. The resolution requiring a year at Folts was reported in *Woman's Missionary Friend* 36 (March 1904): 101. Jeanette Camp Harmount's article for *Life and Light for Woman* on the Moody Bible Institute was reprinted in *Woman's Work for Woman* 10 (August 1895): 229-30.

8. Dennis, "Gleanings," 310-11. Frank Knight Sanders, ed., *The Preparation of Women Missionaries: The Report of a Conference on the Preparation of Women for Foreign Missionary Service* (New York: n.p., 1915).

9. Mrs. O. W. Scott, "What Makes Missionaries?" *Woman's Missionary Friend* 28 (September 1896): 62-64; Isabella Thoburn, "About Missionary Candidates, II," *Heathen Woman's Friend* 19 (November 1887): 118-19.

10. "On Student Work," *Woman's Missionary Friend* 44 (January 1912): 21. See also Valentin Rabe's characterization of the typical female missionary candidate as she appears in the American Board's candidate files in *The Home Base,* 97-107.

11. Louise McCoy North, "Modern 'Schools of the Prophets,' " *Woman's Missionary Friend* 29 (November 1897): 126-30.

12. Samuel Gregory, M.D., "Medical Missionary Women," *Heathen Woman's Friend* 1 (November 1869): 41-43.

13. Mrs. E. J. Humphrey, "Necessity for Female Medical Missionaries," *Heathen Woman's Friend* 1 (October 1869): 33.

14. *Report of the Ecumenical Conference,* 2:199-202.

15. Charles W. Forman, "II. The Americans," *International Bulletin of Missionary Research,* April 1982, 55.

16. *Heathen Woman's Friend* 2 (December 1870): 65.

17. *Life and Light for Heathen Women* 1 (April 1869): 47.

18. *Heathen Woman's Friend* 1 (March 1870): 75; 2 (June 1871): 135-36; 1 (October 1869): 38; 1 (September 1869): 27.

19. Jennie Fowler Willing, *Heathen Woman's Friend* 1 (August 1869): 20.

20. *Heathen Woman's Friend* 8 (August 1876): 35.

21. Jennie K. McCauley, "Why Do We Educate the Japanese?" *Woman's Work for Woman* 3 (September 1888): 234-36.

22. Montgomery, *Western Women in Eastern Lands,* 105, 148, 126.

23. Helen Barrett Montgomery, *Christus Redemptor: An Outline Study of the Island World of the Pacific* (New York: Macmillan, 1906), 8, 12.

24. Ibid., 13, 174.

25. Montgomery, *Western Women in Eastern Lands,* 206, 68-69.

26. For biographical data on Jean Kenyon Mackenzie, see Vivian R. Johnson, "Jean Kenyon Mackenzie," in *Notable American Women,* 2:469-70; Jean Kenyon Mackenzie, *Black Sheep: Adventures in West Africa* (Boston: Houghton Mifflin, 1916), 63, 243; idem., *An African Trail* (West Medford, Mass.: Central Committee on the United Study of Foreign Missions, 1917), 62-63.

27. Mackenzie, *An African Trail,* 32, 22.

28. Ibid., 173, 177.

29. Ibid., 36.

30. Helen Barrett Montgomery, *The Preaching Value of Missions* (Philadelphia: The Judson Press, 1931), 17.

31. *Report of the Ecumenical Conference,* 1:145.

32. Blair, *The Clubwoman as Feminist,* 98-99.

33. *Report of the Ecumenical Conference,* 1:145.

34. On the Woman's Congress of Missions, see *Woman in Missions: Papers and Addresses presented at The Woman's Congress of Missions,* comp. E. M. Wherry (New York: American Tract Society, 1894); and Ellen Parsons, "Woman's Congress of Missions, Chicago, October 2-4," *Woman's Work for Woman* 8 (November 1893): 308-12. On the formation of the Interdenominational Conference of Woman's Boards of Foreign Missions, see *Woman's Missionary Friend* 28 (February 1897): 214.

35. *Woman's Missionary Friend* 27 (February 1896): 230.

36. *Bulletin of the Tenth Interdenominational Conference of Woman's Boards of Foreign Missions* (Central Committee on the United Study of Foreign Missions, 1915), 15.

37. Louise Manning Hodgkins, *Via Christi: An Introduction to the Study of Missions* (New York: Macmillan, 1901).

38. Sales figures for the textbooks are cited in *Woman's Missionary Friend* 37 (March 1905): 91; and in the *Bulletin of the Tenth Interdenominational Conference of Woman's Boards,* 15. For examples of advice on mission study, see

*Woman's Missionary Friend* 34 (January 1902): 15; 34 (March 1902): 77–83; 36 (January 1904): 2–5.

39. On the Keswick Convention and the Mount Hermon Conference, see C. Howard Hopkins, *John R. Mott, 1865–1955* (Grand Rapids: Eerdmans, 1979), 22–30, 114–15.

40. Clementina Butler, "Report of the Sixth Interdenominational Conference of Woman's Boards," *Woman's Missionary Friend* 36 (March 1904): 99.

41. Katharine Weaver Williams, "The Summer School at Northfield, July 12–19," *Woman's Missionary Friend* 36 (September 1904): 305–8.

42. Marcia Kerr, "Northfield Conference," *Woman's Work* 30 (September 1915): 212.

43. "Summer Schools and Conferences," *Woman's Work* 30 (September 1915): 212–13.

44. Mrs. Norman Mather Waterbury, "Report of the Central Committee on United Study of Missions," *Woman's Work for Woman* 19 (April 1904): 90–91.

45. "How We Used the Text-Book," *Woman's Missionary Friend* 38 (January 1906): 12; Mrs. M. H. Lichliter, "The Text-Book and the Meeting," *Woman's Missionary Friend* 41 (October 1909): 351–53.

46. *Woman's Missionary Friend* 39 (September 1907): 316.

47. "How Shall We Pronounce the Names?" *Woman's Work* 24 (August 1909): 187–88.

48. Jane M. Miller, "Duties of the Rank and File of the Missionary Societies," *Woman's Work* 24 (August 1909): 186–87.

49. Estelle M. Ochiltree, "Mrs. Farley's Substitute," *Woman's Missionary Friend* 42 (May 1910): 162.

50. Ibid.

51. Ibid.

52. Ibid., 163.

53. Ibid., 189.

54. Ochiltree, "Mrs. Farley's Substitute," *Woman's Missionary Friend* 42 (June 1910): 203.

55. Carrie M. Wheeler, "Winning New Members," *Woman's Missionary Friend* 42 (August 1910): 276–77.

56. Bertha Procino, "Missionary Societies vs. Women's Clubs," *Woman's Work* 30 (May 1915): 115.

57. See Anastasia Sims, "Sisterhoods of Service: Women's Clubs and Methodist Women's Missionary Societies in North Carolina, 1890–1930," in *Women in New Worlds*, vol. 2, ed. Rosemary Skinner Keller, Louise L. Queen, and Hilah F. Thomas (Nashville, Tenn.: Abingdon, 1982), 196–210; Mary E. Frederickson, "Shaping a New Society: Methodist Women

and Industrial Reform in the South, 1880–1940," in *Women in New Worlds,* ed. Thomas and Keller, 345–61; and John Patrick McDowell, *The Social Gospel in the South* (Baton Rouge: Louisiana State University Press, 1982).

*Chapter 6*

1. The fullest account of the Jubilee is contained in chap. 4 of Louise Armstrong Cattan's *Lamps Are For Lighting: The Story of Helen Barrett Montgomery and Lucy Waterbury Peabody* (Grand Rapids: Eerdmans, 1972). R. Pierce Beaver also devotes a few pages of his *All Loves Excelling* to the subject.

2. Abby Gunn Baker, "The Story of the Washington Celebration of the Woman's National Foreign Missionary Jubilee" (pamphlet apparently published by the Jubilee Committee, 1911).

3. *The Washington Star,* January 28, 1911.

4. *The Washington Star,* February 3, 1911.

5. Helen Barrett Montgomery, "The Trend of Things: Then and Now," *The Herald,* February 4, 1911.

6. Flyer published by the Jubilee Committee (copy preserved in Mrs. Wallace Radcliffe's Jubilee scrapbooks, Presbyterian Historical Society, Philadelphia); *Woman's Missionary Friend* 42 (December 1910): 430.

7. Baker, "The Story of the Washington Celebration."

8. *The New York Observer,* April 6, 1911.

9. Katharine Clark Mullikin, "Eight Women," *Woman's Missionary Friend* 42 (October 1910): 343.

10. Flyer published by the Jubilee Committee (Radcliffe scrapbooks).

11. Lears, *No Place of Grace,* xiv, 10–32, 47–58.

12. Helen Barrett Montgomery, "After the Jubilee, What?" *Bulletin for the Campaign to be Undertaken by Women's Boards of Missions during the Month of October* (Central Committee on the United Study of Foreign Missions, 1911), 11–12.

13. Ibid., 13.

14. Ibid., 15.

15. See Beaver, *All Loves Excelling,* 177–90.

16. See R. Pierce Beaver, *American Protestant Women in World Mission,* rev. ed. (Grand Rapids: Eerdmans, 1980), 202–5, 213–14.

17. *Woman's Missionary Friend* 45 (March 1913): 96.

18. Ibid., 95.

19. "New Recruits," *Heathen Woman's Friend* 22 (May 1891): 259; Isabel Hart, "Consecrated Culture," *Heathen Woman's Friend* 22 (June 1891): 280–82; *Heathen Woman's Friend* 26 (June 1895); Louise Manning Hodgkins, "College Girls in Missions," *Woman's Missionary Friend* 33 (June 1901): 194–95; (August 1901): 267–69; (September 1901): 308–12; (October

1901): 345–48; 34 (May 1902): 153–56; (June 1902): 192–95. On the Student Volunteer Movement, see *Woman's Missionary Friend* 42 (February 1910): 46; and Rabe, *The Home Base*, 90–93, 176–77.

20. "A Life of Service," *Woman's Missionary Friend* 42 (February 1910): 52; Mrs. D. C. Cook, "Our Young People," *Woman's Missionary Friend* 42 (October 1910): 362.

21. *Woman's Missionary Friend* 45 (December 1913): 438; "Student Work," *Woman's Missionary Friend* 47 (August 1915): 285.

22. Mary S. Young, "Mothers and Daughters," *Woman's Work* 30 (July 1915): 163–64; Martha B. Finley, "Choose Leaders to Lead," *Woman's Work* 30 (September 1915): 234–35.

23. *Bulletin of the Fourteenth Interdenominational Conference of Woman's Boards of Foreign Missions* (Central Committee on the United Study of Foreign Missions, 1919), 8–10.

24. Rothman, *Woman's Proper Place*, 5–6, 177–218.

25. Ellen C. Parsons, *An African Trail: A Review* (West Medford, Mass.: Central Committee on the United Study of Foreign Missions, 1917), 4.

26. Jean Kenyon Mackenzie to Mr. Linscott, 11 December 1923, Mackenzie Correspondence, Houghton Library, Harvard University.

27. Jean Kenyon Mackenzie to Mr. Linscott, 4 April 1924, Mackenzie Correspondence.

28. Jean Kenyon Mackenzie to Mr. Linscott, 8 May 1924, Mackenzie Correspondence.

29. Jean Kenyon Mackenzie to Mr. Linscott, 4 June 1924, Mackenzie Correspondence.

30. Jean Kenyon Mackenzie to Mr. F. Greenslet, July 1924, Mackenzie Correspondence.

31. Mr. F. Greenslet to Jean Kenyon Mackenzie, 28 July 1924, Mackenzie Correspondence.

32. Jean Kenyon Mackenzie to Mr. F. Greenslet, 18 August 1928, Mackenzie Correspondence.

33. Jean K. Mackenzie, ed., *Friends of Africa* (Cambridge, Mass.: Central Committee on the United Study of Foreign Missions, 1928), 17–18.

34. Jean Kenyon Mackenzie, *African Clearings* (Boston: Houghton Mifflin, 1924), 259, 50–51.

35. Helen Barrett Montgomery, *The King's Highway* (West Medford, Mass.: Central Committee on the United Study of Foreign Missions, 1915), 8, 17.

36. Helen Barrett Montgomery, *Following the Sunrise: A Century of Baptist Missions, 1813–1913* (Philadelphia: American Baptist Publication Society, 1913), 169.

37. Helen Barrett Montgomery, *The Bible and Missions* (West Medford,

Mass.: Central Committee on the United Study of Foreign Missions, 1920), 21–23.

38. Ibid., 46, 48.

39. Ibid., 80, 88, 11–12.

40. Ibid., 18.

41. Helen Barrett Montgomery, *Prayer and Missions* (West Medford, Mass.: Central Committee on the United Study of Foreign Missions, 1924), 70–71, 11, 189.

42. Ibid., 75, 200, 101, 201, 203.

43. Ibid., 143–44.

44. Ibid., 192–93.

45. Helen Barrett Montgomery, *From Jerusalem to Jerusalem* (North Cambridge, Mass.: Central Committee on the United Study of Foreign Missions, 1929), 39–42.

46. Ibid., 43, 190–93. For Lucy Peabody's tribute, see Montgomery, *Helen Barrett Montgomery: From Campus to World Citizenship* (New York: Fleming H. Revell, 1940), 114–35.

47. Montgomery, *From Jerusalem to Jerusalem*, 208–11.

48. Helen Barrett Montgomery, *The Preaching Value of Missions* (Philadelphia: The Judson Press, 1931), 81.

49. Baker, "The Story of the Washington Celebration," 33.

50. Montgomery, *The Bible and Missions*, 15.

# Selected Bibliography

*Primary Sources*

Allen, Belle J., M.D., comp., and Caroline Atwater Mason, ed. *A Crusade of Compassion for the Healing of the Nations: A Study of Medical Missions for Women and Children.* West Medford, Mass.: Central Committee on the United Study of Foreign Missions, 1919.

Baker, Abby Gunn. *The Story of the Washington Celebration of the Woman's National Foreign Missionary Jubilee.* N.p.: [Jubilee Committee], 1911.

Baker, Frances J. *The Story of the Woman's Foreign Missionary Society of the Methodist Episcopal Church, 1869–1895.* New York: Eaton and Mains, 1898.

Beecher, Catherine E. *An Essay on Slavery and Abolitionism with Reference to the Duties of American Females.* Boston: Perkins and Marvin, 1837; Philadelphia: Henry Perkins, 1837.

———. *A Treatise on Domestic Economy.* 1841. Reprinted with an Introduction by Kathryn Kish Sklar. New York: Schocken Books, 1977.

Bennett, Katharine M., comp. *Status of Women in the Presbyterian Church in the U.S.A., with References to Other Denominations: An Historical Statement.* Philadelphia: General Council of the Presbyterian Church in the U.S.A., May, 1929.

*Bulletin of the Fourteenth Interdenominational Conference of Woman's Boards of Foreign Missions.* Central Committee on the United Study of Foreign Missions, 1919.

*Bulletin of the Tenth Interdenominational Conference of Woman's Boards of Foreign Missions.* Central Committee on the United Study of Foreign Missions, 1915.

Chamberlain, Mrs. W. I. [Mary E. A.]. *Fifty Years in Foreign Fields: China, Japan, India, Arabia: A History of Five Decades of the Woman's Board of Foreign Missions, Reformed Church in America.* New York: Woman's Board of Foreign Missions, 1925.

Commission on Ecumenical Missions and Relations, United Presbyterian Church in the U.S.A. Secretaries' files. Presbyterian Historical Society, Philadelphia.

Davis, Grace T. *Neighbors in Christ: Fifty-Eight Years of World Service by the Woman's Board of Missions of the Interior.* Chicago: Woman's Board of Missions of the Interior, 1926.

Dennis, James S. *Christian Missions and Social Progress: A Sociological Study of Foreign Missions.* 3 vols. New York: Fleming H. Revell, 1897–1906.

Ecumenical Missionary Conference, New York, 1900. *Report of the Ecumenical Conference on Foreign Missions, 21 April - 1 May 1900.* 2 vols. New York: American Tract Society, 1900.

Glasgow, Ellen. *Barren Ground.* Garden City, N.Y.: Doubleday, 1925.

Gordon, Elizabeth Putnam. *Women Torch-Bearers: The Story of the Woman's Christian Temperance Union.* Evanston: National Woman's Christian Temperance Union Press, 1924.

Gracey, Mrs. J. T. [Annie]. *Medical Work of the Woman's Foreign Missionary Society, Methodist Episcopal Church.* Boston: Woman's Foreign Missionary Society, Methodist Episcopal Church, 1888.

Grimké, Angelina E. *Letters to Catherine E. Beecher.* Boston: Isaac Knapp, 1838.

Hart, Isabel, ed. *Historical Sketches of Woman's Missionary Societies in America and England.* Boston: Mrs. L. H. Daggett, 1879.

*Heathen Woman's Friend,* 1869–95. Boston: Woman's Foreign Missionary Society of the Methodist Episcopal Church, North. Publication continued under the name *Women's Missionary Friend,* 1896–1940.

Heck, Fannie S. *In Royal Service: The Mission Work of Southern Baptist Women.* Richmond, Va.: Foreign Mission Board, Southern Baptist Convention, 1913.

*Helping Hand,* 1872–1914. N.p.: Woman's Baptist Foreign Mission Society. Published with the *Baptist Missionary Magazine* and *The Macedonian* in the early years; merged with *Missions.*

Hill, Kate Alexander. Personal papers, 1896–1942. MSS in Presbyterian Historical Society, Philadelphia.

Hocking, William Ernest. *Re-Thinking Missions: A Laymen's Inquiry After One Hundred Years.* By the Commission of Appraisal. New York: Harper and Brothers, 1932.

Hodgkins, Louise Manning. *Via Christi: An Introduction to the Study of Missions.* New York: Macmillan, 1901.

Johnston, James, ed. *Report of the Centenary Conference on the Protestant Missions of the World, London, 9–19 June 1888.* 2 vols. London: James Nisbet and Co., 1888.

Ladies' Board of Missions of New York. *Annual Reports, 1871–1920.* New York: Ladies' Board of Foreign Missions, later Woman's Board of Foreign Missions of the Presbyterian Church (New York). Presbyterian Historical Society, Philadelphia.

*Life and Light for Heathen Women,* 1869–1922. Boston: Woman's Board of Missions, Congregational. Name changed to *Life and Light for Woman* in 1876.

Lyon, Mary. "Letter from Mary Lyon, 1836." Reprinted in *Women of America,* edited by Carol Berkin and Mary Beth Norton, 200–201. Boston: Houghton Mifflin, 1979.

———. "To the Friends of Christian Education, 1835." Reprinted in *Women of America,* edited by Carol Berkin and Mary Beth Norton, 198–200. Boston: Houghton Mifflin, 1979.

McDowell, Mrs. William Fraser [Clotilda Lyon], comp. *Our Work for the World.* Boston: Woman's Foreign Missionary Society, Methodist Episcopal Church, 1913.

Mackenzie, Jean Kenyon. *African Adventurers.* New York: George H. Doran, 1922.

———. *African Clearings.* Boston: Houghton Mifflin, 1924.

———. *An African Trail.* West Medford, Mass.: Central Committee on the United Study of Foreign Missions, 1917.

———. *Black Sheep: Adventures in West Africa.* Boston: Houghton Mifflin, 1916.

———. Correspondence with Houghton Mifflin, 1923–28. Houghton Library, Harvard University.

———. *The Glowing Ember of Prayer.* Boston: Central Committee on the United Study of Foreign Missions, n.d.

———. *The Host in the Hut: A Bulu Treatise on Hospitality.* New York: Women's Board of Foreign Missions of the Presbyterian Church, April, 1917.

———. "My Life in Darkest Africa." *Hearst's International Cosmopolitan* 81 (November 1926): 66–67.

———. *Nana, the Mother.* New York: Woman's Board of Foreign Missions of the Presbyterian Church in the U.S.A., n.d.

———. *Other Children.* New York: Board of Foreign Missions of the Presbyterian Church in the U.S.A., 1925.

———. *The Shadow on the Water.* N.p.: Joint Committee on Women's Union Christian Colleges in the Orient, n.d.

———. "The Silver Cup," *Atlantic Monthly* 130 (November 1922): 608–18.

———. *The Story of a Fortunate Youth: Chapters from the Biography of an Elderly Gentleman.* New York: Fleming H. Revell, 1937.

———. *Talking Woman.* London: Sheldon, 1936.

———. *The Ten Tyings.* New York: Woman's Board of Foreign Missions of the Presbyterian Church in the U.S.A., n.d.

———. *The Trader's Wife.* New York: Coward-McCann, 1930.

———. *The Venture.* Boston: Houghton Mifflin, 1925.

*The Missionary Link,* 1861–93. New York: Woman's Union Missionary Society. Published under the title *Missionary Crumbs,* 1861–1864.

Montgomery, Helen Barrett. "After the Jubilee, What?" *Bulletin for the Campaign to be Undertaken by Woman's Boards of Missions during the Month of*

*October.* Central Committee on the United Study of Foreign Missions, 1911.

――――. *The Bible and Missions.* West Medford, Mass.: Central Committee on the United Study of Foreign Missions, 1920.

――――. *Christus Redemptor: An Outline Study of the Island World of the Pacific.* New York: Macmillan, 1906.

――――. *Following the Sunrise: A Century of Baptist Missions, 1813–1913.* Philadelphia: American Baptist Publication Society, 1913.

――――. *From Jerusalem to Jerusalem.* North Cambridge, Mass.: Central Committee on the United Study of Foreign Missions, 1929.

――――. *Helen Barrett Montgomery: From Campus to World Citizenship.* With Tributes by her Friends. New York: Fleming H. Revell, 1940.

――――. *The King's Highway: A Study of Present Conditions on the Foreign Field.* West Medford, Mass.: Central Committee on the United Study of Foreign Missions, 1915.

――――. *Prayer and Missions.* West Medford, Mass.: Central Committee on the United Study of Foreign Missions, 1924.

――――. *The Preaching Value of Missions.* Philadelphia: Judson Press, 1931.

――――. *Western Women in Eastern Lands: An Outline Study of Fifty Years of Woman's Work in Foreign Missions.* New York: Macmillan, 1910.

Parsons, Ellen C. *An African Trail: A Review.* West Medford, Mass.: Central Committee on the United Study of Foreign Missions, 1917.

――――. *Christus Liberator: An Outline Study of Africa.* New York: Macmillan, 1905.

Peabody, Lucy W. *A Wider World for Women.* New York: Fleming H. Revell, 1936.

――――. "A Woman of Ten Talents: An Appreciation of Helen Barrett Montgomery." *Missionary Review of the World* 57 (December 1934): 580–81.

――――. "Woman's Place in Missions Fifty Years Ago and Now." *Missionary Review of the World* 50 (December 1927): 907–9.

*The Preparation of Women Missionaries.* The Report of a Conference on the Preparation of Women for Foreign Missionary Service held by the Board of Missionary Preparation with the Representatives of the Foreign Mission Boards and of the Missionary Training Schools in North America. 5-7 December 1915. Edited by Frank Knight Sanders. New York, 1915.

Radcliffe, Mrs. Wallace. Two Jubilee Scrapbooks. Presbyterian Historical Society, Philadelphia.

Raymond, Mrs. Maud Mary [Wotring]. *The King's Business: A Study of Increased Efficiency for Women's Missionary Societies.* West Medford, Mass.:

Central Committee on the United Study of Foreign Missions, 1913.

Safford, Mrs. Henry G. *The Golden Jubilee.* New York: Woman's American Baptist Missionary Society, [1922].

Southworth, Emma D. E. N. *Fair Play; or, The Test of the Lone Isle.* Philadelphia: T. B. Peterson and Brothers, 1868.

Wherry, Rev. E. M., comp. *Woman in Missions: Papers and Addresses presented at The Woman's Congress of Missions, Chicago, 2–4 October 1893.* New York: American Tract Society, 1894.

Wiggin, Kate Douglas. *New Chronicles of Rebecca.* New York: Grosset and Dunlap, 1907.

———. *Rebecca of Sunnybrook Farm.* New York: Grosset and Dunlap, 1903.

Woman's American Baptist Foreign Mission Society. *Annual Reports, 1915–1920.* Mission Research Library, Union Theological Seminary, New York.

Woman's Baptist Foreign Mission Society. *Annual Reports, 1872–1914.* Mission Research Library, Union Theological Seminary, New York.

Woman's Board of Missions. *Annual Reports, 1869–1924.* Boston: Woman's Board of Missions. Published in *Life and Light for Heathen Women.*

Woman's Board of Missions. Foreign and home letters. Archives of the American Board of Commissioners for Foreign Missions. Houghton Library, Harvard University.

Woman's Board of Missions. Minutes of the Executive Committee. Archives of the American Board of Commissioners for Foreign Missions. Houghton Library, Harvard University.

Woman's Foreign Missionary Society of the Methodist Episcopal Church, North. *Annual Reports, 1870–1920.* Published in *Heathen Woman's Friend;* after 1895, *Woman's Missionary Friend.*

Woman's Foreign Missionary Society of the Presbyterian Church. *Annual Reports, 1871–1920.* Presbyterian Historical Society, Philadelphia.

Woman's Foreign Missionary Society of the Presbyterian Church. Minutes of the Executive Committee Meetings, 1870–1921. 3 vols. (Handwritten.) Presbyterian Historical Society, Philadelphia.

Woman's General Missionary Society of the United Presbyterian Church of North America. *Annual Reports, 1887–1921.* Presbyterian Historical Society, Philadelphia.

Woman's General Missionary Society of the United Presbyterian Church of North America. Minutes of Annual Conventions. Presbyterian Historical Society, Philadelphia.

*Woman's Missionary Magazine of the United Presbyterian Church,* 1887–1956. N.p.: Woman's General Missionary Society of the United Presbyterian Church of North America.

Woman's Occidental Board of Foreign Missions, Presbyterian Church in the U.S.A. *Annual Reports, 1876–1920.* Presbyterian Historical Society, Philadelphia.

*Woman's Work for Woman,* 1871–85. Philadelphia and New York: Woman's Foreign Missionary Society of the Presbyterian Church. United with *Our Mission Field,* 1886–1889. Continued publication until 1924; name changed to *Woman's Work* in 1905.

Wood, Mary I. *The History of the General Federation of Women's Clubs.* Norwood, Mass.: Norwood Press, 1912.

*Secondary Works*

Agnew, Theodore, L. "Reflections on the Woman's Foreign Missionary Movement in Late 19th-Century Methodism." *Methodist History* 6 (January 1968): 3–16.

Barclay, Wade Crawford. *History of Methodist Missions.* Vol. 3. New York: Board of Missions of the Methodist Church, 1957.

Beaver, R. Pierce. *All Loves Excelling: American Protestant Women in World Mission.* Grand Rapids: Eerdmans, 1968. Rev. ed. (1980) published under title: *American Protestant Women in World Mission: History of the First Feminist Movement in North America.*

———, ed. *American Missions in Bicentennial Perspective: Papers presented at the Fourth Annual Meeting of the American Society of Missiology at Trinity Evangelical Divinity School, Deerfield, Illinois, June 18–20, 1976.* South Pasadena, Cal.: William Carey Library, 1977.

Blair, Karen J. *The Clubwoman as Feminist: True Womanhood Redefined, 1868–1914.* New York: Holmes and Meier Publishers, 1980.

Bledstein, Burton J. *The Culture of Professionalism.* New York: W. W. Norton and Company, 1976.

Bordin, Ruth. " 'A Baptism of Power and Liberty': The Women's Crusade of 1873–74." *Ohio History* 87 (Autumn 1978): 393–404.

———. *Woman and Temperance: The Quest for Power and Liberty, 1873–1900.* Philadelphia: Temple University Press, 1981.

Brereton, Virginia Lieson. "Preparing Women for the Lord's Work." In *Women in New Worlds,* edited by Hilah F. Thomas and Rosemary Skinner Keller, 178–99. Nashville: Abingdon, 1981.

Brereton, Virginia Lieson, and Christa Ressmeyer Klein. "American Women in Ministry: A History of Protestant Beginning Points." In *Women of Spirit,* edited by Rosemary Ruether and Eleanor McLaughlin, pp. 301–32. New York: Simon and Schuster, 1979.

Brown, Arthur Judson. *One Hundred Years: A History of the Foreign Missionary Work of the Presbyterian Church in the U.S.A., with Some Account of Countries, Peoples and the Policies and Problems of Modern Missions.* 2d ed. Bk 1. New York: Fleming H. Revell Company, 1936.

Brumberg, Joan Jacobs. *Mission For Life: The Story of the Family of Adoniram Judson*. New York: The Free Press, 1980.

Brumberg, Joan Jacobs and Nancy Tomes. "Women in the Professions: A Research Agenda for American Historians." *Reviews in American History* 10 (June 1982): 275–96.

Cattan, Louise Armstrong. *Lamps Are For Lighting: The Story of Helen Barrett Montgomery and Lucy Waterbury Peabody*. Grand Rapids: Eerdmans, 1968.

Cott, Nancy F. *The Bonds of Womanhood: "Woman's Sphere" in New England, 1780–1835*. New Haven: Yale University Press, 1977.

Douglas, Ann. *The Feminization of American Culture*. New York: Knopf, 1977.

Entrikin, Isabelle Webb. *Sarah Josepha Hale and Godey's Lady's Book*. Philadelphia: University of Pennsylvania, 1946.

Epstein, Barbara Leslie. *The Politics of Domesticity: Women, Evangelism, and Temperance in Nineteenth-Century America*. Middletown, Conn.: Wesleyan University Press, 1981.

Fairbank, John K., ed. *The Missionary Enterprise in China and America*. Cambridge: Harvard University Press, 1974.

Ferguson, Charles W. *Organizing to Beat the Devil: Methodists and the Making of America*. New York: Doubleday, 1971.

Filler, Louis. *The Crusade Against Slavery, 1830–1860*. New York: Harper and Brothers, 1960.

Finley, Ruth E. *The Lady of Godey's: Sarah Josepha Hale*. Philadelphia: J. P. Lippincott, 1931.

Flexner, Eleanor. *Century of Struggle: The Woman's Rights Movement in the United States*. 1959. Reprint. New York: Atheneum, 1973.

Forman, Charles W. "II. The Americans." *International Bulletin of Missionary Research*, April 1982, 54–56.

Frederickson, George M. *The Inner Civil War: Northern Intellectuals and the Crisis of the Union*. New York: Harper and Row, 1965.

Frederickson, Mary E. "Shaping a New Society: Methodist Women and Industrial Reform in the South, 1880–1940." In *Women in New Worlds*, edited by Hilah F. Thomas and Rosemary Skinner Keller, 345–61. Nashville: Abingdon, 1981.

Freedman, Estelle. "Separatism as Strategy: Female Institution Building and American Feminism, 1870–1930." *Feminist Studies* 5 (Fall 1979): 512–29.

Garrett, Shirley S. *Social Reformers in Urban China: The Y.M.C.A., 1895–1926*. Cambridge: Harvard University Press, 1970.

Garrison, Dee. *Apostles of Culture: The Public Librarian and American Society, 1876–1920*. New York: The Free Press, 1979.

Gordon, Ann D., and Mari Jo Buhle. "Sex and Class in Colonial and Nineteenth-Century America." In *Liberating Women's History*, edited by Berenice Carroll, 278–300. Chicago: University of Illinois Press, 1976.

Harris, Barbara J. *Beyond Her Sphere: Women and the Professions in American History.* Contributions in Women's Studies, No. 4. Westport, Conn.: Greenwood Press, 1978.

Hogeland, Ronald. "The Female Appendage: Feminine Life Styles in America, 1820–1960." *Civil War History* 17 (June 1971): 101–14.

Hopkins, C. Howard. *John R. Mott.* Grand Rapids: Eerdmans, 1979.

Hutchison, William R. Introduction to and Comment on "Evangelization and Civilization: Protestant Missionary Motivation in the Imperialist Era." *International Bulletin of Missionary Research* (April 1982): 50–51, 64–65.

Hyatt, Irwin T., Jr. *Our Ordered Lives Confess.* Cambridge: Harvard University Press, 1976.

Keller, Rosemary Skinner. "Creating a Sphere for Women in the Church: How Consequential An Accommodation?" *Methodist History* 18 (January 1980): 83–94.

Kerber, Linda. *Women of the Republic: Intellect and Ideology in Revolutionary America.* Chapel Hill: University of North Carolina Press, 1980.

Kraditor, Aileen S. *The Ideas of the Woman Suffrage Movement.* New York: Doubleday, 1965.

Latourette, Kenneth Scott. *A History of the Expansion of Christianity.* 7 vols. London: Eyre and Spottiswoode, 1938–1945.

Lears, T. J. Jackson. *No Place of Grace: Antimodernism and the Transformation of American Culture, 1880–1920.* New York: Pantheon, 1981.

Lubove, Roy. *The Professional Altruist: The Emergence of Social Work As a Career, 1880–1930.* Cambridge: Harvard University Press, 1965.

Lumpkin, Katharine Du Pre. *The Emancipation of Angelina Grimké.* Chapel Hill: University of North Carolina Press, 1974.

Lutz, Jessie Gregory. *China and the Christian Colleges, 1850–1950.* Ithaca, N.Y.: Cornell University Press, 1971.

Magalis, Elaine. *Conduct Becoming to a Woman: Bolted Doors and Burgeoning Missions.* N.p.: Women's Division, Board of Global Ministries, The United Methodist Church, n.d.

Massey, Mary Elizabeth. *Bonnet Brigades.* New York: Alfred A. Knopf, 1966.

McDowell, John Patrick. *The Social Gospel in the South: The Woman's Home Mission Movement in the Methodist Episcopal Church, South, 1886–1939.* Baton Rouge: Louisiana State University Press, 1982.

Melder, Keith E. *Beginnings of Sisterhood: The American Woman's Rights Movement, 1800–1850.* New York: Schocken Books, 1977.

Mitchell, Norma Taylor. "From Social to Radical Feminism: A Survey of Emerging Diversity in Methodist Women's Organizations, 1869–1974." *Methodist History* 13 (April 1975): 21–44.

Moran, Gerald R. " 'Sisters' in Christ: Women and the Church in Seventeenth-Century New England." In *Women in American Religion*, edited by Janet Wilson James, 47–65. Philadelphia: University of Pennsylvania Press, 1980.

Neill, Stephen. *A History of Christian Missions*. Harmondsworth, England: Penguin Books, 1964.

Noll, William T. "Women as Clergy and Laity in the 19th Century Methodist Protestant Church." *Methodist History* 15 (January 1977): 107–21.

Norwood, Frederick A. *The Story of American Methodism*. New York: Abingdon Press, 1974.

Perry, Alan Frederick. "The American Board of Commissioners for Foreign Missions and the London Missionary Society in the Nineteenth Century: A Study of Ideas." Ph.D. diss., Washington University, 1974.

Phillips, Clifton Jackson. *Protestant America and the Pagan World: The First Half Century of the American Board of Commissioners for Foreign Missions, 1810–1860*. Cambridge: Harvard University Press, 1969.

Porterfield, Amanda. *Feminine Spirituality in America*. Philadelphia: Temple University Press, 1980.

Rabe, Valentin H. "The American Protestant Foreign Mission Movement, 1880–1920." Ph.D. diss., Harvard University, 1965.

———. *The Home Base of American China Missions, 1880–1920*. Cambridge: Harvard University Press, 1978.

Rothman, Sheila M. *Woman's Proper Place: A History of Changing Ideals and Practices, 1870 to the Present*. New York: Basic Books, 1978.

Ryan, Mary P. "A Women's Awakening: Evangelical Religion and the Families of Utica, New York, 1800–1940." In *Women in American Religion*, edited by Janet Wilson James, 89–110. Philadelphia: University of Pennsylvania Press, 1980.

Shivute, Tomas. *The Theology of Mission and Evangelism*. Helsinki: The Finnish Society for Missiology and Ecumenics, 1980.

Simmons, Adele. "Education and Ideology in Nineteenth-Century America: The Response of Educational Institutions to the Changing Role of Women." In *Liberating Women's History*, edited by Berenice Carroll, 115–26. Chicago: University of Illinois Press, 1976.

Sims, Anastasia. "Sisterhoods of Service: Women's Clubs and Methodist Women's Missionary Societies in North Carolina, 1890–1930." In *Women in New Worlds*, vol. 2, edited by Rosemary Skinner Keller, Louise L. Queen, and Hilah F. Thomas, 196–210. Nashville: Abingdon, 1982.

Sims, Mary S. *The Natural History of a Social Institution—The Y.W.C.A.* New York: The Woman's Press, 1935.

Sklar, Kathryn Kish. *Catharine Beecher: A Study in American Domesticity*. 1973. Reprint. New York: Norton, 1976.

————. "The Founding of Mount Holyoke College." In *Women of America: A History*, edited by Carol Berkin and Mary Beth Norton, 177–98. Boston: Houghton Mifflin, 1979.

Smith, Daniel Scott. "Family Limitation, Sexual Control, and Domestic Feminism in Victorian America." In *Clio's Consciousness Raised*, edited by Mary Hartman and Lois W. Banner, 119–36. New York: Harper and Row, 1974.

Smith, Page. *Daughters of the Promised Land: Women in American History*. Boston: Little, Brown and Company, 1970.

Smith-Rosenberg, Carroll. "Beauty, the Beast, and the Militant Woman: A Case Study in Sex Roles and Social Stress in Jacksonian America." *American Quarterly* 23 (1971): 562–84.

Torbet, Robert G. *Venture of Faith: The Story of the American Baptist Foreign Mission Society and the Woman's American Baptist Foreign Mission Society, 1814–1954*. Philadelphia: Judson Press, 1955.

Ulrich, Laurel Thatcher. "Vertuous Women Found: New England Ministerial Literature, 1668–1735." In *Women in American Religion*, edited by Janet Wilson James, 67–87. Philadelphia: University of Pennsylvania Press, 1980.

Verdesi, Elizabeth Howell. *In But Still Out: Women in the Church*. Philadelphia: Westminster Press, 1976.

Welter, Barbara. "The Cult of True Womanhood." *American Quarterly* 18 (Summer 1966): 151–74.

————. "The Feminization of American Religion: 1800–1860." In *Problems and Issues in American Social History*, edited by William O'Neill. Minneapolis: Burgess Publishing, 1974. Reprinted in *Clio's Consciousness Raised*, edited by Mary Hartman and Lois W. Banner, 137–57. New York: Harper and Row, 1974.

————. "She Hath Done What She Could: Protestant Women's Missionary Careers in Nineteenth-Century America." In *Women in American Religion*, edited by Janet Wilson James, 111–25. Philadelphia: University of Pennsylvania Press, 1980.

Winsborough, Hollie Paxson. *Yesteryears*. Atlanta: Committee on Woman's Work, Presbyterian Church, U.S., 1937.

# Index